The Complete Idiot's R...

tear here

Handy Windows AOL Icons

New Mail (for when you get mail while online)

Compose Mail (when you want to drop someone a note)

Main Menu (takes you to the Main Menu, naturally)

Welcome Screen (also known as In The Spotlight)

Help (opens AOL's help screens online and offline)

Directory of Services (calls up the list of everything there is to do online)

People Connection (the chat areas, see Chapter 10)

Quotes and Portfolios (stock market and financial services and information)

Today's News (today's top news stories)

Center Stage (where many online events happen)

Internet Connection (see Chapter 17)

New Features (see what's been added online lately)

Discover AOL (take the nickel tour of the service)

Keyword (more on this in a second)

Download Manager (see Chapter 12)

File Search (see Chapter 12)

Online Clock (tells you the time and how long you've been online)

Personal Choices (see Chapter 6)

Print (prints the text in the topmost window, if it can be printed)

Save Text (saves the text in the top-most window to your hard drive, if it can be saved)

Quick Keywords

To use a Keyword, press **Ctrl+K** on an IBM-compatible or **⌘-K** on a Mac, or select the **Keyword** item on the **Go To** menu or the **Keyword** icon on the Windows menu bar. When the Keyword dialog appears, type the Keyword you want to use in the text box and press **Enter**. Here are some keywords to get you started (see Chapter 23 for more).

Use This Keyword	To	Use This Keyword	To
2MARKET	Shop 'til you drop	PASSWORD	Change your password
BILLING	Check out last month's bill, this month's bill, or change your payment method	QUICKFIND	Search all Computing Forum Libraries
CLOCK	Display the online clock	SHORTHANDS	Display lists of smileys and common abbreviations, such as ROTFL
GUIDE PAGER	Call a Guide if someone is being offensive or abusive	SOFTWARE	Go to the Software Center (where all the Computing Forums libraries are collected)
INDUSTRY CONNECTION	Find out information from hardware and software companies	TECH LIVE	Get your AOL problems solved by tech support people
INTERNET	Access the Info Autobahn	TITF	Find out what's happening tonight in the forums
NEW	Check out what's been added to AOL recently	TOS	Read the Terms of Service guidelines (good to know when creating a chat room)
NEWSSTAND	Access online magazines and newspapers		

alpha books

Money-Saving Tips

Anything you type online (email, forum posts, even chat or IMs), you can compose just as easily offline, saving you on your phone bill and online charges. These and other time- and money-saving tips are covered in Chapter 22 and throughout the book:

➤ You can write and address email (covered in Chapter 9) offline and then save it for later delivery by just clicking on the **Send Later** button.

➤ *Read* your mail offline, too, by using FlashSessions to retrieve it.

➤ You can write any text you want to post in a message area while offline. Use the **New** command in the File menu to create your message, and then copy and paste it into the form online.

➤ If you visit a forum regularly, add it to your Favorite Places list in your Go To menu; Chapter 22 tells you how.

Common Shorthands

LOL = Laughing Out Loud

ROFL = Rolling On Floor Laughing

ROFLMAO = Rolling On Floor Laughing My A** Off

GMTA = Great Minds Think Alike

IMHO = In My Humble Opinion

IMNSHO = In My Not So Humble Opinion

BTW = By The Way

AFK = Away From Keyboard (so others know you won't answer for a while)

BAK = Back At Keyboard (so they know you're back)

DL/DLing = Download/Downloading

UL/ULing = Upload/Uploading

<g> = Grin

{} = A hug

{{{{{{}}}}}} = A major hug

The COMPLETE IDIOT'S GUIDE TO America Online

by John Pivovarnick

alpha books

A Division of Macmillan Publishing USA
A Prentice Hall Macmillan Company
201 W. 103rd Street, Indianapolis, IN 46290

©1995 Alpha Books

International Standard Book Number: 1-56761-597-X

Library of Congress Catalog Card Number: 95-75190

97 96 95   8 7 6 5 4 3 2 1

Interpretation of the printing code: the rightmost number of the first series of numbers is the year of the book's printing; the rightmost number of the second series of numbers is the number of the book's printing. For example, a printing code of 95-1 shows that the first printing of the book occurred in 1995.

Printed in the United States of America

Publisher
Marie Butler-Knight

Product Development Manager
Faithe Wempen

Acquisitions Manager
Barry Pruett

Managing Editor
Elizabeth Keaffaber

Development Editor
Heather Stith

Production Editor
Phil Kitchel

Copy Editor
Audra Gable

Cover Designer
Scott Cook

Designer
Barbara Kordesh

Illustrator
Judd Winick

Indexer
Greg Eldred

Production Team
*Gary Adair, Dan Caparo, Brad Chinn, Kim Cofer, Dave Eason,
Jennifer Eberhardt, Rob Falco, David Garratt, Erika Millen, Angel Perez,
Beth Rago, Bobbi Satterfield, Karen Walsh, Robert Wolf*

*Special thanks to Christopher Denny for ensuring
the technical accuracy of this book.*

Contents at a Glance

v

Contents

Introduction

Right out of the gate, I have to say one thing: I *love* America Online. You'll have to pardon me if I gush.

I "discovered" America Online way back in 1987, when I bought my first modem for my first computer. It was a time of firsts (computer, modem, online service), and you know how it is with "firsts." The first time you hear a song, you tend to favor *that* version over any other versions of the song you hear—for example, whenever I hear Whitney Houston sing "The Greatest Love of All," in my head I'm hearing George Benson's version at the same time. That's how I am with America Online: unashamedly, unabashedly prejudiced in its favor. Just so you know.

What Is America Online?

I have friends (believe it or not, I have friends) who come over to the house and say "Oh, there's John, piddling away his time on the computer." If I happen to be using America Online, the next thing they usually say is, "What is *that*?"

Invariably, my answer is something like, "It's an online service for computer users," but that doesn't really cover it. Depending on the friend and his or her interests, I follow up with something that I know will appeal to him or her. Teacher-types get, "It's a great educational resource." Lonely hearts get, "It's a great way to meet new and interesting people." Computer geeks get, "This is where I find all that wild software I use." Hobbyists get an answer that appeals to their particular interest (and I haven't run into a hobby yet that wasn't represented on America Online).

Trying to define America Online in a few sentences is like trying to define a big city. You can't really define it without doing it an injustice. No matter how much you say, there's still something left unsaid.

So here's my answer of late: America Online is whatever you make of it. It has resources, information, fun, education, shopping, entertainment, news, gossip, and lots of other stuff to use and explore. Take what you want and do your own thing.

The Life Online

If the description above doesn't satisfy your need for a definitive answer, maybe I can explain it for you by example.

In a typical week, I log onto America Online four or five times. Sometimes I'm just trying to stay current with folks who write to me (through the digital version of letters, called e-mail). Sometimes I'm having a computer crisis, and I log on to get advice from friends or experts, or even from the companies that made the computer-widget that's giving me grief. Sometimes I'm bored and go looking for a fun game to play or fun people to talk with. If I'm doing research, I might log on to find some factoid or another. Sometimes I do all of the above, or other things, or... well, you get the idea.

I think the big city metaphor still works best. Using America Online is like living in, say, New York City, Los Angeles, Philadelphia, or any major city. The city offers you everything it's got, every day. What you *take* from it is whatever your mood and needs dictate.

If that's still too vague, you might want to skip ahead to Chapter 8, which covers all of the various departments of America Online, to get a better idea of what I mean. Meanwhile, back on the ranch....

How to Use this Book

If you've just gotten or are about to get a modem, and you need to know how to get started with America Online (which I'll sometimes call AOL), start with Part 1. It walks you through the process of making sure you have the right hardware and software to get started, shows you how to install the AOL software that's appropriate for your computer, and gets you hooked up and signed on in short order.

If you're just noodling around with the idea of getting a modem and joining America Online, you may want to skip ahead to Part 2, which gives details about AOL's most popular features and how to use them. When you decide to join up (and I hope you do), you can go back to the beginning.

If you're already a member of AOL but want to know what else is available online or how to use it more effectively, just skip around and see what strikes your fancy. Part 1 covers setting up, connecting, and customizing AOL to the way you work and play. Part 2 is about all the various features, departments, forums, and chat areas, and even has a chapter devoted to online etiquette. Part 3 is full of advice and time- and money-saving tips, lists of my favorite stuff online, and information on where to dig up lots of other cool junk.

Assumptions and Conventions

This is a *Complete Idiot's Guide*, so I won't make many assumptions about you or your ability/comfort with your computer. However, some information does fall outside the scope of this book.

I assume that your computer is assembled, works, and that you know how to turn it on and off. I also assume that you know how to perform some basic everyday computer duties, such as formatting a disk, launching an application, and using a mouse. If you don't, you might want to pick up a *Complete Idiot's Guide* about your computer (there are *Idiot's Guides* for PCs, DOS, Windows, and the Mac). It couldn't hurt. So much for assumptions.

The conventions you'll find throughout this book are simple. If I want you to type something, I'll be horribly clever and say Type **this:**, and then give you something to type. If I want you to hit a key, I'll say Press **this** (and tell you what to press). If I want you to click on something with your mouse, I'll say Click on **this**. (I know, you're sitting there thinking: Yeah, click on *this*, pal.)

If there are several steps for what you need to do, I'll list them in order:

1. Do this.

2. Then do that.

3. When this happens, do the other thing.

Other things you'll run into include special boxes of information that are set off from the main text, like these:

Oops! boxes warn you about common mistakes and misunderstandings so you can avoid them. I screw up so you don't have to.

These boxes contain technical information that will try not to hurt you.

EZ boxes, like this one, contain easy tips to help make your life easier. Definitely read these. Who needs extra work?

These boxes contain easy-to-understand definitions of words and terms you may not be familiar with. All of these entries (and a few extras) are also collected at the back of the book in the Speak Like a Geek archive.

They're set off to the side for two reasons. They can either call your attention to important information so you can read it in a hurry, or they put all of the potentially intimidating technical information off to the side so you can ignore it or read it at your leisure. If I were you, I'd definitely read the Speak Like a Geek boxes (because definitions help), the EZ boxes (because they make life easy), and the Oops boxes (because who wants to screw up?). As for the Techno-Nerd boxes, read them or don't read them. The world won't blow up either way.

System Schizophrenia: Windows, DOS, and Macintosh

America Online is for everybody and so is this book. You'll be able to set up, log on, and enjoy AOL no matter which of the three systems you're running.

All three versions of AOL behave in much the same way. They'd probably be identical if differences in the hardware and operating systems didn't demand different handling on different computers. Where the differences are big enough (mostly in Part 1) each of the three versions will have sections devoted specifically to their needs. You'll spot them easily because the name of the section will say **Windows *This***, or **DOS *That***, or **Macintosh *Something Else***. Read the sections that apply to your computer.

Once you get into later sections, the differences are minor. In Parts 2 and 3, the text will generally cover AOL from a Windows perspective. When something differs for Mac or DOS users (say, like key combinations), you'll find that information in boxes like these:

This will tell you when DOS commands differ from those for Windows.

This will tell Mac users what to do to get similar results to Windows users.

When there's a picture of my computer's screen (called a screenshot, oddly enough) the screen on your computer may look a little different if you're using DOS or a Mac. If your screen will look wildly different, I'll give you a screenshot of what you'll be seeing. Fair enough?

Copyrights and Trademarks

Whenever you talk about computer-related junk, everybody's got dibs on certain names, logos, or collections of words. When you delve into a service like America Online, where you can find MTV, *The New York Times*, and thousands of other big companies, there are even more.

Wherever I am aware that a word, name, or whatever is property of someone else, I'll indicate it with the proper capitalization: America Online, Apple Computer, Microsoft Windows, and so on.

However (snide comments from my friends aside), I am human. My editors are human. We make mistakes. If we screw up and don't catch one or two, our lack of capitalization in no way infringes on the copyrights, trademarks, or service marks held by other people or corporate entities. We do that so I don't have to remember what keys to press to make a ®, ©, or ™ after every mention of a company, product, or service. It's a pain.

CompuShow 2000! is copyright ©1994 by Canyon State Systems and Software. It is distributed here by permission of the author.

WAOL Pal 1.1 is copyright ©1994 by Sam Hazan. It is distributed here by permission of the author.

Wedge 0.21 is copyright ©1994 by Tundra Slosek. It is distributed here by permission of the author.

WinZip 5.5a is copyright ©1991-1994 by Nico Mak Computing Inc. It is distributed here by permission of the author.

You've Got Mail! 1.1 is copyright ©1994 by Roald Oines and Rachel Barnot. It is distributed here by permission of the authors.

ZipShell Pro 4.0 is copyright ©1992-1994 by New Vision. It is distributed here by permission of the author.

Love and Bullets

Not gun bullets, typesetting bullets like this: ➤.

➤ Thanks to Dr. Kerry Sharps, dentist and travel maven, for doing half of my airline ticket comparison shopping for me, for the section on EAASY SABRE.

➤ Thanks also to Info-Diva and pal Juliet Cooke for her lunch time suggestions to Aunt Effie in Chapter 7, and just for being the way-cool Goddess-Babe she is.

➤ Another tip of the digital hat to online pal TSaint for the 14,400 baud modem tip in Chapter 6. I was zipping through AOL at light-speed a couple of months before Steve Case let the cat out of the bag in his monthly letter to subscribers. It's so cool when you know a secret.

➤ Special thanks to Jennifer Watson and her merry band of Keyword watchers. Her excruciatingly complete list of Keywords formed the basis for the abridged version of Chapter 23. She freely distributes, out of the kindness of her heart, two versions on AOL: an alpha-betical listing by Keyword and a listing by AOL department. Both lists are updated regularly and are available online. Due to the timetable of publishing, the one in Chapter 23 is already old-ish news; do a file search (covered in Chapter 12) with "SURF" as the search string to find the latest versions.

➤ Still more thanks to all of the software authors who agreed to allow us to include their spiffy applications and add-ins on the enclosed disk and sent me latest-greatest versions at the speed of light.

➤ As always, thanks to the wacky crew at Alpha Books (Faithe, Heather, Martha, Barry, Marie, and everyone) for making work less work-like. And to my pals T. Greenfield, "Dr." Karen Razler, the Rev. Porter, Jackie "Dr. Evil" Yancey, Dr. Ted (the only real Doctor in the bunch), and Mark Yanick for applying liberal doses of coffee and entertainment to keep all work and no play from turning John (nobody calls me Jack) into a dull boy.

What Are You Still Doing Here?

Most people don't read this far unless they think there's a chance their name is mentioned in the thank-yous. If it wasn't, I'm sorry. Please forgive. Now, be on your way. You've got a big adventure in front of you. America Online awaits.

Shoo!

Part 1
Getting It Together

It'd be really nice if you could click your heels together three times (ruby slippers optional) and be ready to log onto America Online. Unfortunately, it doesn't work that way. You've got to click some keys, or click your mouse, to get it done.

This part is all about getting set up to log on. It walks you through what you need, in terms of hardware and software, to access America Online. It'll also hold your hand while you install and configure the AOL software, even help you get through your first session online without breaking a sweat. There are also tips on customizing your America Online software so it works the way you want it to—and no getting funny looks as you stand in front of your PC, clicking your heels, saying, "Oh, Auntie Em, there's no place like AOL, there's no place like AOL..."

Chapter 1

The Least You Need to Know

This is, by no means, exhaustive coverage of everything there is to know about America Online. It's just a quick way for you to stick your toe in and test the waters. In short, it's the absolute *least* you should know before you begin.

1. To use America Online, you need specific hardware and software.

Chapter 2 will fill you in on the details, but these are the basics:

➤ A computer

➤ A modem

➤ AOL software

➤ A telephone line

And that's it, in a nutshell. However, it's nice to have other things such as a mouse, a printer, and a fetching someone to fetch you snacks and beverages while you're online.

2. Signing on is simple.

Signing on is also more fun than humans should be allowed to have. Once your America Online software is installed and set up for your computer (see Chapter 4), you launch it like any other application:

➤ If you're a Windows user, double-click on the **America Online** program group, and then double-click on the **America Online** icon inside.

➤ If you're a DOS user, type **AOL** at the C:\> prompt (you might have to type **CD PCAOL** first, depending on how/where you installed the software). If you use it with GeoWorks Ensemble, AOL is just a double-click away.

➤ If you're a Mac user, double-click on the **America Online** folder, and then double-click on the **AOL** icon inside.

Once your software is running, signing on is as easy as selecting the screen name you want to use (if you have more than one), typing your password, and pressing Enter. Oh, and make sure your modem is turned on and connected to a working phone line—that helps. Chapter 5 reviews this process.

3. While you're online, be polite.

Logging on to America Online (or any online service) is like going to a public place: a mall, the movies, a restaurant. Rules of behavior and etiquette apply.

Chapter 7 has some specific tips, but overall, the Golden Rule applies: treat everyone the way you want to be treated. It works all of the time.

4. All this fun costs money.

Although AOL is (in my opinion) the most reasonably priced online service going, it still costs money. In fact, it costs $9.95 a month, for which you get 5 hours of use. After that, you are charged $2.95 per additional hour. You also have the cost of the phone call, which is a local call in most cases.

Throughout this book, you'll find gobs of time/money-saving tips and tricks; there's a pile of them stacked up in Chapter 22. If you want to find out how much you've spent so far this month online, use the Keyword: BILLING. It will take you to a free area where you can check your current bill, or even see a summary of last month's bill.

5. Keywords take you where you want to be—fast.

Keywords are about as close as we'll get to *Star Trek*'s transporter beam in this century. Type a word and press **Enter**, and you're instantly somewhere else online.

To use a keyword, press the **Ctrl-K** (⌘-K on a Mac) key combination, and then just type the keyword. Press **Enter**, and you're off! Chapter 23 lists oodles of keywords you can use.

6. Sending email is easy.

Chapter 9 covers it in detail, but all you need to do is select Compose Mail from your Mail menu. Fill in the blanks: the screen name(s) of the person(s) you want to receive your mail, a line about what the letter's about, and then what you want to say.

When you're done, click on the **Send** or **Send Later** button (depending on whether you're currently signed on to AOL). You can save some money by composing your mail offline and sending it with FlashSessions (also covered in Chapter 9).

7. Chat rooms can be a riot.

The old saying goes, "You snooze, you lose." On America Online, the new saying is, "You shmooze, you win." Not quite as zippy as the old saying, but it works.

To get to a chat room, select **Lobby** from the Go To menu (or press **Ctrl+L** or ⌘-L) while you're signed on. You land in a lobby. You can stay there and chat, or you can click on the **List Rooms** button and find a room that suits your mood.

To chat, click once in the narrow text box at the bottom of the window to put your cursor there. Type whatever you want to say (the box holds about two lines of type), and then press **Enter**. Your chat appears in the main window in short order, and people all across the country will read it. Very cool.

When you're done chatting, exit the chat room by closing the window (it closes like any other window you've ever closed on your computer). Chatting is covered in more detail in Chapter 10.

8. If knowledge is power...

...then AOL will make you powerful. You can find all manner of information online: everything from current events and computing news and information (see Chapter 13) to education resources like the online encyclopedia and an online university (Chapter 14). Even if you aren't in a "learning" mood, you can get the latest Hollywood gossip, entertainment news, sports, and other scoop to help you while away your idle hours. Check out Chapter 13 for more details.

9. Signing off is a 2-step operation.

When you're done poking around online, do this:

1. Click on your Go To menu.

2. Select **Sign Off**.

3. Click on the Yes button.

Your AOL software will disconnect you from the service and even hang up your phone. If you're finished using AOL, you can exit the application by selecting Exit (**Quit** on a Mac) from the File menu. Chapter 5 reviews how to sign off.

10. The disk at the back of the book contains information and useful add-ons that will help you customize and accessorize AOL.

As my friend Teresa is fond of saying, "Life is cheap—it's the accessories that kill you." The disk is full of accessories to help Windows users sail through AOL with style and panache. The disk's contents and instructions for use are in Chapter 24.

DOS and Mac users, don't frown. Chapter 24 also contains a map and directions for you to put together your own disk from the millions of files available online.

ON YER' MARK...

What You Need to Get Started

Take a good hard look at the computer you want to use to access AOL. Make sure it's up to snuff and that you've got all the fiddly bits together and connected.

System Requirements

America Online isn't too fussy about what hardware you can use with it, but there are some basic requirements you should at least meet before you try to install your software. (We'll talk about installing software in the next chapter).

A good computer geek can tell what your computer's attributes are; normal folks are better off looking in the manual that came with your computer, or on a sticker on the computer's box (if you still have it). Here are some other hints:

➤ **Computer type:** To find this, look for no-brainers such as a sticker or label on the case. For example, my Gateway 200 486DX2/50 is a 50 megahertz 486. The manual that came with your computer should definitely have this info, too.

➤ **Memory (RAM):** If you're a PC user, just pay attention to the memory test your computer performs every time you start up. (For instance, mine says 640 base memory, 7096 extended. That adds up to 8 megabytes, more or less.) Or, you can type the command **MEM** at any C:\ prompt. Mac users can select **About This Macintosh** from the menu.

➤ **Monitor:** Again, look at the manual that came with the computer. For IBM-compatibles, most 386, 486, and Pentium computers have VGA or Super VGA monitors, while most XTs and 286 computers have EGA monitors. For Macs, don't worry about it; any Mac monitor will do.

➤ **Hard disk space available:** For IBM-compatibles, type **DIR** at any C:\ prompt, and the last line it displays will be **xxx,xxxx bytes free**. That's how much room is left on your hard disk. For Macs, check your hard drive's window; the info should be there. If not, check the Show disk info in header option in your Views control panel.

➤ **Operating system version:** For IBM-compatibles, type **VER** at the C:\ prompt to find out what version. For Macs, you can find out by choosing the **About This Macintosh** item from the menu as described above.

Windows Requires...

The latest version of America Online for Windows (called WAOL for short) is version 2.0. It requires that you have:

➤ A 386-based PC or higher (486 or Pentium)

➤ 4MB of RAM

➤ Hard drive

➤ Windows 3.1 or later

➤ A color monitor (and controller card) capable of displaying 256 colors

➤ A mouse

➤ A Hayes or Hayes-compatible modem

These are *minimum* requirements. If you have more/better hardware than is required, don't worry about it. If you don't meet the requirements, you're going to need to try an earlier version of WAOL or the non-Windows version (those requirements are coming right up).

DOS Requires...

The current version of America Online for DOS (without Windows) is called PCAOL 1.6. It will run by itself on an IBM-compatible or an IBM-compatible running GeoWorks Ensemble (a graphical interface program that's somewhat like Microsoft Windows) with the following hardware requirements:

➤ Any old IBM-compatible (even an XT)

➤ 640K of RAM

➤ A hard drive

➤ An EGA (or better) monitor and video controller

➤ MS-DOS 2.0 or higher

➤ A mouse is recommended

➤ A Hayes or Hayes-compatible modem

Again, these are minimums. If you have better equipment, you should have no problems.

Macintosh Requires...

America Online for Macintosh (the current version is 2.5.1) requires that you have:

➤ A Macintosh computer with a hard drive and monitor

➤ System 6.0.7 or higher

➤ 4MB of RAM

➤ A Hayes or Hayes-compatible modem

These are (do I have to say it again?) minimum requirements: "more is good—less is *bad.*"

9

Modems Demystified

In addition to the basic hardware you need (as explained above), you also need a *modem* that's appropriate for your computer—that is, one that's DOS or Mac-compatible depending on which computer you own.

A modem is a device that turns the information and commands from your computer into sounds that can travel through telephone lines to another modem-equipped computer at a remote location. When the information and commands from your computer reach the other computer, the other computer's modem turns those sounds back into information and commands it can use. The name modem is a contraction of the words **mo**dulating and **dem**odulating, which is science-speak for the process of turning information into sound and back into information again.

Hayes-compatible A modem that conforms to the standard set of modem commands developed by the Hayes Corporation. Hayes compatibility is fairly standard among modems. I wouldn't mess with one that isn't Hayes-compatible; it will complicate your life unnecessarily.

In order to use America Online, you have to have a modem, preferably a *Hayes-compatible* modem (but don't sweat it, most are). Beyond that, AOL isn't very finicky. If you already own a modem, make sure it's connected to your computer properly (check your manual for details), and you may skip ahead to the next section.

If you don't have a modem, here are some considerations you should weigh before you purchase one.

Inside or Out?

Modems come in two varieties: internal and external. Internal modems go inside your computer; external modems sit on the desk near your computer. Internal modems tend to be a little less expensive than external models because you don't have to pay for frills like a pretty protective case. However, installing an internal modem means actually opening up your computer (*oh, ack!*) and tinkering with its gizzards.

You also need to be sure that the internal modem you choose will physically fit inside your computer: do you have an open *expansion slot*? And is the case big enough to hold the modem? (Generally the latter is only a problem with laptop computers, but you should check before you buy.)

Generally speaking, an external modem is easier to set up and install; you just plug it in. You don't feel like you're performing surgery on your computer just to install it.

Speed Concerns

The other major thing to consider when selecting a modem for use with America Online is its speed. Modem speed is often discussed in terms of *BPS* (bits per second), for how much information the modem can send. A *bit* is the smallest unit of information a computer can deal with, like a molecule of information. Faster modems send more bits per second. Fast modems are more expensive, but you can save time (and therefore money) while online, which may save you money in the long run.

> **Expansion slot** The area inside your computer that accepts an expansion card, which adds new functions and/or features to your computer. An expansion *card* is a circuitry board that fits into an expansion slot inside your computer. The video controller card mentioned earlier is an expansion card.

What are we talking about when we say fast and slow here? Well, 1200 bps or 2400 bps is pretty slow. 9600 bps is the average these days, and 14,400 is fairly fast (it's what most of the serious modem geeks use). Recently, 28,800 bps modems have begun to hit the market, and who knows what's next?

The speed limit, if you'll pardon the expression, on America Online at this time is 9600 BPS, with 14,400 access promised in the near future. If you're buying a modem only for use with AOL, save yourself some money and buy a 9600 or 14,400 BPS modem.

You might hear the term baud being used interchangeably with bps. Baud is the speed at which the modem operates. BPS (bits per second) is the amount of data that is transferred between the two computers.

Up to 9600 bps/baud, the two are the same. Modems that advertise 14,400 or 28,800 bps are really only operating at 9600 baud, but they use data compression to achieve a higher bps. Data compression is the process of compressing data to make it smaller so it takes less time to send over the phone lines. Then the receiving modem un-scrunches it.

Obviously, this doesn't work if both modems don't speak the same compression language. My 14,400 modem uses v32.bis as its compression language, for instance. If it's talking to a 9600 bps modem or a 14,400 modem that doesn't use v32.bis, it can't do any better than 9600 bps.

More than you wanted to know? Well, I warned you.

If you think you may want to do other things with your modem (and there are a lot of other things to do), you may want to think about getting as fast a modem as you can reasonably afford. Fast modems can always slow down if circumstances demand it, but slower modems can't go beyond their maximum speeds. I'd avoid a 28,800 modem until the dust settles and a standard compression scheme emerges (see the preceding Techno Nerd sidebar). V.34 seems like the winner right now, but who knows?

At the time of this writing, AOL was in the process of adding 14,400 baud access. In some metropolitan areas, you *can* use 14,400 with a 9600 baud local access number. It isn't official yet, and it won't work for everyone, but it doesn't hurt to try.

Other Bells and Whistles

You'll also see modems that are *send fax* or *send-and-receive fax* modems. These modems give you the ability to send documents from your computer to a regular fax machine. If it's capable, it will also let a regular fax machine send a document to your computer.

If you know you'll never want to do anything but use America Online, don't worry about fax capability. Otherwise, you may want to think about getting a fax modem. Fax capability doesn't increase the price too much, and—if nothing else—faxing is a *very* techno-chic way to order a pizza.

The Telephone Line

Man, I just got a flash of Glen Campbell singing "Wichita Lineman" in my head. Scary. In order for your computer and modem to work the magic that is America Online, your computer needs to be connected to your modem, and your modem needs to be connected to a telephone line. If you can plug a telephone into a wall jack, you can connect your modem to one as well, Jack. No sweat.

Beyond that, there aren't many concerns about your phone line. You do need to know if it is a touch-tone line or a pulse dial (touch-tone lines beep once for each number you press; pulse lines sort of click the same number of times as the number you dialed). You'll have to tell your modem and AOL software so they know what kind of noises to make to dial.

When you're using America Online, your telephone line will be busy. You can't receive incoming calls or make outgoing calls—which could be traumatic if there are telephone junkies in your home. If you find it *is* traumatic, you may want to consider getting your local phone company to either hook you up with their Answer Call service (which will take messages while your line is busy) or put in another phone line just for your modem. Both cost money, though, so consider the dollars-to-trauma ratio before you spring for either.

Another thing you need to know is whether you have call waiting service (where if you're on the phone with someone, your phone clicks to let you know there's another call coming in).

The last thing you need to know is if you need to dial an additional number (usually a 9) before you can dial an outside phone number. Most home users won't have to, but many office workers will.

Got it all? Good. We'll put all this phone line information to use in Chapter 4.

The Right Software

Finally, the very last thing you need to get connected with America Online is the right software for your computer. If you just purchased a modem or are about to purchase one, you'll probably find AOL software in the modem box—along with a ton of other software or special offers for online services. This is also true if you just bought a computer that came with a modem (a Mac Performa, for example).

If you didn't get it, can't find it, or lost it, don't panic. The right software is as close as your phone. Pick it up and call 1-800-227-6364. You'll get one of those "If you want software, press 1" setups, so listen closely and ask them to send you a starter kit for your computer. Have the following information handy:

➤ Make and model of your computer

➤ Amount of RAM installed

➤ Your operating system version

➤ Whether or not you're running Windows

➤ The size (3.5 or 5.25 inch) and capacity (low or high density) of your floppy drive(s).

They'll get a kit in the mail to you on the double. When you have your software, move on to Chapter 3. It's all about installing the software on your computer.

The Least You Need to Know

In order to painlessly get connected to America Online, you need to know some basic information and have some basic hardware.

➤ You need to know your computer's configuration. Look in the manual that came with your computer if you're not sure.

➤ You need a modem.

➤ You need a telephone line.

➤ You need the right AOL software for your computer.

Chapter 3

The Installation Tango

In This Chapter

➤ Windows installation

➤ Plain ol' DOS installation

➤ Macintosh installation

➤ Installing dual carbs in an '83 Pulsar

As the saying goes, "It takes two to tango." This chapter actually gives you three ways to do the installation tango with America Online.

Installing AOL under Windows

Installing the Windows version of America Online (also known as WAOL) is much the same as installing *any* application under Windows.

You begin by inserting the WAOL disk in your A: or B: drive. Select **Run** from under the Program Manager's **File** menu, and you'll get the Run dialog box. In the Command Line text box, type **A:\SETUP**, and press **Enter** or **click OK**.

The America Online setup application launches. Your computer will churn for a few minutes and you'll see a window that says "Initializing Setup." Then WAOL scopes out your system to see what you have and how to best install itself. When it's finished you'll see a Welcome window that gives you three options:

➤ The **Install** button will (*duh*) install America Online with no further ado. Most users will probably use this. The default drive is C:, and the setup program creates a directory called **AOL20**.

➤ The **Review** button will let you review and/or change the directories where the WAOL software is installed. If you want to install the software on another hard drive or with a different directory name, use this option. After you've made whatever changes you care to make, click on the Install button.

➤ The **Exit** button will quit the Setup application, leaving your hard drive untouched.

For the sake of clarity, I will always assume that you're working with your A: drive. If you're working with B:, or another floppy drive, substitute the correct drive letter wherever you see A: in the text.

The same goes for your hard drive, C:. If you're using a different hard drive, or a logical drive, substitute the appropriate drive letter wherever you see C: in the text.

If you choose the Install button, just watch the installation proceed. If you choose the Review button, review and/or change the drive where the software will be installed and the name of the directory the setup program creates.

A little window tells you what the installer is doing while it's doing it. You'll also see a thermometer that tells you how far along it is. The whole thing only takes a few minutes. When the installation is complete, a message appears saying that the installation was successful, and that you launch your new WAOL software by double-clicking its icon in the Program Manager.

When the Setup application goes away, the America Online program group window is open, and you'll see a triangular icon called "America Online Double-Click to start."

Double-click on that icon to launch America Online and begin the setup procedures covered in Chapter 4. You may want to skip ahead now.

Installing the DOS Version

The DOS version of America Online (called PCAOL, for short) is also easy to install, but it involves a few more steps than the Windows procedure. The Windows version can snitch information about your computer right from Windows. In DOS you need to tell America Online about your system. The first part is installing the software.

Installing for DOS

The installation part is simple.

1. Insert the America Online disk in your floppy drive.

2. At the C:\> prompt, type **A:INSTALL**.

3. The installer launches, and you see a screen something like the one shown here. Read this screen and press **Enter** to continue.

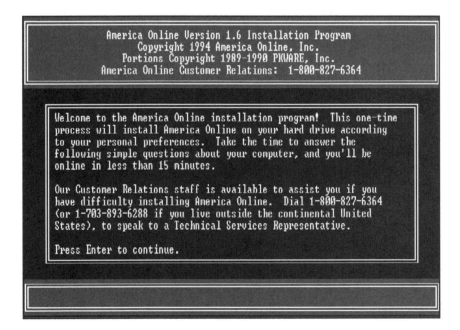

America Online's DOS version installer.

4. Next, you see a screen asking if you have another copy or an earlier version of PCAOL installed. Use your up and down arrow

keys to select the answer that's right for you (most, I suspect, will say NO). Then press **Enter**.

If you tell the installer that you have another copy of PCAOL installed, it will install a new copy but keep any customized settings, mail, and screen names from the old version.

5. Next you'll be asked if it's okay for the installer to create a directory on your C: drive called C:\AOL. Unless you know you want to install PCAOL on another hard drive or in a directory with another name, just press **Enter**. Otherwise, change the drive and directory information to meet your needs before you press Enter.

6. Then the installer asks if you want to install your PCAOL software to run under plain DOS or as a GeoWorks Ensemble application. If you don't have Ensemble, choose **DOS**. If you have Ensemble, you can choose either. Make your selection and press **Enter**.

GeoWorks Ensemble A DOS shell application, that functions like Windows, giving you the benefits of a graphical user interface (GUI, pronounced "goo-ey"). However, unlike Windows, GeoWorks runs on even the lowliest XT IBM-compatible computer. If you've been frus-trated because you can't run Windows, GeoWorks Ensemble is a viable alternative.

7. The installer goes through its installation thing. Take five.

8. When the installation is finished, you may get a message suggesting that you make some changes to your AUTOEXEC.BAT and/or CONFIG.SYS files so America Online will run better on your computer. At this point you have three choices:

➤ Select **Make All** to have the installer make all of the suggested changes.

➤ Select **None** to skip the changes altogether.

➤ Select **Files and Buffers Only** to have the installer make *some* of those changes.

If you're at all squeamish about tinkering with your AUTOEXEC.BAT and CONFIG.SYS files, choose **Make All**, and you won't have to mess with them yourself.

9. You'll be asked if you want to alter your AUTOEXEC.BAT file so you only have to type AOL at the C:\> prompt to launch the application. If you select Yes, it will save you the step of typing CD AOL before typing AOL to launch America Online. Choose it or not, at your own discretion.

At this point, your America Online software is installed on your hard drive, but it isn't quite ready for you to run it yet. As I mentioned earlier, you need to provide it with some specific information about your PC.

Setting Up the Software for Your PC

The first thing the installer asks you about is your video display. It chooses what it thinks is the best display your monitor is capable of giving. If you agree, press **Enter**. If you disagree, press the **F10** key, and you can select a new video choice. Press the **Esc** key to return you to the previous screen, or press the **F3** key to quit the installer and return to DOS.

The next screen gives you the chance to calibrate your monitor's alignment with PCAOL. You'll see arrows at the corners of your screen. Fiddle with your monitor's control until they're just right, and then press **Enter**. If you can't get the arrows into the corners, press **F10** to choose a new video setup and try again.

After the alignment is right, you are asked to confirm that your monitor is actually displaying the number of colors you selected. If it is, press **Enter**. If not, press **F10** to choose a new video setup.

> These four options, by the way, remain constant throughout the rest of the procedure. For every step described, you can press **Enter** to accept an option and continue; press **F10** to make a different selection from the one showing (if available); press **Esc** to return to the previous screen; or press **F3** to quit the installer and return to DOS. Just so you know.

Next, the installer asks you to select the kind of mouse you have, if you have one. Scroll through the list until you find your mouse make and model, and press **Enter**. If you don't know, select **None** or take a guess. The program will ask you to test your mouse, so you can be sure your selection works before you proceed. When your mouse is set up, you'll be able to use it to select the rest of the information about your system.

The next thing Installer needs to know is where your modem is connected (to which COM, or **com**munications, port) and its highest speed. PCAOL only supports speeds up to 2400 baud. If you aren't sure where your modem is connected, select **COM2**, which is the most common. If it's wrong, you can change it later (Chapter 6 tells you how). If you aren't sure of your modem's speed, select 2400. Most modems will step down to the proper setting automatically, and you can change this setting later, too (again, see Chapter 6).

The last thing it needs to know is what kind of printer you have and what port it's connected to. Scroll through a list of printer names until you find yours, and then click on it. If you don't have a printer, select **None**. Then you need to tell the software what port your printer is connected to. Most use LPT1; if you don't know where yours is connected, choose **LPT1**. You get a chance to test the printer and change the settings if it's wrong.

After you set up your printer and test it, you're asked if you want to delete the extra driver software from your hard drive. Drivers are the bits of software that tell AOL how to print to your printer, to send stuff to your monitor, and so on. If you think there's a chance you might have guessed wrong in the configuration set up, keep the drivers—you may need some of them later.

Now PCAOL launches automatically, and you can begin setting it up with your member and payment information. That's all covered in Chapter 4, so why not jump ahead to that chapter now?

Installing on a Macintosh

Installing your America Online software on your Mac is much the same as for any software you may have installed, if it used an installer program.

Begin by inserting the AOL disk in your drive. When the disk's icon appears on your desktop, its window may open automatically (most do). If it doesn't, double-click on it. In the window that opens, you'll see an icon named Install America Online. Double-click on that icon to launch the install program. You'll see a dialog box like the following one.

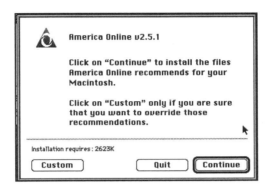

The America Online installer for Macintosh.

At the bottom of the dialog, there are three buttons. Click on the **Continue** button to install all the files America Online thinks it needs for your Mac model. Most users will probably use this option. You can click on the Quit button to quit the installer without doing anything to your Mac, or you can click on the Custom button to select what parts of the AOL software are installed. Don't select Custom unless you're absolutely sure you know what parts of the software you need and don't need.

When you're asked to select where the software will be installed, the Installer automatically chooses the hard drive where your System software is installed. If you want AOL installed somewhere else, navigate to the new location using the Desktop button and the drive and folder icons in the display window. (This is just like navigating to a particular disk or folder when you want to open or save a file.) Press **Enter** when you're set.

The installer will churn for a second or two. Then you'll get a thermometer-type display by which you can keep tabs on its progress. When it's finished, press **Enter** to quit the installer.

Now you can launch America Online by double-clicking on its icon in the newly created America Online folder on your hard drive. When it starts up, it asks you to configure the software for your Mac. That's covered in the next chapter. Get cracking.

The Least You Need to Know

Always remember these things (at least until after you've installed your AOL software):

➤ You must install the America Online software on your computer (whatever type you have) before you can use it.

➤ Carefully follow the installation instructions here, and on your screen. You'll have help and information every step of the way.

➤ If the installation program asks you for information you're unsure of, just press **Enter**. The installer provides you with the most common answers, and, if they're wrong, you usually have an opportunity to change them.

Chapter 4

It's a Set Up!

In This Chapter

➤ Launching AOL

➤ Getting connected

➤ Filling in the blanks

This chapter is all about doing the initial setup and registration for your newly installed America Online software. (So if you haven't installed AOL yet, jump back to Chapter 3 and do that first.) You might want to read through this chapter before you actually go through the process. There are some tips here to help speed things along, but you need to do them *before* you're online.

Let's Do Launch

If you just finished the installation process, your America Online software may be running and ready to go, in which case you don't have to launch it again. However, if you quit after installing, you need to launch the application (that is, start it up) again, before you can proceed. Start the application by following the instructions specific to your computer type.

Windows Startup

In Windows, double-click on the **America Online** program group in the Program Manager window. When the America Online window opens, double-click on the **America Online** icon (it's the only one in the window, so there's no guesswork involved). AOL starts right up.

DOS Startup

For the PC version of America Online, you need to type one or two things at the C:\> prompt. If you told the installer software to modify your AUTOEXEC.BAT file so you can start America Online by entering just one command (that was covered back in Chapter 3), you need only type **AOL** at any DOS prompt (C:\>, A:\>, or whatever).

If you didn't say "Yes" to the easy start question, you need to type *two* things. First, at the C:\> prompt, type **CD AOL** (or whatever name you gave the AOL directory, if you changed the default name). Then press **Enter**. The C:\> prompt changes to C:\>\AOL (or whatever name you gave the AOL directory). Then type **AOL** and press **Enter** again. America Online fires right up.

Mac Startup

With the Mac version of America Online, you need to locate the America Online folder. Unless you told the installer to put it some-where else, it will be in the same window as your System folder. If you put it somewhere else, I hope you remember where (actually, if you *can't* remember where, you can use the **Find** command on the **File** menu).

Double-click on the **America Online** folder icon to open its window. Then double-click on the **America Online** icon (it's shaped like a triangle) in that window. Your Mac will churn for a moment or two, and AOL launches.

The Three Faces of AOL

This is one of those chapters where I'll basically be showing you the Windows version of AOL, with side references to any differences peculiar to the PC or Mac versions. Here's why:

The Windows Version.

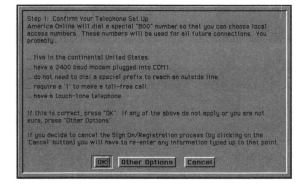

The DOS Version.

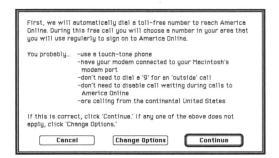

The Macintosh version.

If you look at the three figures—really look closely—you'll see that (superficial differences aside) all three do the same thing: they give you the opportunity to accept or change the software's assumptions about your computer and telephone setup. While the three buttons at the bottom of each screen may say something a little different, they mean the same thing:

Yes, you're right.

No, you're wrong.

"Help, Jane! Stop this crazy thing!"

You'll find, as you go along and learn more about America Online (both here and on your own), that the similarities between the three versions far outweigh the differences.

Okay, let's proceed.

Assumptions

You remember the old saw about "never ass-u-me?" You and I should never assume, but your AOL software does. It assumes five things about you and your computer setup. If it assumes incorrectly, you need to set it straight. In order of appearance, those assumptions are

1. That you live in the continental U.S. (meaning not in Alaska or Hawaii, or another country).

2. That you're calling from a direct phone line (as opposed to one where you need to dial "9" to get an outside line).

3. That you have a 2400 baud (or higher) modem connected to your COM1 port. The software checks your modem's speed automatically, but sometimes it guesses wrong.

 For Mac users, question 3 will say, "Have a modem connected to your Macintosh's modem port," and won't have a baud rate specified. The AOL software checks your modem directly for baud rate.

4. That you need to dial "1" before calling a toll-free 800 number.

5. That you have a touch-tone telephone.

If these five assumptions are right, you merely press **Enter** and go on your merry way. This will be the case for most users. If any of them are wrong, click on the **No/Other Options/Change Options** button and correct them. It's a simple process, so don't sweat it.

I've Got Your Number

When you tell the software to continue, the next thing it does is dial a toll-free number so you can select a *local access number*. Because America Online's central computers are located in Vienna, Virginia, calling in would be a long distance call for most people. So that you don't get hit with outrageous long distance charges, you access AOL by calling a local phone number.

The first thing you'll see is a variation on the screen shown in the following figure. All you have to do is type your local area code—mine's 215—and press **Enter** or click on the **Continue** button. When you do, the computer you've called sorts through its database of local access numbers looking first for those that start with the area code you've entered, and then for those that start with nearby area codes.

Local access number The local phone number you call to access AOL. The computer at that location (called a *node*, if you care) connects you to America Online.

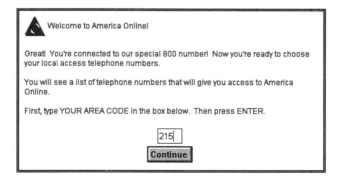

> ⚠ Welcome to America Online!
>
> Great! You're connected to our special 800 number! Now you're ready to choose your local access telephone numbers.
>
> You will see a list of telephone numbers that will give you access to America Online.
>
> First, type YOUR AREA CODE in the box below. Then press ENTER.
>
> 215
>
> Continue

Type your area code here.

You'll see the results of that search in a dialog box that looks like the one in the figure below. In fact, you'll see it twice because you need to select *two* local access numbers. One for your first try, and a second number to try if the first number is busy.

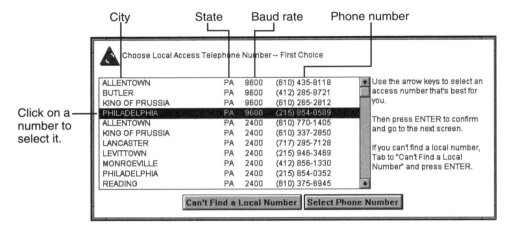

Local access numbers in the 215 area.

Scroll through the list of phone numbers to find one that's a local call for you and that will accommodate your modem's highest baud rate. If you use a 9600 baud modem on a 2400 baud access number, you won't be able to use your modem to its full speed potential.

Right at this moment, 9600 baud is the highest "official" speed modem you can use with AOL. However, 14,400 baud modems might work if you live in a big(ish) city. Give it a shot (with a 9600 baud access number). It might work.

In some areas, you may have to connect with a long distance call, but it will still be less (probably) than a call all the way to Virginia, and you can look for a closer number once you get online (Chapter 18 shows you how). America Online is always updating their local access numbers and adding new ones. Don't give up hope.

When you've clicked on a number to select it, press **Enter** or click on the **Select Phone Number** button. You've made your first choice. If you can't find a second number, you may choose to use your first choice number as your second choice, too. You won't have an alternate if that number is busy, but you can try to find a second number once you get online.

Once you've selected both numbers, AOL asks you to confirm your choices, and then you're disconnected from the toll-free number. Your AOL software dials your first choice local access number and connects you directly to America Online for the rest of the registration process.

If you're trying to register yourself during a heavy usage period (say from about 7 PM to 11 PM, Sunday through Thursday, later on Friday and Saturday) both of your access numbers may be busy. It can happen. Just take five and try again in a few minutes.

The Password Is: Cranky-Tuna

While your computer is trying to connect you to America Online, locate the registration certificate that came with your AOL software. It will say something like **This is your registration number and password. DO NOT DISCARD.** It will also have a little label in the center of it with two lines of type. The top line is a series of numbers; that's your registration/certificate number. The second line is a two-word combination such as CRANKY-TUNA; that's your temporary password.

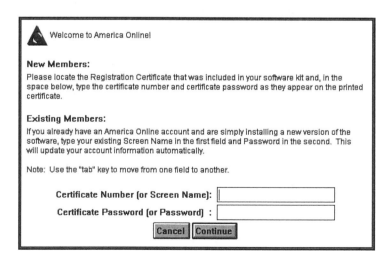

Enter your certificate information here.

When you connect to AOL, a screen like the one in the preceding figure appears. Very carefully type the line of numbers into the first box (you can use your Backspace and Delete keys if you make a mistake). Make sure it's right, and then press the **Tab** key. Then type the password into the second box. Check to make sure you typed it correctly, and then press **Enter**. AOL's computers check the information you entered to make sure it's valid (if it isn't, you'll be asked to enter it again), and then move you on to the next stage of the registration process.

If you're already registered as a member of America Online, but you've upgraded or reinstalled your software, you won't need to use the registration certificate. Just type your screen name in the top box and your password in the bottom box. AOL then updates the new copy of your software with all of your account information.

The next thing you'll see is an informational screen telling you how to get around in the next few screens, where you'll be asked to enter information about yourself. To move from box to box, either use your Tab key (which will move you to the next box in line) or use your mouse to click in the next box you want to type in. When you've filled in all of the requested information, press **Enter** or click the **Continue** button.

State Your Name for the Record

In order for the folks at America Online to know who they're dealing with and to mail you information and updates to the AOL software you're using, they need to know who you are and where you live. You enter this information in a screen that looks like the following figure. Fill in all of the boxes with accurate information. If you make a typing mistake, double-click on an information box to select that information, and re-enter it.

```
┌─────────────────────────────────────────────────────────────────┐
│  ⚠  Please be sure to enter ALL of the following information accurately:  │
│                                                                   │
│  First Name: │John            │   Last Name: │Pivovarnick      │  │
│  Address:    ││                                               │   │
│  City:       │                                               │    │
│  State:      │    │        Daytime Phone: │                 │     │
│  Zip Code:   │        │     Evening Phone: │                 │     │
│                                                                   │
│  Note:  Please enter phone numbers area code first, for example, 703-555-1212, and enter │
│  state with no periods, for example, VA for Virginia.             │
│                                                                   │
│                      │ Cancel ││ Continue │                       │
└─────────────────────────────────────────────────────────────────┘
```

Tell us about yourself...

This information is *very* important because it's setting up your Master Account (that is, the account that will be billed for all the screen names and users that are registered under it). When the information is complete, press **Enter** or click on **Continue**.

Talkin' About Money, Honey...

After you enter your name, address, and telephone number(s), you'll see two informational screens that explain your billing and payment options. You'll be asked to select a payment method. The most popular method is by credit card. America Online accepts Visa, Mastercard, and American Express. If you want to use one of these credit cards, click on the card's name to select it, and then press **Enter.**

If you *don't* care to use one of these cards, click on the **More** button. You can then choose from the other two payment options: the Discover Card or payment from your checking account. The Discover Card option, like the other credit cards, bills your AOL charges to your Discover Card account each month.

The checking account option authorizes your bank to deduct the amount of your monthly online charges from your checking account and send it to America Online. This option is potentially dangerous because (like any automatic deduction from your account) if you forget to deposit enough money into your checking account, you could wind

31

up bouncing checks and incurring all manner of outrageous bank charges. (Where I bank, the bounced check charge is $30 per check—*ouch!*) If you can use one of the credit cards, I recommend that you do so (unless it's maxed out). I know how forgetful *I* can be.

When you select your payment method, you'll get a screen like the one shown here. It will be slightly different, depending on which credit card you choose. (If you choose the checking account option, it will look very different. You'll need to enter the name and address of your bank, plus your checking account number and other information.)

Enter your credit card information here.

Again, enter the information carefully. You can cancel the process by clicking on the **Cancel** button, or change your billing method by using the **Other Billing Method** button. When you're done, check the information to be sure it's correct, and then press **Enter**.

SAFETY ALERT! SAFETY ALERT!

This is the *only* time you will be asked to provide America Online with personal information (like your address) or financial information (like your credit card number)—except if you're ordering from a shopping area. If anyone *ever* asks you for such information while you are online, they're probably trying to rip you off. Do not give them the information, and report that person's screen name immediately to an on-line Guide or Customer Service representative (Chapter 8 will explain how).

Pick a Name, Any Name

After you register your payment method, you'll be asked to enter a screen name for yourself. Your screen name has a couple of functions: it's your mailing address, for when people want to send you email or other messages (Chapter 9), and it's your online name. In addition, when you're in a chat room (Chapter 10), your screen name appears on the screen of every person in that chat room whenever you "speak."

The screen name you choose must be at least three characters long, but can't be more than ten characters. It must begin with a letter, but after that it can be any combination of letters, number, or spaces. Your screen name should be representative of you. You can go with a variation of your real name (mine is Piv, for Pivovarnick), or a fictional character you like ("Godzilla" has been taken, though), or perhaps your favorite band, television show, or hobby. You can use just about any name you want, as long as it's more than three characters and fewer than ten.

You might want to make your first screen name, the one for your Master Account, some harmless version of your own name (like mine). That way, you have one name that's appropriate for use in any situation. If you care to, you can use one of your four remaining screen names to express your frivolous, funny, or wild side as you see fit. (I have one of those, too, but I'm not going to tell you what it is.) Just a thought.

Your screen name cannot be obscene (or even a form of masked obscenity, like d*mn), offensive, or insulting. Keep in mind that just because your name isn't obscene, offensive, or insulting to you, it may be offensive to someone else. Likewise, if you want people to feel free to talk to you, you should also try to avoid scary or intimidating names (oh, like Cannibal or Insane1). Otherwise, you'll have to spend a lot of time (and, therefore, money) convincing people you aren't the maniac your name implies.

Come up with a few choices before you start the registration process. Be flexible, and have some alternative choices handy. The name you want may already be taken, and if so, you won't be able to use it.

Enter the screen name of your choice in a dialog box like the one shown here. Then press **Enter** or click on **Continue**. AOL's computer checks to be sure no one else is using that name. If no one is, it's all yours.

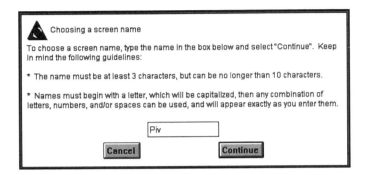

Choosing a screen name.

If your name is being used by someone, AOL will suggest a variation, usually by adding a number to the one you entered. If you entered "Godzilla," it might suggest "Godzilla99." If 99 people are already using "Godzilla," you're out of luck; a higher number will push it over the ten character limit for screen names.

You can't have the same screen name as someone else for a very simple reason: your screen name is your mailing address online. You don't want someone else getting your mail, do you? You don't want to pay for some stranger's online charges, do you? I didn't think so.

Others online will be *very* impressed if you can come up with a cool screen name without any numbers in it: that means you're the first one to think of that name, ever. It isn't easy, but it can be done.

When you finally get a name that satisfies both you and the AOL computer, it creates your master account under this name. Your master account is the main account to which your sub-accounts (other screen names you create, if any) will be billed. You won't be able to delete that name or change it, but you can add up to four additional screen names under your master account (Chapter 7 tells you how). You might want to add screen names for other members of your family/household, or even other screen names for yourself—perhaps a work name, and a play one.

Pick a Peck of Pickled Passwords

Finally, you'll be asked to select a password for your account. A password should be a word, words, or number that only *you* know. That way, no one can log on with your account, run up your bill, read your private mail, and so on.

Your password can be from four to eight characters in length, and it can be anything you choose. It should be something you can remember without writing it down, but not *so* obvious that anyone can figure it out. Don't use your phone number, your middle name, your social security number, your dog's name, or other easily obtained information.

You'll need to enter your password twice, as shown in the figure, because (for security reasons) you don't see the password as you type it; you just see a line of asterisks (****). Typing it twice ensures sure that you enter the same password both times. If they don't match, you have to start over. Type carefully.

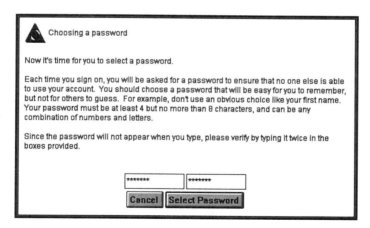

Carefully type your password twice.

If, by some chance, someone does learn your password and use your account, you will be responsible for the online charges the evil-doer incurs. So, for security's sake, you should change your password regularly. Chapter 7 tells you how.

TOS=Terms of Service

The last step in the registration process doesn't involve anything but reading. Before America Online will let you access the service, you must read and agree to the Terms of Service (TOS). They outline what is unacceptable behavior online and what are unacceptable uses of the service.

The only thing that everyone who uses America Online has in common is an interest in, or at least access to, a computer of some kind. The TOS guidelines are therefore intended to ensure that all these varied users can have a pleasant and safe time online. Read them and follow them.

You signify your acceptance of the TOS by pressing **Enter**. You are then disconnected from America Online so that you may sign on under your newly created screen name with your brand new password. For some help and advice with your first time online, turn to Chapter 5.

The Least You Need to Know

➤ You have to register with America Online before you can use the service.

➤ The registration process will go faster if you have your registration certificate, credit card or checking account information, a few screen name ideas, and a good password handy.

➤ Use your Tab key or your mouse to move from box to box when entering information. And type carefully.

➤ Your screen name must be at least three characters, but no more than ten.

➤ Your password must be at least four characters, but no more than eight. It shouldn't be something obvious; it should be something you can remember.

➤ Really *read* the Terms of Service before you agree to them.

Your First Time (I'll Be Gentle...)

Folks who've read computer books on other subjects may be scratching their heads over why I want you to jump right into America Online without some long, boring introduction to the menus, features, and such. Frankly, because it's long and boring. You'll get all that as you need it.

Pre-Launch Drill

In all my years of using AOL (and it's nearly 10 years now), I've found that before you sign on for a serious session, you should do a few things to make your sojourn online a little more pleasant:

➤ If you're so inclined, get yourself a beverage. Put it in one of those spill-proof travel-type mugs (because spilled liquids and computers are bad news).

➤ Go to the bathroom.

➤ If you have a music source nearby, play some good tunes for background.

➤ For your first few online sessions, you may want to have a pen and paper handy for jotting down Keywords (more about those in a bit) for online areas you think you'll want to explore later.

➤ Dress comfortably.

These tips will save you from having to walk away from your computer during your session (which wastes time and money) or from having to sign off, take care of business, and sign back on (which is annoying). If you've got all that together (or if you're choosing to ignore my advice), launch your AOL software by the method appropriate for your computer setup (as explained in Chapter 4).

Signing On

When your copy of AOL launches, you'll see a variation of the sign-on window shown, depending on which version you're running. The basic components remain the same.

AOL's sign-on window.

DOS screens are very different from those shown here. The plain DOS version of AOL hasn't been brought up to the same multimedia interface as the Windows and Mac versions. However, the same elements exist in your screens, and the keyboard commands are the same as for Windows; everything just looks different.

The screen name box will display the name you created during your online setup session (see Chapter 4). You'll only have one name (plus a "Guest" entry) right now, but you'll be able to add more later. When you have more (after Chapter 6 for sure), you can choose which name from the pop-up list you want to use to sign on.

You have a Guest screen name so that someone else who already has an AOL account of their own can sign on from your computer using their existing screen name and password. If your guest doesn't have an account, they have to sign on under one of your screen names with your password. Or you may want to create a new screen name for privacy's sake (both yours and theirs).

Type your password in the Password text box. Click on the Setup button to change your modem information or your local connection number. The Help button calls up AOL's Help system. We'll talk more about using the Setup button in Chapter 6 and about the Help system in Chapter 21.

To sign on:

1. Make sure the Screen Name box is showing the one you want to use (if you have more than one).

2. Type your password in the Password box.

3. Click on the **Sign On** button or press **Enter**.

Your software goes into its song-and-dance. You'll see a little screen that shows you what's happening. The software talks to your modem and then dials the first of your access numbers (if your modem has a speaker and it's turned on, you'll hear it dial). Your call is answered by the computer at the other end. You may hear some high pitched squeals; that's just the two modems getting to know each other. At this point, you are connected to your local node, and the computer there tries to hook you into America Online. You can cancel your connection at any time by clicking on the **Cancel** button.

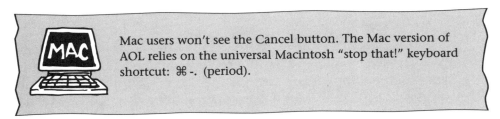

Mac users won't see the Cancel button. The Mac version of AOL relies on the universal Macintosh "stop that!" keyboard shortcut: ⌘ -. (period).

When you finally get to AOL (it takes a minute or so), your software talks to their software, they check your password, and then they let you in.

Welcome! You've Got Mail!

When you officially connect to America Online, you'll hear (yes, *hear*) a hearty "Welcome!" followed by an announcement that you've got mail. You'll also see the screens shown below.

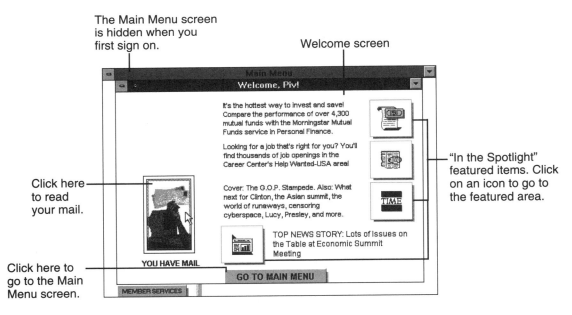

Main Menu (hidden) and Welcome screens.

Whenever you sign on to AOL, they want you to know what's happening online, so the Welcome screen shows you what areas of the service are "In the Spotlight" that day. These change almost daily, so the ones you see will be different than the previous figure. You can visit a featured area just by clicking on the icon next to the description—but don't wander off yet. Let's get through the organized portion of our tour first.

First, click on the **You Have Mail** icon to display the New Mail window. Your window will show that you've got actual *email*: Steve Case, the big kahuna of AOL, welcoming you to the service. Everyone gets a welcome letter the first time he or she signs on. To read it, click on the mail entry to select it (if it isn't already selected), and press **Enter** or click on the **Read** button. Alternatively, you can just double-click on the piece of mail you want to read. Another window opens to display the message. (This is the simplified first-look treatment on mail, so don't worry about the other buttons in any of these mail screens. Chapter 9 is devoted to the fine points of online communications.)

After you read your welcome letter, you can double-click on the **Control-menu box** or press **Ctrl+F4** to close the window. Then do the same to the New Mail window. You'll be back at the Welcome screen.

 Mac users click in the window's close box (it's in the same spot as the one indicated in the figure) or use the ⌘-**W** combination to close the mail and any windows.

Discovering America Online: The Nickel Tour

In order to painlessly introduce new users (also known as "newbies") to the variety of features and services available online, AOL provides a quick, eight-part tour of the service. To begin, click on the **Go to Main Menu** button at the bottom of the Welcome screen. It will take you to the Main Menu as shown on the following page.

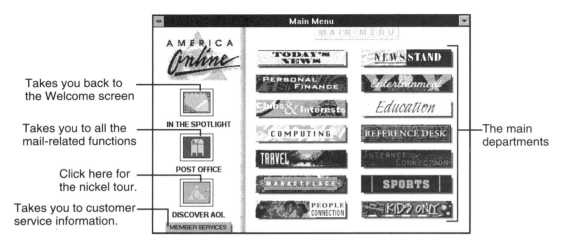

Takes you back to the Welcome screen

Takes you to all the mail-related functions

Click here for the nickel tour.

Takes you to customer service information.

The main departments

The Main Menu: AOL's Main Street.

The Main Menu is the crossroads of America Online: you can get anywhere from here. The right side of the screen contains the 14 general departments. Click on an icon to go to a department that interests you—but not yet. The left side of the screen has four icons. The top one, In the Spotlight, takes you back to the Welcome screen. The Post Office icon gives you access to all of the mail-related facilities. The Discover AOL button is the one we're interested in; it takes you on the tour. Below that is a teeny-tiny icon (Member Services) that, when you click on it, takes you to a free area where you can get help, information, and other useful stuff. We'll talk about Member Services in Chapters 6 and 21. For now, click on the **Discover AOL** icon. The following screen appears.

The nickel tour.

You can take the tour in any order and go as deeply into the areas discussed as you care to. The following list briefly explains what each area is all about, in the order in which they appear on-screen. To go to an area, just click on its icon. When you're through with each area of the tour, just close that area's window(s) as you did the mail windows earlier, until you're back at the Discover America Online window. When you're finished with the tour, close the Discover America Online window, and you'll be back at the main menu. Ready? Let's go.

➤ **A Letter From Steve**   Every month, head honcho Steve Case writes an open letter to all the members of America Online, bringing them up to date on new developments, features, and services online. The letter is usually featured on the Welcome/In the Spotlight screen, but if it isn't, you can find it here.

➤ **America Online Highlights**   The Highlights area is a somewhat more expanded tour, showing you twelve of the popular areas (from the thousands). To take the expanded tour, click the **America Online Highlights** button. Click on the **Start** button on the Highlights screen, and then follow the on-screen instructions.

➤ **New Features & Services**   Click on the **New Features & Services** icon to see a listing of the features and services that have been recently added to America Online. You can use it to read a description of each of the new areas or to actually go to them.

➤ **Directory of Services**   You can use the Directory of Services to search for areas that match your interests. Read the "How to Search the Directory" text before you search (you'll need to double-click on it in the scroll box); it gives you valuable tips.

You can also check out the Calendar of Events for special events and guest appearances by major and minor celebrities. Double-click on the **Calendar of Events** item in the scroll box. Then double-click the calendar of your choice (there are several).

➤ **The Best of America Online**   The "Best of" area gives you information about 25 of the most popular features and services. Double-click on any list item for information and/or access to the area described.

➤ **America Online Store**   Part of the shopping extravaganza available online, the America Online store gives you the opportunity to buy stuff with the AOL logo on it. All of the online shopping opportunities are covered in Chapter 16.

➤ **America Online Press Releases** Can't get enough information about AOL? Go to the press release area to read every bit of press that AOL has released about itself—ever.

➤ **What's Hot This Month** This area gives you information about the hot files to download, new areas, and any contests that are running online. Double-click on any topic to read more about it.

Getting Around

At this point, you may be champing at the bit to explore. That's cool, and you'll have your chance. But first let me explain some of the ways you can get around the service, and how to find your way home should you get lost.

Menus

The most helpful menus in your initial exploration will be the Go To and Window menus (we'll look at the other menus in upcoming chapters as you need them). The Go To menu takes you to ten popular areas (listed at the bottom of the menu) and takes you back to the Main Menu or the Welcome/In the Spotlight screen should you get lost somewhere. In Chapter 22, we'll use the Edit Favorite Places command to change these ten areas to your favorites.

You can also use the Go To menu to perform some of the more common searches online by choosing the Search Directory of Services, Search Software Libraries, or Search Today's News commands. The Lobby menu item takes you to a general chat area (discussed in Chapter 10). Network News shows you an information screen that tells you if something interesting is going on *right now*. The Online Clock item tells you what time it is (in military time) and how long you've been online—very handy for knowing your online time and charges.

The Window menu is handy for your exploration because it helps you keep track of the windows you have open. The top portion lets you arrange your windows for easy access (personally, I find the Cascade option handiest). It also lets you close all of the open windows in one fell swoop, in case you get incredibly confused. (Then you can use the Go To menu to get back to the Main Menu or wherever.)

You'll only use the Exit Free Area command when you use Member Services. (That's discussed in Chapter 20.) The Remember/Forget

Window Size and Position commands will tell your AOL where and how you like your windows displayed. So far, I've only used these for email (Chapter 9) and chat room (Chapter 10) windows. You may find other uses.

The bottom part lists all of the windows you have open. Selecting one of them brings that window to the front of your screen—very handy if you get lost in a sea of windows.

The Windows Menu Bar

Mac and DOS users can skip this section—you don't have it.

Windows users, beneath your menu headings is a row of colorful icons that you can also use to get around AOL and/or do stuff. Clicking on any of the menu bar's icons gives you access to an area or function of America Online. The following table describes the menu bar icons from left to right.

Icon	Name	Description
	New Mail	For when you get mail while online
	Compose Mail	When you want to drop someone a note
	Main Menu	Brings the Main Menu front and center on your screen
	Welcome Screen	Also known as **In The Spotlight**
	Help	Opens AOL's help screens on- and off-line
	Directory of Services	A list of everything available online
	People Connection	The chat areas (see Chapter 10)
	Quotes and Portfolios	Stock market and financial services and information
	Today's News	A list of today's top news stories

continues

Continued

Icon	Name	Description
	Center Stage	Where many online events happen
	Internet Connection	(See Chapter 17)
	New Features	New services and areas online
	Discover AOL	An introductory tour
	Keyword	(More on this in a second)
	Download Manager	(See Chapter 12)
	File Search	(Also Chapter 12)
	Online Clock	Tells you the time and how long you've been online
	Personal Choices	(See Chapter 6)
	Print	Prints the text in the topmost window, if it can be printed
	Save Text	Saves the text in the topmost window to your hard drive, if it can be saved

If you can't use a menu bar function, the icon for it will fade out.

Keywords for Rapid Transit

As you were going through the Discover AOL section, you may have noticed that many of the areas had the word "Keyword:" (followed by a word or two) at the bottom of their screens. Keywords provide you with an easy way to get where you're going. To use a Keyword, click on the **Keyword** icon in the menu bar or select **Keyword** from the **Go To** menu. You can also use the keyboard shortcut **Ctrl+K**. You'll see the Keyword dialog box shown in the following figure. On a Mac, the keyboard shortcut for Keywords is ⌘-K.

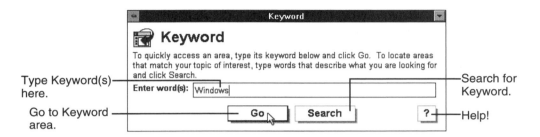

The Keyword dialog box.

Type the Keyword you want to use in the text box and press **Enter** or click the **Go** button.

You'll find Keywords all over AOL. They're at the bottom of most department screens. You'll also find a list of all the current Keywords (from the time of this writing) in Chapter 23. If you find an area you think you'll want to visit often, write down the Keyword for it. You can use the Keyword to get there in a hurry, and you can even use it to add that area to your Go To menu (which I'll show you in Chapter 6).

Signing Off

Once you've explored all the bits of AOL that you care to explore, end your session by signing off. Signing off disconnects you from the service and your local access node. You can sign off in a couple of ways:

➤ Select **Sign Off** from the Go To menu. This disconnects you from AOL but leaves your AOL software running.

➤ Select Exit from the File menu. This disconnects you from AOL and shuts down your AOL software.

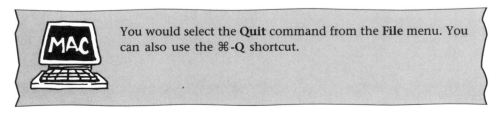

You would select the **Quit** command from the **File** menu. You can also use the ⌘-Q shortcut.

Whichever method you choose, you'll get a dialog box asking whether you're sure you want to sign off. You'll have the option of signing off, staying online, or signing off and exiting the AOL application. Click on the one you want, and you're out of there.

The Least You Need to Know

The information you picked up in this chapter is pretty important. Aside from the Discover AOL tour, it's all information you'll use every time you sign on.

➤ Signing on is as simple as selecting a screen name, entering a password, and pressing **Enter**.

➤ The Welcome (or In The Spotlight) screen highlights the latest developments online and gives you speedy access to your new email, if any is waiting for you.

➤ The Main Menu gives you access to all of the departments online.

➤ The Windows menu bar gives you fast access to popular features.

➤ Use Keywords to get to your favorite areas quickly. Press **Ctrl+K** on on your keyboard (⌘-**K** on a Mac), type in the Keyword, and press **Enter**. You're there!

➤ Signing off is easy, too. It's the first option on the **Go To** menu.

Chapter 6

Preferential Treatment: Setting Preferences

In This Chapter

➤ Changing your setup

➤ Preferences you can change offline

➤ Preferences you have to change online

➤ Parental control

Now that you've had your first session online, you have more of an idea (though probably not a complete idea) of what AOL is and how it works. You may not care for some of what it does, but you'll be happy to know that you can change a lot of it. This chapter shows you how.

Network and Modem Stuff

There are a number of America Online features you can tailor to suit your needs while you're *off*line, thereby saving yourself some money on your phone bill. Let's start with two of the more important ones: your network and modem configuration.

Network The "network" of Network & Modem Setup refers to the telephone network (SprintNet, Tymnet, and so on) that you use to connect to America Online.

Offline means that you aren't connected to America Online (or any other online service) and, therefore, are not being charged.

Online means that you are connected to AOL (or another online service) and are being charged for your connection time and any long-distance charges you're incurring.

You might want to change your network and modem setup for any number of reasons: you're buying a new, faster modem; you're moving and need to change your local access number; or your current access number is always busy. To change your setup, begin by launching AOL. When it's running, and you see the sign-on screen, click on the **Setup** button. The Network & Modem Setup dialog box appears.

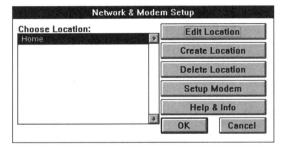

AOL for Windows Network & Modem Setup window.

Mac users won't get this intermediate screen. When you click on Setup, you'll go directly to a screen like the one coming up next.

DOS users won't get this intermediate screen. When you click on Setup, you'll go directly to a screen like the one coming up next.

We aren't going to concern ourselves with the Create and Delete Location buttons here. You'll only use them when you're traveling and want to access AOL from different places on the road. All that's covered in Chapter 18.

Changing Your Network Settings

From the Network & Modem Setup dialog box, click on the **Edit Location** button. AOL displays the Network Setup screen. From this screen, you can change the type of phone line you have (from pulse to touchtone), and you can enter a new local access number (AOL adds new ones all the time). You can change your modem's baud rate (speed) if you get a faster modem. (You may also have to change your Modem Setup; that's coming up next.)

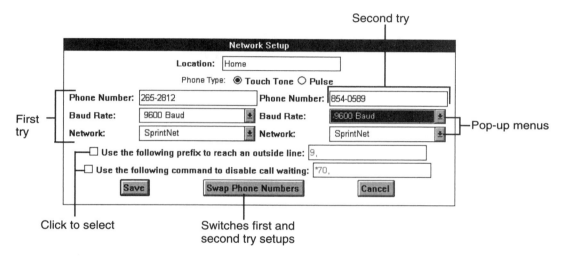

America Online for Windows Network Setup dialog box.

If you enter a new access number, you may have to pick a new Network entry from the pop-up menu (where it says "SprintNet" in the figure). The correct network information will be right next to each phone number when you look up new ones online (Chapter 18 explains how). Just choose the same network from the pop-up menu.

You can also make your AOL software dial a "9" or other number if you need to dial a certain number to get an outside line. (Most users won't need this unless they use America Online at work or where all outgoing calls are routed through a switchboard of some kind.) To do this, click on the check box in front of **Use the following prefix to reach an outside line** option. Change the number in the text box if you need to; the default is 9.

The highest "official" modem speed for AOL right now is 9600 baud. However, if you have a modem that goes 14,400 or faster, you *might* be able to use 14,400. In the Setup window, set your modem speed to 14,400 baud. Make sure you have a 9600 baud SprintNet number entered as your local access number. Try signing on.

If you live in or near a big city (New York, L.A., San Francisco, Philadelphia, Atlanta, and so on), you might just be able to bluff your way through at the higher speed. Most 9600 lines are also capable of handling 14,400 baud communications. AOL's modems can also handle it. It's sneaky right now but will probably be "official" by the time you read this.

Keep your eyes peeled—AOL is in the process of testing a new way of accessing the service that will allow speeds up to 28,800 baud. Woof, that's fast.

If you have call waiting, select the Disable call waiting option in this dialog box to disable it whenever you sign on to America Online. The clicking noise that an incoming call makes can disrupt the flow of information to your computer. You might find yourself suddenly disconnected—and that's no fun.

If you always seem to get a busy signal on your first attempt to connect to AOL, but you usually get through on the second attempt, click on the **Swap Phone Numbers** button. Your second try phone number magically becomes your first, and vice versa.

Bummer. Mac users don't get the Swap Phone Numbers button. If you want to swap them, you have to do it manually. No one said life is fair.

When you've made all the changes you care to make, click on the **Save** button to make your changes permanent. If you don't want to save your changes, click the **Cancel** button.

Pick a Modem

If you've upgraded to a new, zippier modem, you need to tell your AOL software what kind it is. To do that, click on the **Setup Modem** button. You'll see a screen like the one following.

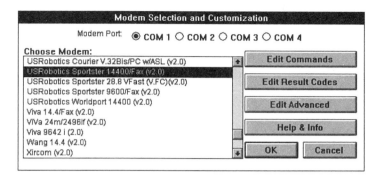

Modem selection is as easy as clicking on a name.

Mac users won't have this screen either. You can change your modem and port selection at the bottom of your Setup screen. From the pop-up lists, choose your modem's name (or one that's compatible) and the port where it's connected.

DOS users: your modem setup screen is a little harder to find. Here's how:

1. Click **Setup** in the sign on window.

2. Click on the **Advanced Setup** button at the bottom of the setup screen.

3. Click on the **System Preferences** button at the bottom of *that* screen.

4. Click on the **Modem** button (bottom center) of that screen. Here you can change the port where your modem is connected, and the type of phone line (pulse or touch-tone).

5. To change your modem speed, click on the **Speed and Format Options** button. Check your modem's manual for the proper settings here.

Then you have to dig your way out by clicking a lot of **OK** buttons, closing screens, and getting back to where you started.

When computer equipment is **compatible** to another similar piece of equipment, it means they work pretty much the same. Specifically, Hayes compatible means that a modem conforms to the standard commands set by the Hayes Corporation. Most modems are Hayes compatible.

If you changed the port where your modem is connected, click on the appropriate radio button at the top of the dialog box. If you also changed modems, you need to scroll through the list on the left side of the dialog box until you see the name of your modem (or a compatible one—check your modem's manual). Click on the name of the modem to select it.

If your modem (or a compatible modem) is listed, you won't need to fool with the three Edit buttons beside the scroll box. If not, you really need to read your modem manual and enter all of the information requested in the screens brought up by the Edit Commands, Edit Result Codes, and Edit Advanced buttons. Don't panic, though—most popular modems *are* listed. When you're done, click on the **OK** button.

Which Do You Prefer?

The next set of preferences makes your AOL software behave the way you want it to. Once again, you don't have to be online to change the preferences covered here. Save yourself some cash and do it offline. To begin, select **Set Preferences** from the Members menu. The Preferences window appears.

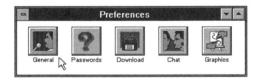

America Online for Windows Preferences.

On a Mac, selecting Set Preferences from the Members menu brings up a window with two scrollable lists. The left side of the screen lists all of the general categories of things you can change; the right side of the screen lists the individual items you can change in each category.

On the whole, simply double-clicking an item on the right side of your screen will turn that item on or off. (It's turned on when a check mark appears before the entry.) Font preferences, however, call up a dialog box where you can select the actual fonts used for a number of features. Let your taste and your eyesight be your guides. Although you access them differently, the features you can change remain comparable to the Windows version of AOL, so read on for more details.

 DOS users have a simplified version of the preferences screen that doesn't involve opening other screens (probably to compensate for the modem settings being so difficult to access). Simply click on the preference items you care to turn on or off. A preference is activated (on) when the diamond in front of the entry goes dark. Although you access them differently, the features you can change remain comparable to the Windows version of AOL, so read on for more details.

General Preferences

To access the General Preferences screen, click the **General** icon in the Preferences box. The General Preferences screen lets you display the Main Menu at sign on, receive Network News and close your mail after it's been sent (which can keep you from accidentally sending mail twice). This screen also enables you to set the size of text to small, medium, or large. You can also enable chat and event room sounds, which are a lot of fun but can slow things down. (You'll hear more about sounds in Chapter 10.)

The last item in the General Preferences screen sets AOL so that incoming documents scroll as you receive them. I leave this one turned off, because it means that you wind up at the end of all the text you get. You may want to try it both ways before you decide. To select any of these preferences, just click in the check box before each entry or in the radio buttons before the font sizes, and then click **OK**.

The Password Is...

Click on the **Passwords** icon in the Preferences box to open the window that lets you store passwords for each of your screen names.

Simply click in the text box after the screen name and type the correct password. Click **OK** when you're finished.

If you store your passwords, you won't ever have to enter a password when you want to sign on or use a FlashSession (more about those in Chapters 9 and 12). However, it also means that anyone with access to your computer can sign on with your account and run up your phone bill and online charges. Think carefully about your computer's security before you store your passwords.

Mac users don't have a Password option in their Preferences screen. To store your password(s), select **Edit Stored Passwords** from the Members menu. You can specify whether a user can use the selected screen name and password to sign on, to use a FlashSession, or both.

DOS users can't store their passwords. Sorry.

Download Preferences

Click the **Download** icon to open the Download Preferences dialog box. In this dialog box, you can set what happens to and with files you're *downloading* (copying from the AOL computers to your own). Although this box won't make much sense until you read Chapter 12, here are the options:

➤ Display image (picture) files on download

➤ Automatically decompress files at sign off

➤ Delete ZIP and ARC files after decompression

➤ Confirm additions to my download list

➤ Retain information about my last 20 downloads (you can adjust the number of files, too)

In my software, all these options are turned on. You may want to wait until you've read Chapter 12 before you fiddle with them. Click on **OK** when you're done setting these options.

Mac users only have three downloading options: you can decompress files at sign off, delete compressed files, and confirm additions to the download list.

DOS users have the same options, except for the Display image files on download option. The DOS version of AOL can't display images.

Chat Preferences

To access the Chat Preferences dialog box, click the **Chat** icon in the Preferences box. The Chat Preferences you can set to your liking include: notification of when members enter your room, notification of when they leave, double-spacing of incoming messages (otherwise, it's single-spaced), an alphabetical member list, and enabling (turning on) chat room sounds.

You might not want to adjust these until you've read Chapter 10 or spent a little more time in chat rooms online. Click on **OK** when you're done.

Mac users only have two Chat options: double-space text and enable chat room sounds.

The only option DOS users have is whether chat text appears double-spaced.

For Your Graphics Viewing Pleasure

The final preference screen is the Graphics Viewing Preferences screen. To get at it, click the **Graphics** icon in the Preferences dialog box. You can choose to display image files on download (again) and can set JPEG (a type of graphic format) compression quality.

The more you compress JPEG images, the worse they may look on your screen. JPEGs lose detail and can become very spotty looking when highly compressed (so do I, for that matter).

If you find your displayed or downloaded images look like someone's been playing with the color knob on your television, you may want to use the **Set Color Mode** option. It lets you tell your software specifically how many colors your monitor can display (from 16 to over 256). If you don't tell your software how many colors your monitor can handle, the software guesses, and it may guess incorrectly. So, you might want play with some images online before you fiddle with these settings.

Mac users only have two Graphics Viewing options: display on download and Use System Colors. The second uses your Mac's normal color assortment (8 colors) for the picture files displayed. Try it to see if you like it.

 DOS users don't have Graphics Viewing Preferences, because you can't view graphics online or while downloading.

And that's it for the preferences you can set without signing on. Okay, okay, to be honest, you can also edit your Go To menu. That's a time/money saving tip, and it's covered in Chapter 22.

Preferences Online

You can change other features and functions of America Online, but you have to be signed on to change them. Once you've signed on, select **Personal Choices** from the Members menu. You'll see a window like the one shown below.

Here's a money-saving tip: You can access all of the online preferences in the Member Services area, which is free of online charges. Just click on the Go To menu and select **Member Services**. Click **Yes** when asked if you really want to enter the free area. Then select **Personal Choices** from the Members menu.

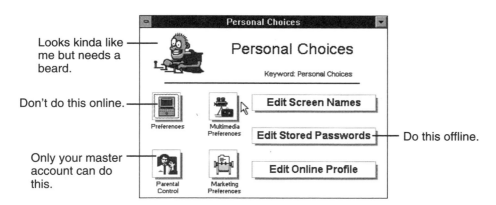

The Personal Choices dialog box.

If you're a DOS user, you don't have a Personal Choices menu item, nor can you fiddle with the multimedia preferences (since you're not multimedia capable). However, you can edit your screen names and online profile, as described here, by selecting the appropriate item from your Members menu. To exercise Parental Control, use the Keyword: PARENTAL CONTROL.

Let's look at each function in the Personal Choices dialog box, starting with the buttons on the left side of the window.

Preferences

Don't waste your time here. These preferences are the same ones we just fiddled with offline. Unless you decide while you're online that one of them desperately needs to be changed, do it after you've signed off. Why spend the money?

Multimedia Preferences

AOL's new multimedia interface lets you look at picture files while you're online—you couldn't do that before. It's very cool, but it can take time on slower computer systems. Clicking the Multimedia Preferences icon opens a dialog box that lets you turn off pictures so you only see the ones you want, or so they're only displayed when you connect to AOL at 9600 baud or higher. You may want to try AOL with multimedia turned on just to see how it works; if it's annoying or if it's too slow on your computer, then decide.

Don't bother with the Other Graphics Options button in the Multimedia Preferences dialog box unless you need to. It accesses the same graphics options we set offline. Click **OK** when you're finished fiddling.

Parental Control

This option is NOT about controlling your parents. Give it up. I already tried. It's for parents to control their child's access to some of the features of America Online. Kids—don't read this. Now that it's adults only...

You can only activate Parental Control with your master account (the screen name you created when you first joined America Online). Click the **Parental Control** icon to open a dialog box in which you can restrict other accounts' usage of the following four parts of the service. You can restrict any or all of these parts.

➤ **Block All Instant Messages** This keeps the specified screen name from receiving instant messages (IMs) from other users while online. (IMs are covered in Chapter 9.)

➤ **Block All Rooms** Check this option to prevent the specified screen name from entering *all* of the chat rooms in the People Connection. (The People Connection area is covered in Chapter 10.)

➤ **Block Member Rooms** Click this option to prevent the specific screen name from entering member-created rooms in the People Connection. He or she can still enter AOL sponsored rooms such as LaPub and Teen Chat.

➤ **Block Conference Rooms** Select this option to block entrance to conference rooms, chat-type rooms located in most forums (see Chapter 11).

Just click the appropriate box(es) after the screen name(s) for which you want to restrict access. Click **OK** when you're finished.

Marketing Preferences

In an age in which enormous quantities of junk mail fly around, many companies (America Online included) make a few extra bucks by selling lists of their clients' names and addresses. In the Marketing Preferences window, you can specify whether you want AOL to pass your name around. This window even gives you tips on how to cut down on the number of sales phone calls and the amount of junk mail you generally receive. Check it out by clicking on the **Marketing Preferences** icon.

Edit Screen Names

Selecting the Edit Screen Names button accesses a window with a scrollable list of options. The first few will be information about screen names, the screen name policy (definitely read it), and how to create and delete screen names.

To create a screen name, double-click on the (*duh*) **Create a Screen Name** item in the list. You'll see a screen exactly like the one you used to create your very first screen name (back in Chapter 4, if you need a refresher). You can add up to four more screen names to your account, each with its own password (which you'll create in a minute). A screen name can be 3 to 10 characters long and contain any combination of letters, numbers, and spaces—as long as the first character is a letter.

Type the screen name you want to create, and press **Enter**. If the screen name is not in use, it's yours. If someone got to it first, you'll be offered a reasonable facsimile. Keep trying until you're happy with it. Once AOL accepts your screen name, you'll be asked to set a password for it (also as you did back in Chapter 4). Make sure the password is one that the user can spell and one that others won't be able to figure out easily.

To delete a screen name, double-click on the **Delete a Screen Name** item in the scrolling list. Type in the screen name you want to delete, and press **Enter**. That screen name is gone forever (really—you can't get it back), so be sure you mean it before you delete it.

Edit Stored Passwords

Been there, done that. Don't do this online—it's a waste of money since you can do it offline for free (it's covered earlier in this chapter).

Edit Online Profile

Your online profile is a short-and-sweet autobiography with bits of information about you. If other folks online are curious about you, they can read it using the Get Info command on the Members menu, and you can read theirs, too.

If you want to create one, click on **Edit Online Profile.** You'll get a Profile window with a scrollable list of options. You might want to read the About Member Profiles information before you create your own; just double-click on it to read it. When you're ready to create your profile, double-click on **Create/Modify Your Member Profile** (this also works if you want to change an existing profile later on). You'll see a screen like the following figure.

```
┌──────────────────────────────────────────────────────────────┐
│ ▬              Edit Your Online Profile                 ▼ ▲   │
├──────────────────────────────────────────────────────────────┤
│ To edit your profile, modify the category you would like to   │
│ change and select                                             │
│ "Update." To continue without making any changes to your      │
│ profile, select "Cancel."                                     │
│                                                                │
│ Your Name:          │John Pivovarnick                       │ │
│                                                                │
│ City, State, Country:│Philadelphia, PA                      │ │
│                                                                │
│ Birthday:           │12/01/60                  │               │
│                                                                │
│ Sex:           ● Male        ○ Female        ○ No Response     │
│                                                                │
│ Marital Status:   ● Single  ○ Married  ○ Divorced/Separated    │
│                   ○ No Response                                │
│                                                                │
│ Hobbies:     │ues, Collecting, Cooking/Dining, reading,      │ │
│              │Movies/TV, Music, Science/Nature              │ │
│                                                                │
│ Computers Used: │Mac II, IBM PC, Other Macs                 │ │
│                                                                │
│ Occupation:    │Writer, MacHead, looking for love in all    │ │
│                │the wrong places                            │ │
│                                                                │
│ Personal Quote: │Complete Idiot's Guides to Macs and        │ │
│                 │CD-ROM, Home Computer Companion            │ │
│                                                                │
│                 [Update] [Cancel] [Help]                      │
└──────────────────────────────────────────────────────────────┘
```

My online profile. No giggling.

Just click in each text area to activate it and type in what you want to say. Tab to the next area and type, then tab and type, and so on until you're done. You can be as vague or specific as you care to be. You may also leave any area blank that you don't care to answer (it's better to leave it blank than to resort to a lie—*I* think, anyhow).

When you're done, press **Enter**, and your profile is saved to the AOL computer. From then on, when people call up your profile, they'll see the information in a window.

Billing Information

When, in the course of human events (like holiday shopping) you run up your credit card past the credit limit, you may need to change your method of payment. You can do that by going to Member Services (covered in detail in Chapter 20) with your Go To menu, or by using the Keyword: BILLING.

You can use the Billing area to review last month's bill, check the current month's bill, and/or change your method of payment, should you want to. You follow the same process you did when you provided your payment information for the first time back in Chapter 4. Go back there if you need the details again, but it's easy enough.

Passwords

As a security precaution, every AOL user in your home should change passwords regularly—once a month, if not more often. The longer you use a password, the more likely someone will figure out what it is and be able to use it. To change your password, use the Keyword: PASSWORD. It will take you to the Password section of the free Member Services area.

You'll be asked to type in your old password, and then type in your new password twice (to make sure you can type it twice exactly the same). Click on **Change Password**, and your password change is completed. Just don't forget your new password. You can only change the password for the account you signed on with, so you need to sign on under each of your screen names to change all those passwords.

The Least You Need to Know

Everything should be set to your liking now (or at least you know what your options are), so you're good to go. Anything you set, changed, or otherwise tinkered with in this chapter can be changed back at any time (except the deletion of a screen name). So don't be afraid to try different settings on for size until you find the set of preferences that works best for you. Here's what you should keep in mind:

➤ To change your modem or network preferences, click the **Setup** button in the sign-on window. You can do this before you go online to save some money.

➤ You also can tinker with some other preferences while you're offline by choosing **Set Preferences** from the Members menu.

➤ Some preferences have to be set online (creating screen names, creating member profiles, changing passwords). Go to the *free* Member Services area so you don't have to pay online charges while tinkering.

➤ Change your password frequently, especially if a lot of people have access to your computer. Use the Keyword: PASSWORD to go to the Password section of the free Member Services area.

Part 2
Cruisin'

Part 1 got you set up and signed on to America Online. Like a first swimming lesson, it was a chance to hold your nose and stick your face in the water without feeling too threatened. Now you're ready to do some real swimming—or "cruisin'" as the name of this part implies.

In the next chapters, you'll learn your way around the major (and minor) AOL departments, as well as how to chat, correspond with email and IMs (immediate messages), find and download files, upload your own creations, and do piles of other stuff.

Before you begin, though, there's a fun little chapter about the etiquette of this brave new world called America Online. You should definitely read it. In the online world, as in the "real" world, politeness counts. So turn the page and let's get this party started.

THE HONESTY OF AMERICA ONLINE

Chapter 7

Aunt Effie's Guide to Online Etiquette

In This Chapter

➤ Safety tips

➤ Public and private behavior

➤ Rules for gracious living in the digital world

Aunt Effie's a lovely woman with whom I sometimes consult over Earl Grey tea and finger sandwiches. She mediates the complexities of life online the way Emily Post and Miss Manners have done for the non-digital world. If you run into a nagging point of online etiquette, you can send questions for Aunt Effie to the author at the screen name **Piv**. The following letters and responses from the Aunt Effie Archives deal with some of the most common etiquette issues.

Safety First!

Dear Aunt Effie:

I hear horror stories on the news about people who are victimized via online services in the form of credit card scams, child pornography, and even stalking. Is this stuff really happening, or is the media just trying to scare us?

Signed, Afraid to turn on my computer

Dear Afraid:

Is this stuff happening? Yes. Is the media trying to scare you? Yes again. Have you noticed how you only hear these stories during ratings or "sweeps" periods? I think broadcasters will use any excuse to get sexually explicit or frightening matter on the news.

But, dearie, the digital world is just a smaller version of the rest of the world. In today's world, there's crime, child abuse, discrimination—you name it, it's out there. And it's also online. The same folks who do unkind, rude, or misguided deeds out there also do them online. Even though you're using an online service from the safety of your own home or another comfortable location, you should behave just as you would traveling the streets of any large city. Protect yourself by following some basic safety tips:

You don't have to avoid talking to strangers. However, don't give out any information online that you wouldn't want people offline to have, such as your phone, long distance, or credit card numbers; home address; work address; and anything that you wouldn't want generally known.

If someone harasses you in any way and by any means (live chat, email, IMs), you don't have to take it. Report the offending person to the nearest Guide, or use the Guide Pager (see Chapter 10). Get the offender's screen name, the name of the room in which the incident occurred, the time the offense took place, and a sample of the offensive language or behavior (as distasteful as it may be for you to repeat it, it *must* be done). When you've got all that together (and it's very easy if you know how to use the Copy and Paste commands), you might want to ignore the offensive person with the **Ignore** command (that's in Chapter 10, too). Don't allow yourself to be a victim—it's no fun.

Signed, Aunt Effie

Be Polite and Courteous

Dear Aunt Effie:

I was online the other night with my buddy, and we were goofing around the way we usually do, you know, calling each other names (booger breath, doody brain, and so on) when suddenly other people in the chat room started getting on our cases, calling us names that really hurt. Why? We were just fooling around.

Signed, Not a booger brain

Dear Boog:

When you talk to someone in person, that person and others can tell whether you're kidding by your tone of voice, the look in your eyes, or the smile on your face. These are all *visual clues* that help people figure out what you're really trying to say. But when you're online, no one can see you. So that rich source of visual information is cut off. The onlookers who picked on you may have thought there was a real fight brewing and either wanted to stop it, egg it on, or join right in. That's probably why you got the response you did.

The rule of thumb online is the tried and true golden rule: treat everyone the way you want to be treated. If you and your buddy have a thing for calling each other "doody brains" in fun, you need to learn how to use shorthands and smilies (as discussed in Chapter 10) to let other folks online know that you're having harmless fun.

However, I feel I must comment on the use of words like "doody" in general. Even sanitized scatological references (such as "doody," "poopy," and the like) may make other chatters uncomfortable. Just as others online can't see the visual clues that let them in on your joke, you also can't tell what age other chatters might be, or whether your off-color comments are embarrassing or angering them. I would refrain from using such language; if you can't resist, confine it to private communications such as IMs (discussed in Chapter 9). When in doubt, don't.

Signed, Aunt Effie

NO SHOUTING!!!!

Dear Eff, bubeleh:

I'm an older single gentleman of comfortable means, but with poor eyesight. I occasionally use AOL to rendezvous with a certain Alaskan lady friend to chat. She's a retired person who also has eye trouble. When we are in a chat room, we type in ALL CAPITAL LETTERS so we can easily pick out each other's chat from the general chat. We've repeatedly been asked not to type in capitals. Why?

Signed, SHLOMO S.

Dear Shlo, my little kugel:

TYPING IN ALL CAPS IS LIKE SHOUTING AND IS CONSIDERED RUDE. You and your lady friend's visual concerns are legitimate, but there are other ways of going easy on your eyesight than resorting to all capital letters. You can highlight each other's chat, so you can spot it easily. You may also want to increase the size and spacing of the fonts (the letters on your computer screen) that you use online generally, and for chat especially. Chapter 10 explains highlighting. Chapter 6 explains how to change the font size and other customizable features of AOL.

And just for your information, since you're both "of a certain age" and apparently enjoy computers, you might want to check out the SeniorNet area on AOL (Keyword: SENIORNET). It's a group of folks aged 55 and older who are using their later years to learn whatever they can about computers and computing.

And, Shlo, darling, should anything (God forbid) happen to your lady friend, call me—we'll talk.

Signed, Your Maiden Aunt Effie (wink, wink)

Public Behavior

Dear Aunt Effie:

I'm a twelve-year-old girl. I was in a chat room the other night and all the other teens (at least I think they were teens, grownups don't act like this, do they?) wanted to talk about, like, oh, you know—mushy and dirty stuff. And someone kept calling me a "MorF!"

Signed, Sweet Polly Pureheart

Dear Sweet PP:

I know some fifty-year-olds who act like randy teens. Don't assume they were all teens—and don't assume that one who speaks like a grandmother is a grandmother either. You just can't tell for sure. That's one of the nice things about being online: not being able to "see" puts everyone on a level playing field. But it's one of the hazards, too.

I suggest that if you don't care for the general conversation in a room, move on until you find one you *do* like. If it's really offensive (people using words they couldn't say on television), you might want to report it to a Guide.

As for people calling you a "MorF," they weren't calling you a name, my pet, they were asking your gender. "MorF" is a typing shorthand for "Male or Female?" Most people prefer to flirt with a specific gender, and the MorF in question wanted to be sure you were his/her type before the eyelash batting began.

Some folks with genderless screen names get awfully tired of being "MorFed" as it is called and of the seemingly endless "Age and location checks" where everyone is expected to state their name, gender, age, and location for general consumption. I think it's perfectly acceptable to avoid answering the question. If you don't care to disclose your gender, a simple "yes" is the most evasive answer. When asked my age, I generally say it's "Under the speed limit—except in a school zone." However, I think it is *totally* inappropriate to chat under an assumed gender (or age, or ethnic background, or anything). Either don't say anything, or be honest.

Signed, Aunt Effie

Privacy, Please!

Dear Aunt Effie:

The other night online, someone I didn't know asked me if I "wanted to go private." I don't know what that means, so I said "No, thank you." Did I miss out on something fun?

Signed, Cautious in Carlisle

Dear CC:

You've discovered, all on your own, one of Aunt Effie's favorite mottoes: "When in doubt, don't." Good for you! As for whether you missed out on something fun, it depends on how old you are and what your idea of "fun" is. Here's how it works.

Chatting in public rooms (where anyone can walk in and join the conversation) is regulated by the somewhat strict, but fair and necessary, Terms of Service agreement that everyone should have read when they first joined. That means strictly G-rated, or at most PG-rated, conversations. Conversations are kept on track by the Guide Staff and other members, and you can be fairly sure that you won't encounter anything too offensive for too long. That's in a public room.

When someone asks you to "go private," they're asking you to enter what's known as a private room, where only the people who know the room's name can enter. These rooms are not moderated, and conversation is pretty much "anything goes."

There are private rooms where Alcoholics Anonymous-type groups meet (while maintaining their own anonymity) without strangers wandering in. HIV+/AIDS patients meet in a private room to frankly discuss their condition and offer support and advice. And sometimes friends get together in a private room simply so they can converse without having to keep up (or put up) with a dozen other conversations going on around them.

However, on the other hand, there are people who use private rooms as a sort of 900- number, to talk in explicit sexual language to each other. Depending on how you feel about such conversations, you may want to politely refuse invitations to "go private," or you may not.

If you care to go private, Chapter 10 tells you how to create and/or enter a private room. If you are concerned about young people getting an eyeful in a private room, Chapter 6 covers the use of Parental Control, which enables you to restrict their access to member-created rooms.

Signed, Aunt Effie

For (Whatevers) Only

Dear Aunt Effie:

I was online last night looking for chicks to chat up. I found a room called "Women Only" and thought it would be an ideal place to meet babes. I wasn't in there for two minutes when they were asking me to leave. Is that completely rude or what?

Signed, A Babe Magnet

Dear Magnet:

Aunt Effie has only one good nerve left, and you're getting on it. While I, personally, do not care for the exclusionary nature of Public Rooms with "Only" as part of the name, I do understand the reasoning behind them.

Not only women, but ethnic, religious, or sexual minorities, and even hobbyists, create Only-type rooms so they can discuss topics of relevance to their group without the distraction of having to sift through lots of unrelated chat. If I were in a room aimed at specific members (in this case, women) and you simply barged in and started blathering "Hey, baby what's your sign? Where you from?" and other singles-bar babble, I would have no choice but to call the Politeness Patrol myself and have you taken to the Romance Connection. That's what it's there for (see Chapter 15).

On the other hand, if you are truly curious and open to learning about whatever group is meeting in the room, you should ask politely if you can listen in and ask questions before you join in. If you are asked to leave because you are a non-whatever, I would have to sic the Politeness Patrol on the room members. How else are the curious going to find out about people who aren't like themselves, unless by some sort of open exchange of information and ideas?

If you're going to enter a room aimed at a group to which you are not a member, be polite, don't disrupt, and let them know that while you may not be whatever they are, you would like to know more about them. Most often, they will be pleased and impressed, will ask you to stay, and will answer all your questions.

Signed, Aunt Effie

Email Mania

Dear Aunt Effie:

My friend Doug (not his real name) is always doing fancy stuff to his email. He uses fonts that I don't have and colors I can't see on my grayscale monitor, and always makes the email window twice the size of my screen. This makes it very difficult for me to read his letters. I don't want to embarrass him (or myself) by complaining, but what else can I do?

Signed, Hate to Whine

Dear Whine:

What you can do (without whining—that's *very* unattractive) is send him a note the next time he sends you an illegible piece of email. It might say something like:

Dear Doug:

I just received your lovely note. I can tell by all the different fonts and colors (or whatever) that you put a lot of time into it. However, your embellishments don't translate well on my computer, and I can't really make out what you're trying to say. My computer isn't nearly as big and powerful as yours.

Could you please send me a plain copy? As much as I appreciate your efforts to pretty up your note, I'm much more impressed by what you have to say....

Trust me, dear, he won't ever do it again. In general, you shouldn't mess too much with your email unless you know the recipient's computer and what it's capable of. If you're sending email to an Internet address or to someone using a laptop computer, you should definitely keep your text plain and keep the window size smaller than your desktop computer's monitor is capable of showing. Otherwise, your mail will look all screwy when it gets where it's going. There are many more tips on email etiquette in Chapter 9.

Signed, Aunt Effie

File Foibles

Dear Aunt Effie:

I have an acquaintance online who is forever sending me files that she thinks I might find interesting. I don't know if I'm interested or not—I can never open the files because I don't use the same software as she does. What should I do?

Signed, Interested in Being Interested

Dear IBI:

For goodness' sake, *say something* to your friend! Send her a note on the order of the one in the email section above, telling her that you might be interested in what she sent if only you had the application she used to create it. Send her a list of the appropriate software you own and ask if she has that program or one that can export a file in a format you can open.

When you want to send someone a file, you should do the following things to make the process as painless as possible:

➤ **Ask.** Ask the recipient what format she'd like the file in. It's the easiest method all-around.

➤ **Stick to basics.** If you're sending a word processing document, send it as a plain text file. If the file is short enough, you may want to use America Online's basic word processing powers to create it (see Chapter 22).

➤ **Use standard formats.** If you're sending another type of file (like a picture file), stick to a basic format like GIF since just about any computer can open one of these created on any other computer.

Chapter 9 covers the details on how to send a file to someone. Chapter 12 covers files in general.

Signed, Aunt Effie

Export The process in which one application saves a file in the format of another application (or one that another application can import, at least). Exporting is usually done with the **Save As** command, but check your manual.

Import The process in which one application opens a file created in another application with a minimum of fuss. In the process, the first application translates the file into its own format so you never have to bother with the translation again.

The Least You Need to Know

Generally, all of the advice given here boils down to a few basic tenets, which I call Aunt Effie's Guide to Gracious Living:

➤ *Always* be polite. "Please" and "Thank you" go a long way in this world.

➤ Public room behavior should be kept above-board and appropriate for members of all ages and levels of sensitivity.

➤ Private room behavior can be whatever the folks in the room want it to be, as long as everyone knows and agrees to it beforehand.

➤ Never make assumptions about the people you meet online. Don't assume anything about them personally (race, creed, gender, and such) or about their computers (hardware, software, or other peripherals).

➤ When in doubt, ask. That applies to new terms, new situations, or anything you're unsure of.

➤ If you're still in doubt, *don't*.

Chapter 8

Broadstrokes: The Departments at a Glance

In this chapter, you'll get a quick look at all of America Online's main departments, plus a little more detail. When you're done, you should have a pretty good idea about where most things are—certainly enough to get you started. Bear in mind that AOL is growing and expanding faster than this universe of ours, so things will probably look different (at least a little) from the figures in this book. Be brave and explore.

The Main Menu

The Main Menu is a good place to start your explorations. It appears automatically behind the In the Spotlight (or Welcome) screen when you first connect to AOL. To get at the Main Menu, click on the **Go To Main Menu** button at the bottom of the In the Spotlight screen. The Main Menu jumps to the front, looking a little like the next screen.

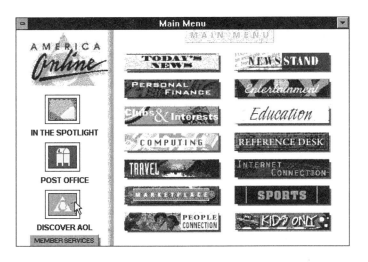

Main Street, AOL.

On the left side of the Main Menu, you'll notice the America Online logo at the top with four icon-buttons below it. You can click once on any of these icons to immediately go to that particular service or area.

➤ The In the Spotlight button takes you back to the Welcome screen, which shows the day's online highlights.

➤ The Post Office button takes you to all of the email-related functions in one tidy window.

➤ The Discover AOL button starts up that tour you took in Chapter 5 (you did take it, didn't you?).

➤ The little rectangle that says "Member Services" takes you to the free customer service area, the place where you change your billing information or create and delete screen names, as well as get help, make suggestions, and generally learn a lot of useful information about AOL. Member Services is *so* important, it rates a chapter of its very own (Chapter 20).

The Main Menu is dominated by the 14 department buttons on the right side. You can click on each of these buttons (as with most buttons) to go to the specified department—quick as a flash. The following section describes all of the departments, plus the Post Office, in detail.

Departmental Details

When you've read a few of these sections, you'll notice that most of the departments have a similar layout; that's so you won't be puzzled by how a new area works. Most departments offer a list of all the different forums that make up the department, plus icons you can use to access the more popular features.

As a way to keep you from getting lost, most department screens have three buttons at the bottom of the window that you can use to get back to the Main Menu, Member Services, or the Index of everything online with a single mouse click.

Playing Post Office

AOL's Post Office is a centralized location where you can deal with the varieties of mail you can send online—which makes sense. (Remember that you can also access all the options discussed here through your Mail menu. Just select the appropriate menu item.) Click the **Post Office** icon, and you'll see a window like the one shown here.

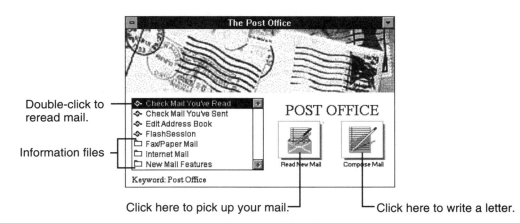

The Post Office: email central.

You can use AOL's Post Office, like your neighborhood Post Office, to write and send mail (by clicking on the Compose Mail icon) and to pick up mail that's been delivered to you (by clicking on the Read New Mail icon).

You can reread mail you've already read by double-clicking the Check Mail You've Read item in the scroll box. You can also see whether mail you sent has been read by the recipient by double-clicking the Check Mail You've Sent option. Other things you can do via the Post Office include editing your AOL address book, scheduling a FlashSession to automatically send and receive your email, sending a fax or paper mail through AOL, and sending mail to someone via the Internet. Email is explained in greater detail in Chapter 9.

Today's News: Read All About It

Clicking on the Today's News button takes you to the screen pictured here. The top of the window displays a scroll box containing today's headlines. To read an item of interest, just double-click on it.

Scrollable list of today's top news stories

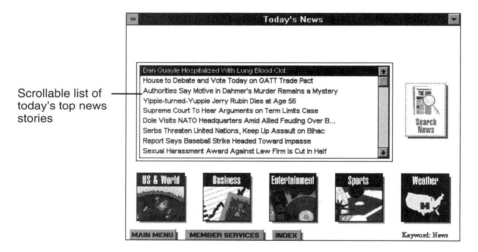

Get news and weather as the stories happen.

If you want some specific news coverage, click on one of the subject icons lined up across the bottom of the window. Select US & World, Business, Entertainment, Sports, and/or Weather for just the news you need.

If you want to find news stories about something in particular, click on the **Search News** icon. You can then enter the word(s) or

80

phrase you want to find. America Online scours the news and presents you with all the news stories that contain the word or phrase you entered (if there are any). AOL gets its news from top news services and gives you all the news you can use.

Personal Finance: Dollars and Sense

Have a bundle o' bucks you want to invest? Look for sound investment advice by clicking on the Personal Finance icon on the Main Menu.

On the right side of the Personal Finance window is a scrollable list of all the finance-related departments that are available online—and that's a lot of stuff. Browse through and see what strikes your fancy.

The left side of the screen has icons for some of the more popular features: Financial News, Financial Forums, Morningstar Mutual Funds, stock market Quotes and Portfolios, Reference and Resources, and an online version of the *Investor's Business Daily* newspaper.

Clubs & Interests

Clicking on Clubs & Interests on the Main Menu takes you to the area shown on the following page. Every online forum that is a club, hobby, interest, or way of life is available. This screen contains the standard scroll box containing all of the various forums in the department, plus six icons to help you get to the more popular areas in Clubs & Interests.

Make sure the search word or phrase you enter is specific. If you want to know what's going on in England's government, *don't* enter the word "England"; you'll get a lot of unrelated news (probably about Princess Di). If you enter "Government," you might get news on the goings-on in Washington D.C. and other seats of government. Enter the word "Parliament" instead, and you'll only get news related to the actual seat of English Government. I suggest that you double-click on the Help & Info button in the Search News window before you search the first time. It contains a lot of helpful tips.

Forum A self-contained area online devoted to one broad topic (Macintosh Computing, say, or a particular hobby). Generally, all AOL forums have informational text you can read, a file library, a message area, and often a chat room. Chapter 11 covers forums in detail.

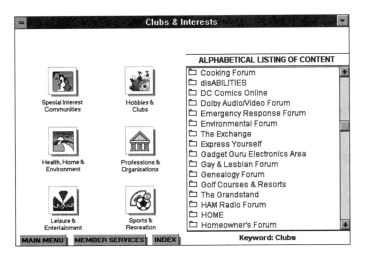

What are you interested in?

Special Interest Communities gives you immediate access to forums for the African-American, Christian, Gay and Lesbian, and disABILITIES forums. Health, Home & Environment takes you to related forums, including cooking and pet care forums. Leisure & Entertainment gives you a choice of fun and leisure-related forums. I think you get the idea.

Computing

Clicking on the Computing icon in the Main Menu takes you to the computing area appropriate to your computer. As always, there are the standard elements: a scroll box with an alphabetical list of all the computing forums available online, and the six icons to highlight popular features.

Of note here are the icons for the Software Center (which we'll search through in Chapter 12), the Industry Connection (which keeps you up to date with what's hot and happening with your favorite hardware and software companies), and Tonight in Computing (which gives you a list of all the various meetings and happenings taking place today in the computing forums). Computing is the department I, personally, visit more than any other online—but I'm a geek.

Traveling to the Travel Department

The Main Menu's Travel icon sends you first class to the Travel department. In my humble opinion, the coolest thing in the Travel department is EAAsy Sabre, which you can use to search for, reserve, and book airline flights to just about anywhere. I'll talk about it more in Chapter 16, "Shopping."

If you're not actually about to travel, you may want to share past travel experiences. So head for the Travel Forum or Traveler's Corner. If you're planning a trip, you can check out Bed and Breakfast-type lodgings at your destination, check the weather while you're at it, and find out what there is to do when you arrive. To access the topic you want, click on the appropriate icon on the left side of the window, or double-click on the listing in the Travel Resources scroll box. *Vaya con Dios!*

A Mall of One's Own: The Marketplace

Clicking on the Marketplace icon on the Main Menu takes you to the central listing of shopping opportunities online. You can buy everything from flowers for your sweetie to new and used computer hardware. You can even become an informed shopper by checking out *Consumer Reports* magazine online. But don't whip out those credit cards yet, we'll be shopping in Chapter 16—and don't you *dare* start without me.

People Connection

Unlike most of the other Department icons on the Main Menu, which take you to a listing of all the forums available in that Department, the People Connection icon zaps you right into the middle of a live chat room.

There are two reasons why People Connection doesn't take you to a listing of chat rooms. The first is that because the number and variety of rooms is changing all the time, there is no list of rooms that are available all the time. The second reason is simple: When you want to chat, you want to chat—so why waste time? Plop, you're in. Chat away. The ins and outs of chatting and chat rooms are covered in Chapter 10. Until then, you may talk quietly to yourself.

Read More About It in the Newsstand

If you aren't content with the short clips about today's headlines that you get when you click on Today's News, and you want to read more in-depth and insightful coverage of current events, click on the **Newsstand** icon on the Main Menu. It takes you to the Newsstand, shown below.

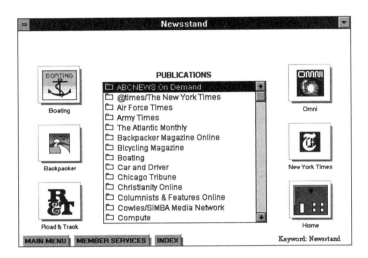

Pick a magazine or newspaper.

Here you can choose from dozens of online versions of your favorite magazines or newspapers, and even transcripts of ABC News stories you may have missed. As always, Mr. Phelps, you should click once on an icon or twice on an entry in the scroll box to access the publication's forum.

In addition to copies of articles from current issues of these publications, many of the forums also offer you the chance to look at and/or download related photographs. Chapter 11 talks about looking at photos online. Chapter 12 tells you how to download files.

That's Entertainment!

With one click of your mouse button on the Main Menu's Entertainment icon, you can find yourself hip-deep in Hollywood. You can get more than you ever wanted to know about movies, television, games, comic books, the Grateful Dead, and tons more. If it's at all entertaining to someone, somewhere, you can probably read, see, or learn about it here.

A few of the many forums you might find interesting include:

➤ **NBC Online**   Ask them what happened to "TV Nation" or whose bright idea it was to put "Frasier" up against "Home Improvement."

➤ **MTV Online**   Get clips of the latest videos, ask Eric Nies to your prom or get "Beavis and Butt-head" pictures.

➤ **Bulls & Bears Game**   Build a pretend stock portfolio and see if you can make yourself a millionaire.

➤ **AD&D Online**   Maybe swords and sorcery are more your cup of mead. Get Advanced Dungeons and Dragons tips and tricks until you run out of spells, or get your head chopped off by a Balrog in a woodpile.

That's Education

Since all play and no (home)work make Jack a *really* dull boy, the students in your family might want to (or you might want them to) check out the Education department. Click on the **Education** icon on the Main Menu, and you are whisked to the online equivalent of a little red schoolhouse.

Chapter 14 covers all of the education resources available online. But if you're curious now, you may want to check out the Smithsonian Institute's forum, C-SPAN Education Services, or perhaps the Academic Assistance Center for help expanding your horizons or just finishing your homework.

That's Information!

If you need to know something in a hurry, click on the Main Menu's Reference Desk icon. You land in information heaven, as shown in the following figure.

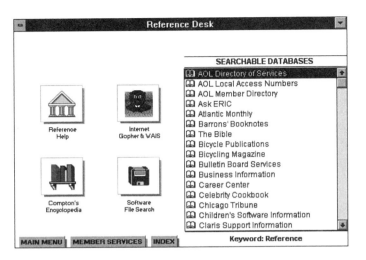

More information than you can shake a disk at...

Database A database is a great big pile of information that you can look through (search) according to a search string (a keyword or phrase). You search an online database with a general topic, and (maybe) a keyword to help you narrow the search to the information you need.

Although many of the forums on America Online contain huge libraries of information that you can search (like the Search News function discussed earlier in this chapter) for particular words or phrases, the Reference Desk gives you one-stop searching ability by putting access to all of those searchable databases in one central location. You can look for a job, recipes from the Celebrity Cookbook, local AOL access numbers, and more.

Finding the right word or phrase to search for the information you need is nearly an art form—at least it takes practice. Click on the **Reference Help** icon and read the information there before you try a search.

Surfing the Internet

In case you've never heard of it, the Internet is a world-wide network of computers through which people exchange information, files, and bad, bad jokes with each other. There was a time when you needed all sorts of techno-geeky knowledge and access to a government, college, or military computer to get hooked into the Internet (or "the Net" as some call it). Not anymore.

Clicking the Main Menu's Internet Connection icon takes you to the department shown below. America Online was one of the first major commercial services to offer Internet access to common folks like you and me. It will *probably* be the first of the major services to offer complete access (but it'll be a close race).

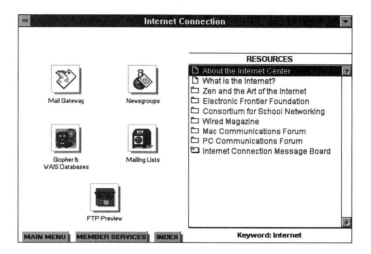

The Internet brings the world to your computer.

The Internet is wild, wide, and wacky. It also takes a lot of explaining, which is why I devote Chapter 17 to it. Be warned, though: using the Net can be quite habit forming.

Sports, Of Course

If you're one of those folks who is disappointed when you don't get your usual subscription to *Sports Illustrated* for a holiday gift, take heart. Click on the **Sports** icon on AOL's Main Menu, and you'll have all the sports you can stand: professional and amateur, all the coverage, all the statistics, all the color commentary, baseball, basketball, even golf.

Click on the **Grandstand** icon, and you'll be able to *play* just about any sport you can imagine, too. Click on the **ABC Sports** icon, and you can post a message to Roone Arledge and other ABC TV sports honchos. It will be a great comfort to you should more professional athletes ever decide to strike.

Kids Only

If you've got children (aged about 5 to 15 years), you'll definitely want to click on the Main Menu's Kids Only icon. It takes you to the KOOL (Kids Only OnLine) world shown here.

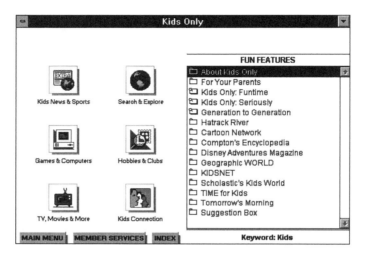

Not for grownups.

Kids Only is a kid-size version of America Online, complete with its own kid chats, special events, and forums of interest to kids. Chat areas are supervised by KO staff, and while adults are allowed to enter and watch what goes on, they cannot participate. It's Kids Only, after all. Kids Only is covered in more detail in Chapter 15. You might want to snoop through, just to satisfy your parental instincts, before you let your youngster(s) log on. But after that, it's hands off.

Watch This Space

America Online is adding new features and forums almost every day. Although the departments described here are the main departments now, the contents of each can change at any time.

If you're curious to see what new stuff has been added recently, use the Keyword: NEW. (You remember how to use Keywords, don't you? Skip to Chapter 23 if you don't.) You'll also see new additions featured on the In the Spotlight screen that you see when you first sign on. Nothing on America Online is kept secret.

The Least You Need to Know

The contents of the various departments may differ—or even change—from day to day. But these things remain true most of the time:

➤ The Main Menu is your gateway to all the various departments and the forums in each department.

➤ Most departments present you with a list of all the forums in that department. Just double-click on the entry you want to visit.

➤ Most departments also have a few icons for featured or popular areas of the department. Click on the icon to visit that area.

➤ You can get back to the Main Menu at any time by clicking on the Main Menu button at the bottom of most windows, or by selecting **Main Menu** from your Go To menu.

➤ The Index button, found in most main department screens, calls up a listing of all the forums and services offered online. It's a great tool to help you find what you're looking for.

Chapter 9

Love Letters Straight from Your Heart

In This Chapter

➤ Receiving, reading, creating, and sending email

➤ Using FlashSessions to save $$$

➤ An Address Book you probably can't lose

Blast! Now I've got that song stuck in my head—don't you hate it when your brain turns into musical Velcro?

Anyhow, where was I? There are four main ways to communicate with other folks on America Online: email, Immediate Messages (IMs), chat rooms, and message board postings. This chapter is about the first one: email. (The other three will be covered in Chapters 10 and 11, by the way.)

You had your first experience with email the very first time you signed on to AOL. You got a lovely note from AOL's CEO SC welcoming you to the service. (For the initial-impaired, that's America Online's Chief Executive Officer, Steve Case.) In all likelihood, that's only the first of hundreds, maybe even thousands, of pieces of email you'll receive. You need to know how to read it, respond to it, and create some of your own. This chapter gives you the facts.

You've Got Mail!

Whenever you have email, you'll hear that thrilling announcement—
"You've Got Mail!"—and you'll see the mailbox icon flashing. The mail
might be waiting for you when you first sign on, or you might receive
it during your adventures online. Either way, to read it, you can do one
of the following:

➤ Click on the big **You Have Mail** icon on the left side of the In The
Spotlight screen if you happen to be there (that's what you did
back in Chapter 5).

➤ Click on the **Post Office** icon on the left side of the Main Menu
(you saw that in the last chapter) if you happen to be there, and
then click on the **Read New Mail** icon in the Post Office.

➤ Windows users can click on the mailbox icon (the first one) on
the Windows menu bar. (You learned about this bar in Chapter 5.)

➤ Select **Read New Mail** from the Mail menu.

Regardless of how you decide to get at your mail, once you select
Read New Mail, you'll see a window something like this, with all your
new mail listed.

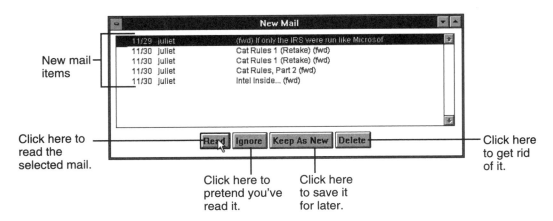

Lots of mail for me.

When the New Mail window opens, the first item in the list is automatically selected. To read the first piece of mail, click on the **Read** button or double-click on the piece of mail in the list. The mail opens in a window like the following figure.

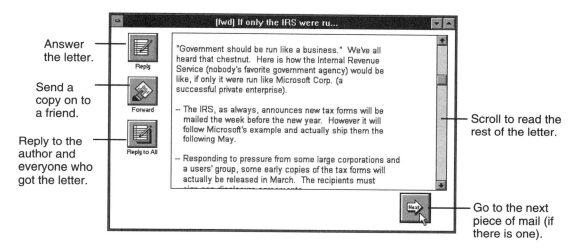

Answer the letter.

Send a copy on to a friend.

Reply to the author and everyone who got the letter.

Scroll to read the rest of the letter.

Go to the next piece of mail (if there is one).

You must be reading my mail...

Read the mail. You may have to use the scroll bar at the right of the window to read it all. When you're done, you can reply to the letter by clicking on the **Reply** button. This opens a blank email form already addressed to the person who sent you the first letter, with the abbreviation Re: (business-speak for "regarding") in the Subject box, followed by the name of the original letter. All you have to do is type your reply and send it off. (You'll learn more about that in a moment.)

You can also forward the letter to someone else who might be interested by clicking on the **Forward** button. You'll get another blank letter form, but you must type in the screen name of the person you want to get it. The subject box will say "(fwd)" instead of "Re:," followed by the original letter's name.

If this piece of email was sent to multiple recipients, you may want to send a response to everyone who got it. To do so, click on the **Reply to All** button. Your return mail will go to everyone who received the original.

However, you may want to think about the letter and answer later. In that case, you might want to save the letter to your hard drive. To do that, click on the **Save** menu bar button (the last one on the right) or select **S**ave from the File menu. You'll get a typical Save dialog asking you where you want to save the letter and what you want to call it. The letter will be saved as a text file that you can open and read later with the Open command (also in the File menu).

Mac users can save their mail just by clicking on the **Save to Flashmail** button below the Reply to All button. (Windows users don't have this button.) The mail is saved without any further ado, and the letter's window closes, returning you to the New Mail window. Just double-click on the next piece of mail you want to read. To read your saved mail later, select **Read Incoming Mail** from the Mail menu, and you'll get a list of all your saved mail.

On the other hand, the letter may not need (or be worth) responding to, in which case you can click on the Next button at the bottom of the window. This automatically opens the next letter waiting for you. If there isn't a next letter, you won't see the button.

Mac users have not only a Next button, but also a Prev button (for Previous). The Prev button returns you to the previous letter in the mail list (if there is one).

Just for giggles and yucks (and to keep this chapter moving along), let's say you want to reply to a letter *right now*.

Replying to Mail Online

First, one piece of advice: you don't really want to reply to mail online; it eats up your time and money. You're better off answering your mail offline and sending it the next time you sign on or with a FlashSession. But I'll tell you more about all this later. For now, just remember that this is an example.

While you are reading your mail, if you click on the Reply, Forward, or Reply to All button, you get a window like the one shown here.

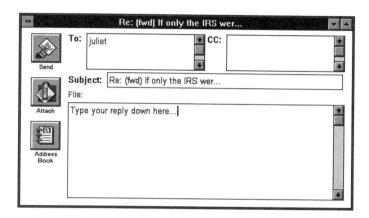

A snappy answer.

The To: and Subject: boxes will be filled in automatically, as described earlier. If you care to, you can edit them to your heart's content. In the CC: box, you enter the screen names of folks who should receive copies of the letter.

Type your response in the large box at the bottom of the window. Just click in it once to put the cursor there, and then type away. When you're done, click on the **Send** button, and your mail is sent on its way (without a stinking 32-cent stamp).

Composing Mail from Scratch

You probably won't get much email until you send a little yourself. To start, select **Compose Mail** from the Mail menu. You'll get a blank mail form something like the one shown on the following page. I say *something* like the one there because this one was composed offline (which is why the Send button is grayed-out—you can't send mail offline). You'll also notice a file attached to this one. I'll tell you what that is and what to do with it in just a bit.

The Send button is
grayed out when you
compose offline.

Click this button to
save the message
for later delivery.

Click this button
to detach the
attached file.

Name of the
attached file

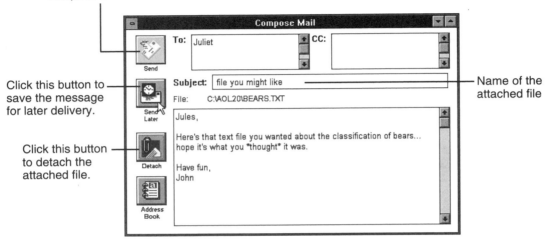

A letter written from scratch.

To move from box to box when composing mail, you can use your Tab key, or just click once in the box you want to fill in next. Tabbing takes you to the next box, so you may have to tab a few times to get where you're going.

Mac users have an additional box on their mail form, marked Return Receipt. If you check that box, when the recipient opens and reads your mail, the program generates a little memo telling you the date and time he read it. Personally, I think it's fairly rude to use Return Receipt unless it's extremely important to know that your mail was received. Otherwise, just use the Check Mail You've Sent option in the Post Office or Mail menu to see if and when your mail was received. I think Aunt Effie would agree.

In the To box, type the screen name of the person you're sending the mail to. If you're sending it to more than one person, type them in like this: *screen name1, screen name2,* and so on. If you're sending a copy to someone else, type that person's screen name in the CC box. If you want to send "carbon copies" to multiple people, type the names just as you did in the To box.

In the Subject box, type the subject of your letter (up to 32 characters/spaces). Then write your letter in the big text box at the bottom. When you're done, you can click on the **Send** button (if you're signed on to AOL), or click the **Send Later** button.

FlashSession An automated way to send and receive mail and files from AOL. You can start a FlashSession while online or off.

You're done—just remember to send your mail. You can send it manually (select **Read Outgoing Mail** from the Mail menu, and then click **Send All**) or using a FlashSession. If you try to log off with mail waiting to be sent, AOL reminds you that you have files to be sent and gives you the chance to do a FlashSession before letting you disconnect. There's more about FlashSessions coming up shortly.

Attaching Files to Email

Sometimes you have a file on your computer that you want to share with one of your friends online. You could write a letter explaining what the file is, and then attach the file and send it. For example, the last figure showed a letter I was sending that had a file called BEARS.TXT attached to it. To attach a file to your letter, click on the **Attach** button on the left side of the mail window. The Attach File dialog box appears.

The Attach File dialog box works like Windows' Open and Save dialog boxes. Use it to specify the drive and folder that contain the file you want to send. Then click on the file name to select it and click **OK**. The specified file is attached to your mail. You can send only one file with each piece of mail.

The Attach File dialog box looks slightly different on a Mac. Use the list box on the left to navigate to the file(s) you want to attach to your mail. Click on the file to select it, and then click on the **Add** button. That file is moved to the window on the right side of the screen. Mac users can send multiple files by repeating the process. You can also *compress* the files (make them smaller, so it takes less time to send and receive them) by clicking on the **Compress Files** check box. (File compression is explained in detail in Chapter 12.)

Upload To send a file to a remote computer for storage or distribution.

Download To retrieve a file from a remote computer for use on your own computer.

When you send mail with a file attached, it goes through an extra step as the attached file is *uploaded* to America Online for delivery. When you receive a file attached to mail, you need to *download* it before you can do anything with it. Both uploading and downloading are discussed in Chapter 12.

That's about all you need to know about email, except for some fast, easy money-saving tips and tricks.

Saving Time and Money with FlashSessions

To use FlashSessions, you have to do two things:

➤ Do a little planning.

➤ Remember to leave your computer on with your America Online software running.

DOS and GeoWorks users don't have FlashSession capability, only Mac and Windows versions do. Sorry about that, but I don't write the software.

Here's the scenario. You're offline, composing some mail to your online friends. As you finish each letter, you click on the **Send Later** button. When you do, you get a message that says, "Your mail has been saved for later delivery. If you would like to schedule a session to deliver this mail, select FlashSessions from the Mail menu." When you're done writing all your mail, that's just what you'll do.

You continue working until you've written letters to all your pen pals and colleagues. Done? Good. Select **FlashSessions** from the **Mail** menu, and you see the following window.

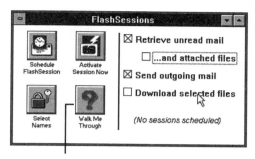

Click here if you need help.

The FlashSessions window.

By clicking on the appropriate check boxes on the right side of the window, you can set your FlashSessions to retrieve new mail, retrieve any files attached to that mail, send all your outgoing mail, and download any files you may have in your download manager. (Don't worry about this last one for now, Chapter 12 will put it in perspective.)

Because a FlashSession will actually log on to AOL with any or all of your accounts, you must click on the **Select Names** button on the left side of the window. You'll get the dialog shown in the next figure.

You need to enter each password—but SHHH! It's secret.

Click in the check box beside the screen name(s) for which you want to do a FlashSession, and then carefully enter the password for each name in the box beside it. Be careful—you'll only see asterisks (***) on-screen as you type (passwords *are* supposed to be secret, you know). When you're done, click **OK** and you're returned to the FlashSessions window.

Now you can either click on **Activate Session Now** if you can't wait, or schedule a session for a regular time and day by clicking on the **Schedule FlashSession** button. If you click on Activate Session Now, you'll see a quick dialog that says, "Now? You mean it?" (I made that up, but it's about right.) If you mean it, click **Begin**, and it will. You can also tell the program not to log off when it's done by clicking **Stay Online When Finished**. If you don't want to activate the session now, you can click on the Schedule FlashSession icon. You'll get the following dialog box.

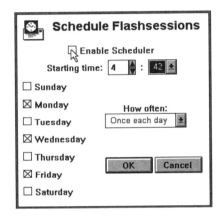

Scheduling FlashSessions.

Click on the **Enable Scheduler** check box to tell your computer that you really want it to do a FlashSession at the time and days indicated below. If you don't enable it, nothing will happen (sounds like serious codependency, doesn't it?).

Next, set the time (in military time, where 1:00 PM is 13:00). I usually set the time for some ungodly hour like 4:42 AM, because I'm less likely to get a busy signal in the wee small hours. Then click the check boxes beside the days of the week you want the FlashSession to happen. In the figure, I've selected Monday, Wednesday, and Friday.

When you've specified the days and time, click on the **How Often?** pop-up menu and select how many times a day you want a FlashSession. To me, no mail is so important it can't wait a little while, so I only do one session on each selected day. However, I know folks who check their mail hourly. Do what pleases you.

100

You're set. Click **OK**, and your AOL software begins counting the minutes until it's time to spring into action. Remember your computer must be turned on, the AOL software must be running (even if it's minimized), and you must have enabled the scheduler, or this won't work.

When the appointed time rolls around, your software calls AOL, retrieves any new mail you have, sends any mail you've saved with the Send Later button, and downloads files with your mail and in your download manager (depending on the options you selected). Then it logs off. And can you believe it does all this automatically? The next time you go to your computer, you'll have mail and files and whatnot waiting for your amusement and edification.

Using the Address Book

The Address Book is a great little feature that can save you lots of time if you write to a lot of people one at a time or send the same letter to a bunch of folks at once. After you've been online a few weeks or months, you'll get into a pattern where you correspond with the same folks on a regular basis. When you find yourself sending, oh, the third or fourth email to the same person, add him to your Address Book. The following steps will walk you through it.

The Mac version of the Address Book is slightly different. If you click on the Address Book icon while composing mail, you don't have the option of editing the entries. To do that, you must select **Edit Address Book** from the **Mail** menu. Mac users also don't get the To: and CC: buttons in the Address Book. Simply click in the appropriate address box (To: or CC:) before you open the Address Book, and the name you select will be put into that box.

1. While you're penning your latest missive, click on the **Address Book** icon. This opens the Address book, which looks something like the figure below (but without Juliet Cooke's misspelled name in it).

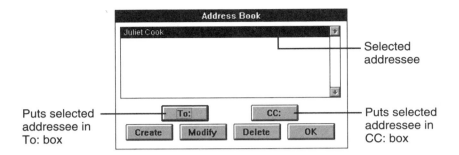

A little black book.

2. To create a new entry, click the **Create** button. The Address Group dialog box appears.

3. Type the "real name" of the person (if you know it) in the box marked Group Name. If you're creating an entry to send mail to a group of people, enter a name that will remind you who the group is, such as "Writer's Club" or something similar.

4. In the Screen Names box, type the person's screen name (Juliet in the example). If the entry is for a group mailing, enter the screen names of all the people you want included in this group, separated by commas and spaces: Juliet, TKirk, and so on.

If you don't want everyone who is getting your mail to know that they're getting a mass mailing, or you don't want them to know the screen names of everyone else on your mailing list, type the screen names in parentheses: (Juliet, TKirk, and so on).

That sends your mail as *blind carbon copies*, abbreviated BCC. Only the recipient's name appears in her copy's address portion. Some people find BCCs rude; others think they're cool. You be the judge.

5. When you're done (and you've checked the names for accuracy) click **OK**. Your new entry appears in your Address Book.

From then on, when you want to send mail to that person or group, click on the **Address Book** icon. Click on the name of the person or group to whom you want to send the mail, and click on the To: or CC: button. The screen name(s) magically appear in the appropriate address box in your mail.

To change an existing entry, open the Address Book, click on the entry you want to change, and then click on the **Modify** button. Make your changes and click **OK**.

To remove an Address Book entry, open the Address Book, click on the entry you want to remove, and click on the **Delete** button. You are asked if you're sure you want to delete the item. If you're sure, click **OK**, and the entry is deleted.

General Mail Factoids

Here's some general information about mail that I couldn't work in elsewhere, so it's just kind of *here*....

➤ AOL only holds your mail for about 30 days. If you don't read it, it disappears. You'll still get the "You've Got Mail!" message, but there won't be anything in your mail box.

➤ AOL only stores mail you've read for about 30 days as well. If you want to keep it, save it.

➤ Online, you can reread any mail you've already read, even if you didn't save it. Use the **Check Mail You've Read** option in the Mail menu.

While online, select **Check Mail You've Sent** from the Mail menu to see a list of recently sent mail. Click on the mail you want to check and click on **Status**. It will tell you if and when the mail was received.

➤ If you get ticked off and fire off an angry letter to someone, you can **Unsend** it if you calm down before the addressee reads it. While online, select **Check Mail You've Sent** from the Mail menu. You see a list of recently sent mail. Click on the mail you want to recall and click on **Unsend**. If the mail hasn't been read, it is deleted from the addressee's mailbox. If it has already been read, you might want to fire off an apology instead.

➤ You can send email to folks on the Internet or other online services that have Internet access. That's all covered in Chapter 17.

➤ When you are replying to specific statements in someone's letter,
it is polite to quote the relevant parts of the original message (just
copy and paste them) so everybody knows what you're talking
about without having to dig up the original. Offset the quoted bits
on their own line, with some indication that it's a quote, like this:

>>If Windows crashes in a forest, and there isn't anyone around,
does it make a sound?<<

➤ While it's polite to quote salient snippets from a letter, it's kind of
rude and lazy to just tack your answer onto a copy of the whole
original letter (unless the letter was just one or two lines). Don't be
rude.

➤ If you use FlashSessions to get your mail, you can wind up with a
lot of mail saved on your hard drive. To delete some/all of it,
select **Read Incoming Mail** from the Mail menu. You'll get a list
of your saved mail. You can reread it and delete it if you care to
with the Read and Delete buttons.

The Least You Need to Know

That's about it for email and related fun factoids. You'll get the hang of
it in no time. Meanwhile, keep these concepts in mind:

➤ You can get at all of your mail functions (offline)
through the Mail menu. Online, you can use the Mail
menu or go to the Post Office.

➤ Save time and money by composing, reading, and
answering your mail offline, and using FlashSessions to
deliver it in one fell swoop.

➤ The Address Book will also save you time, especially if
you send the same letter to a lot of people.

➤ You can unsend potentially embarrassing mail—but
only if the addressee hasn't read it yet.

➤ If you care to, drop me a note: my screen name is PIV.
It'll be a pleasure to hear from you.

Chapter 10

Your Chat Room or Mine?

In This Chapter

➤ The nickel tour of a chat room

➤ Going public and keeping things private

➤ Instant (message) gratification

➤ Let a :) be your umbrella

As cool as the file libraries are, and as much fun as the fun and games stuff, the forums, and everything else online is, chatting is at the heart of the online community. If you're a social animal, you're gonna *love* it.

L Is for Lobby

When you're online and you need to chat, head for the People Connection. You can get there a couple of ways:

➤ Click on the **People Connection** icon on your Main Menu.

➤ Select **Lobby** from your **Go To** menu.

➤ Use the keyboard shortcut **Ctrl+L** (⌘ **-L** on a Mac).

A lobby in the People Connection is like the lobby of a really big hotel. It's where you enter the People Connection and make your way to the room of your choice—but you don't need a reservation.

For your first chat session, you may want to hang out in a lobby for awhile until you get a feel for what goes on and how things work. There's often a Guide present; the Guides are great sources of help and information should you feel dazed and confused. More about the Guides in a bit.

Anatomy of a Chat Room

When you arrive in the lobby, your screen will look something like the figure shown below. Most of the action takes place on the bottom half of the window, so let's start there.

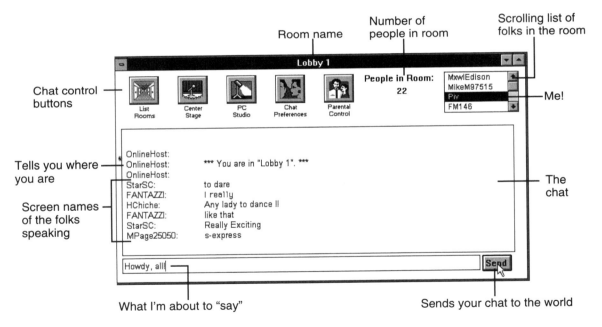

Welcome to the lobby.

 The main difference in Mac-based chat rooms and lobbies is that the Control Buttons (List Rooms, Center Stage, and so on) go down the side of the window, not across the top. You also have an extra button called People and a different kind of list of people entering and leaving. Otherwise, things work pretty much the same.

The Chat's the Thing

When you first enter a lobby, you may not see anything more than the Online Host announcing, "***You are in 'Lobby 32.'***" (or whatever lobby number or room name you're entering). Just wait a second. Before long, lines of chat will begin to scroll up your screen.

Etiquette demands that when you first enter a new room you send a general "Howdy" (as I'm doing in the figure) or some other greeting to the room. That does two things for you: it puts your name and message up on the screens of everyone in the room to let them know you're there, and it shows that you aren't a *lurker*.

> A **lurker** is someone who enters a chat room and drifts off into a corner, not speaking to anyone publicly or participating in the chat in any way. Some folks are unnerved by lurkers; they wonder what you're up to, and it makes them nervous. At least say hello to someone from time to time.

To say "Hello," click in the thin text box at the bottom of the window to put your cursor there (if it isn't already). Type whatever you care to say, and click the **Send** button or press **Enter**. Your chat, preceded by your screen name, magically appears in the general chat display.

You'll probably get a few replies. If there's a Guide in the room, you'll definitely be greeted, welcomed, and otherwise made to feel at home. You can then feel free to hang back and get a sense of the room. Does there seem to be a topic open for general discussion? Is it a free-for-all of random babble? Give it a minute or two before you pass judgment. Walking into a chat is like walking into the middle of a movie: it can take you awhile to make sense of things.

Button-y Button

There's a row of five buttons in every chat window. The following list describes those five buttons in order of appearance.

> ➤ **List Rooms** brings up a list of all the active public rooms online. (More on that in a bit.)

> ➤ **Center Stage** gives you access to the *huge* meeting room where many online events are held. (More about that in Chapter 15.)

> ➤ **PC Studio** gives you access to a calendar of all the events happening online, another entrance to Center Stage, and games, cartoons, and other fun activities. It's sort of "Fun Central" and is also covered in Chapter 15.

> ➤ **Chat Preferences** enables you to change the preferences you set while offline, back in Chapter 6.

> ➤ **Parental Control** gives you access to the Parental Control options you learned about back in Chapter 6. Parental Control can only be turned on/off by the Master Account screen name.

Getting Info

While you're watching the chat scroll past, one person may pique your curiosity. Locate the interesting/alarming person's screen name in the scroll box at the upper right corner of the window and double-click on it. You'll see a handy-dandy little dialog box like the one below.

Ye olde curiosity stop.

Mac users don't have that scroll box of screen names on-screen all the time. To see it, you have to click on the **People** button. The list appears, showing information buttons similar to those shown in the figure.

You can also highlight one or more chatters by selecting their screen name(s) and clicking on **Highlight**. From then on, their chat will appear in boldface type so you can easily pick it out from the rest of the chat. Highlighting works until you turn it off, or the highlightee leaves the room.

If you want to learn more about the person, click on the **Get Info** button. You'll be able to read the person's online profile if he or she created one. If that person is being unbearably rude, feel free to click the **Ignore** check box, and the rest of the rude commentary from that person will not appear on your screen. If you want to talk to the person, click on the **Message** button, and you'll be able to send an IM (Instant Message) to that screen name.

IMs Away!

If you're checking out this person's profile because you think she is witty and intelligent, you may want to let her know. Of course, you can simply say so in the general chat, the same way you said "Hello" to the room.

> **IM** is short for Immediate Message. It's a little note that pops up on the recipient's screen (with a musical accompaniment, no less) right after you send it.

However, you may be interested in, say, *flirting* with the person in question or using an embarrassing pet name (Pookie, perhaps). If so, you might not want the rest of the room seeing you bat your eyelashes and talk baby talk. Send it in an IM (and thanks for *not* sharing).

To send an IM, you can double-click the recipient's name in the scrolling list of people in your room, and then click on the **Message** button in the dialog box that appears. Or you can simply select **Send Instant Message** from the Member menu. The Send Instant Message dialog box appears.

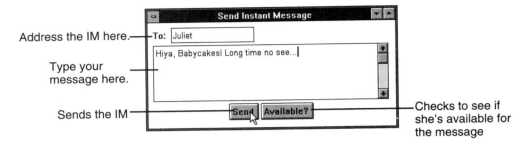

Address the IM here.

Type your message here.

Sends the IM

Checks to see if she's available for the message

Sending an IM. (She hates when I call her "Babycakes" in public.)

Most of the screen names I'm using here are made up. Others are real people whose names I've changed. Please don't bother trying to IM or e-mail these folks. If the messages get delivered at all, they'll probably reach the wrong person. If you want to practice with a real person and haven't met anyone online yet, practice on me—PIV.

If you're sending an IM from the member information dialog box, you won't have to type the screen name. However, if you're sending the IM with the Send Instant Message command from the Member menu, you will have to type it. Type the screen name in the To: text box, type your message in the bigger box, and then click on **Send**.

Your message is on its way. In a moment or two, the recipient will probably respond. When she does, you'll hear what sounds like a sprinkling of fairy dust, and the IM will pop to the front of your screen.

An incoming Instant Message.

110

The top half of the IM window contains all the messages that have gone back and forth between you and your friend—as long as you *don't* close the window. If you want to hide the IM window so you can see the chat again, just click on the lobby or room window behind it, and the IM slips into the background. To bring it forward again, open the Window menu and select the **IM From (***screen name***)** item, or click on any exposed portion of the IM window.

The bottom half of the IM window is where you'll type subsequent IMs, but you won't see it at first. To open it, click the **Reply** button; it pops right up, and the Reply button changes to a Send button.

Locating Your Digital Pals

If you've already made some friends online and they aren't in the lobby or chat room you've entered, how do you find them? Use the **Send Instant Message** command in the Member menu. Enter your friend's screen name in the To: box, and then click on the **Available?** button. AOL checks to see if your friend is signed on and able to receive an IM. It won't tell you anything more.

If you want to find your friend so you can join him in a chat room, you need to use the Locate Member Online command (also in the Member menu). When you select the **Locate Member Online** command from the Member menu, type your friend's screen name in the dialog box that appears and click **OK**. AOL's computer snoops around for you and comes back with the information.

You'll get a message that says your friend is "...not currently signed on," or "...is online, but not in a chat area," or "...is in 'Lobby 1' in People Connection" (or whatever forum or chat room). Depending on the answer you get, you can send an IM asking your friend to meet you somewhere, or you can go to the chat room where your friend is hanging out. The next section explains how to go to another chat room. WAOL PAL on the disk that came with this book also helps keep tabs on your friends; see Chapter 24 for details.

Going to Another Room

To leave the room you're in and go to another, start by clicking on the **List Rooms** button. This brings up a list of all the public rooms currently active online (like the one shown here) but the names of the rooms will be different, of course.

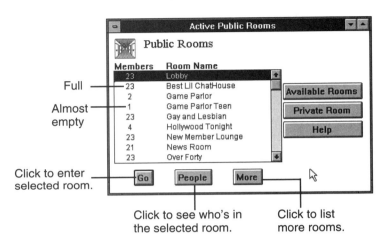

Full ———

Almost empty ———

Click to enter selected room. ———

Click to see who's in the selected room.

Click to list more rooms.

All of the active rooms, at your fingertips.

If you're having trouble online, go to one of the help rooms in the People Connection, which are staffed by Guides who are there to help you. Look for a help room specific to your computer—WAOL HELP ROOM, MAC HELP ROOM, or PCAOL HELP ROOM. The names will be capitalized online so you can easily pick them out of the list. To find out more about getting help, read Chapter 21.

Scroll through the list. When you see one that looks interesting, click on the room and click on the **Go** button. You'll land in the selected room. If none of the rooms strike your fancy, click on **More** to see more room names. When the More button fades to gray, there aren't any more rooms to be seen.

Some of the rooms in the list will be full, and you won't be able to enter them. The maximum number of people allowed in a Chat room is 23. So in the picture, you wouldn't be able to get in the New Member Lounge (unless you're using Wedge from this book's disk; see Chapter 24).

You can click on the **Available Rooms** button, and the list of rooms changes to show only the rooms that aren't full. This saves you some time scrolling through the list.

112

If you do select a full room and click on the Go button, you'll get a message saying something like, "That room is full, would you like to go to a room like it?" If you click OK, you'll land in a room with the same name as the one you selected, but with a number after it (Best Lil ChatHouse 2, for example). You may be the only person in there when you arrive, but don't panic. It sometimes takes a little while for folks online to discover that a new room has opened. Wait a minute or two before you abandon the room. Some people are uncomfortable entering a room with only one other person in it, so they may hang back until a few other brave souls have entered.

A Room of Your Own

If none of the available rooms appeal to you, click on the Member Rooms button in the Available Rooms window. The list changes to show all of the rooms created by members like yourself. You'll also get a new button, Create Room, with which you can create a room of your very own. Here's how:

1. In the Member Rooms window, click on **Create Room**. The Create a Member Room dialog box appears.

2. Type the name of your new room. Keep it within the Terms of Service guidelines (use Keyword: TOS if you forget what they are).

3. Click the **Create** button.

As long as the name you've entered isn't already in use, your room will be created and you will be the only one in it. Sit back, relax, and wait for throngs of adoring members to enter your domain and chat with you. Since it's "your" room, play host(ess) and politely greet the folks as they enter. If the name you chose is already being used, AOL will suggest the same name with a number after it, to differentiate your room from the other(s).

I Vant to Be Alone...Sort Of

Sometimes it seems like the folks online don't want to cooperate with you when you chat. You and a friend or two want to have a nice conversation, and everyone else keeps butting in and/or disrupting it. You can avoid all that by creating a private room.

Remember what Aunt Effie said about private rooms back in Chapter 7. Because they are not supervised, *some* people use them for some very adult chat, indeed. If you're inviting someone to go private with you, make it clear what your intentions are.

If someone asks you into a Private Room for a pleasant chat and then starts sending chat of an explicit nature, that's sexual harassment—and it's not allowed. Report that jerk to a Guide. The next section tells you how.

Creating a private room is just like creating a public room, except you start by clicking the **Private Room** button on any of the Room dialog boxes. The Enter Private Room dialog box looks *exactly* like the Create a Member Room dialog box, except the name is different. Type the name of the room you want to create and click **Go**. If that name isn't in use, you'll go right to it, and you will be alone.

The thing with private rooms is that the names don't appear in any of the room lists. That's what makes them private. To get people to join you, you have to ask them in and give them the name of the room you've created. You'll probably want to use a private form of communication (an IM or email message to invite them). Otherwise the room won't be very private.

To enter a private room, follow these steps:

1. Click on the **Private Room** button in any Room display.

2. Type in the name of the private room you want to enter.

3. Click **Go**, and you're there. Chat away.

Meet the Guides

Guides are extensively trained in the ins and outs of AOL, and if they don't personally have the answer to your question, they will at least be able to tell you who does. You can spot a Guide by his or her name: it will always be Guide *Something*. You'll find Guides in lobbies, roving through member rooms, and staffing the help rooms. Have a question? Ask a Guide.

Since public rooms are open to every member, Guides are also charged with keeping public chat within the guidelines of the Terms of Service (TOS) and warning members who cross the line. If you find yourself online without a Guide in sight, and someone is being somehow abusive or offensive (in chat, email, or through IMs), you can use the Keyword: GUIDE PAGER to summon a Guide. A Guide will respond shortly, usually in five minutes or less (unless it's a *very* busy night).

;) A Wink and a Smile

As Aunt Effie mentioned back in Chapter 7, there is such a thing as online shorthands you can use either to save typing (abbreviations) or to show facial expressions that wouldn't be seen otherwise (smileys). The first time you see one of these, you may be scratching your head in puzzlement; but you'll catch on fast enough. The one in the section name, the ;), is a wink and smile. If you turn your head to the left (or turn the book to the right), you'll see it. You can find lists of tons of online shorthands by using the Keyword: SHORTHANDS.

Using the Guide Pager Keyword is like calling 911 or setting off a fire alarm. It's serious business. You don't use it just to ask a simple question or because someone calls you "cheese breath" or another harmless (if stinky) name. Don't use it frivolously. If you just need a Guide to answer your questions, find a Help room or a lobby with a Guide in it and ask. In other words, use an alternative method to get help (like those in Chapter 21). Don't use the pager.

ROFL!

Say what? ROFL is an often-used shorthand that you'll run into a lot. It stands for Rolling On Floor Laughing. To explain, one person types something hysterically funny, and someone else types the shorthand ROFL to let him know it was funny. However, the second person is saving himself having to type it all out, as well as saving time (and time equals money online). Here are some common shorthands (though this is by no means a complete list):

LOL = Laughing Out Loud

GMTA = Great Minds Think Alike

IMHO = In My Humble Opinion

IMNSHO = In My Not So Humble Opinion

BTW = By The Way

AFK = Away From Keyboard (so others know you won't answer for awhile)

BAK = Back At Keyboard (so they know you're back)

115

DL/DLing = Download/Downloading

UL/ULing = Upload/Uploading

<g> = Grin

{} = A hug

{{{{{{}}}}}} = A major hug

If someone uses a shorthand you don't understand, just repeat the shorthand with a question mark or two (IMNSHO??), and someone will explain it to you. Then you can spring it on someone else later.

A Smiley's Worth a Thousand Words

The other kind of shorthand uses your keyboard's punctuation and number keys to make a reasonable facsimile of a face, called a *smiley*. Smileys let others online know whether you're just playing, kidding, or being evil. To understand a smiley, turn your head to the left or turn this book to the right.

Usually, there are eyes, a nose (optional), and a mouth. Note all the different symbols for the eyes, noses, and mouths shown in these smileys.

:-)	Basic smile
;-)	Wink and smile
:-o	Shock
=8O	Very shocked
:-x	My lips are sealed
0:-)	I'm an angel
}:->	I'm a devil
:-/	Chagrin
:-(	Frown
:-P	Sticking my tongue out
:-D	BIG smile

116

:-*   A kiss

:~(I'm crying...or my nose is broken

There are as many smileys as there are people thinking them up. Some have come up with smileys that resemble themselves, like this one:

[8-)>X   A man with a crew cut, glasses, smile, beard, and bow tie.

Some of them are so complicated they look like an editor exploded.

Sound Off!

Every now and then while you're cruising a chat room, you'll see something like {Welcome} scroll past your screen. What's even stranger is when you see it *and* hear it. Ever since the first Mac version of the software, America Online has given members the opportunity to send sounds to other members' computers (that have the same sound installed) in a chat room.

If you look in the folder where AOL is installed (it's probably called WAOL, or something similar), you can see that you already have some sound files installed. They end with the extension .WAV. You've got the files done.wav, goodbye.wav, gotmail.wav, im.wav, and welcome.wav. These are the sounds AOL uses when you log on (Welcome), log off (Goodbye), download a file (File's Done), get email (You've got mail!), or get IMs (that tinkling sound).

To send a sound in any chat room, just type {S WELCOME.WAV} where you'd normally type your chat, and press **Enter**. Everyone in the room will hear "Welcome!" because everyone who uses AOL has that sound. You must use the curly brackets { } and a capital S (for sound) or it won't work.

You can also add sounds to your library. Just do a file search with the phrase WAV, and you'll turn up piles of sounds. Download them and move them into your AOL folder. You may want to keep a list of your installed sounds handy, so you don't have to scrounge around for the right name to type.

Mac users use the same method for sending chat sounds, but leave off the .WAV extension. So you would type {S Welcome}. But there's an easier way. Here's how:

1. In a chat room, select **Send Chat Sound** from the **Chat** menu. This gives you a list of all the installed sound files on your Mac.

2. From the list of available sounds, click on a sound to select it.

3. Click **Send**, press **Enter**, or double-click on the sound name.

4. The sound name appears in proper format {S *Sound Name*} in the area where you type your chat. You can type some text to send as well or just press **Enter**.

The DOS version of AOL isn't sound-capable, so DOS users won't be able to hear the sounds. However, you can *send* sounds like a Windows user, using the format {S WELCOME.WAV}. You won't be able to hear them, but they will play on other sound-capable machines.

Captain's Log

Sometimes when you're online, you wind up in the thick of a very informative, interesting, or otherwise engaging chat. Or you might get a set of important IMs that you want to keep. Or you might just want a record of everything you did while online. You can do all of these things with a process called *logging*.

You can create a log file easily. Select **Logging** from the **File** menu. The Logging dialog box appears.

In the top half of the dialog box, you can open a Chat Log, which saves everything everyone says in every chat room you enter. In the bottom half, you can open a Session Log, which saves all of the text files and anything else you read online. If you open a Session Log, you can also click on the Log Instant Messages check box to save any IMs you get.

To open a log, click **Open**. You'll get a standard Save File kind of dialog box, asking you to tell AOL where to save the file and what to call it (it suggests a name automatically). Change any data you care to, and then press **Enter**. AOL begins logging (if you're already online) or waits for you to sign on before it starts.

When you've recorded everything you care to record or when you sign off, select **Logging** again from the **File** menu. You'll get the same dialog box, but the Close button will be activated. To turn the log off, click **Close**. You can open and read your log(s) like any text file with AOL or your favorite word processor. It's a very handy feature, especially in a help room.

Logging works the same for DOS users as for Windows users, but the dialog box calls the "Chat Log" a "Conference Log." It's the same thing. You don't, however, have the Log Instant Messages option.

Mac users have three separate logging options: System (which logs everything), Chat (which logs just chat room conversation), and Instant Messages (which logs only IM text). The logging feature on Macs is located in the File menu, but it's called Logs.

The Least You Need to Know

All the stuff you've read here will make more sense and be easier to remember once you've been chatting for a while. Until then, remember these pointers:

➤ All chat rooms are accessed through the People Connection.

➤ Your first stop is always a Lobby.

➤ To go to another room, click the **List Rooms** button and choose your new room from the list.

➤ You have to know the name of a private room to enter it or to give the name to someone you want to join you in private.

➤ The format for typing the send sound command is {S NAME.WAV}.

➤ Don't be a lurker.

Chapter 11

A Funny Thing Happened on the Way to the Forum(s)

In This Chapter

➤ Forums defined

➤ What goes on here?

➤ Forum events

➤ Forum message boards

If you're a little shy and don't want to face a crowded public chat room right now (or ever, for that matter), you may be more inclined to try posting your messages to one of the hundreds and hundreds of forum message areas on America Online. In most forums, you can find lots of information, download software, and even chat—if you feel like it.

So, What's a Forum?

Inside each department (except the People Connection, which is all chat) are dozens of individual areas geared to specific topics, interests

Don't forget that the make of your computer determines which Computing department you'll land in. If you're on a Mac, you'll get a listing of all the Mac forums, not the DOS-based forums shown here. Of course, Mac users can also access the DOS/Windows forums.

services, or publications. Each one of these individual areas provides a forum where members can speak out, learn, and generally kibitz about the subject at hand.

For example, look at the main screen for the Computing department, shown below. In the list box on the right, you can access any one of 14 forums—actually more, because the item called Apple Computing Forums gives you access to all the Macintosh and Apple II forums, just by double-clicking on it. That's in case you need to know what's going on with Macs from your PC.

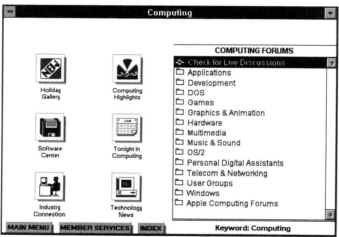

The Computing Department, with forums.

If you read down the list, you can see that each forum entry is devoted to one broad category, such as Development (programming) or Graphics and Animation. Let's look at one.

Parts of a Forum

If you double-click on Windows in the list, it will take you to the Windows Forum, shown on the following page.

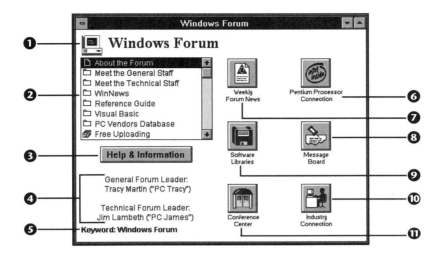

Anatomy of a forum.

The Windows Forum is fairly representative of all the forums you'll see online in terms of what's available in each and how they work. Although the parts may be arranged a little differently, they'll be similar. I've numbered the various parts in the figure so they're easier to sort out. Let's go through them.

1. The forum name (in this case, Windows Forum) always lets you know where you are.

2. This scroll box provides access to informational files (About the Forum, in this figure), folders of information (Meet the Staff folders), and all the features of the forum (including software libraries and upload areas).

3. The Help & Information button (strangely enough) gets you help and information. Use it if you get stuck or confused.

4. The names and screen names of the forum leader(s). In the figure, there are two (for the Technical and General Forums). Some forums only have one forum leader.

If you look at the names of the forum staff in the figure, you'll notice they're both called "PC *Something*." That shows they work in the PC Computing forum. All forum staff members' names begin with letters to help you identify what forum they work with. The GeoWorks Forum staff names all start with GW, for instance. This helps you figure out who the players are when you don't have a scorecard; this can be especially helpful in a crowded forum chat room.

5. The Forum Keyword (in the figure, it's WINDOWS FORUM) enables you to sidestep the Main Menu and Department screen and go right to the forum of your choice. (Chapter 23 is bursting with Keywords.)

The right half of the forum screen has buttons. Some of these will change from time to time; others will always be the same.

6. The Pentium Processor Connection takes you to a forum of related interest (if you're interested).

7. Weekly Forum News tells you what's hot and happening in the forum this week, so you can plan to attend online events or get the latest information.

8. Message Board takes you to the forum's message area, where you can read what other members think about the subject at hand, post your own thoughts, and even get help with problems. (More on this coming up.)

9. Software Libraries takes you to the various libraries of software related to the forum subject. (Chapter 12 is all about software and other files: finding them, downloading them, and uploading your own.)

10. Industry Connection takes you to the area where all of the hardware and software companies online have their own forums. You can get advice and software straight from the horse's mouth (or the other end, depending on how you feel about the company).

11. Conference Center is the forum's chat area. It might be host to guest speakers, moderated forums on a specific subject, or just general chat. Not all the forum chat areas are called Conference

Centers, but you can figure out from the name that it's a chat room of some kind. All chat rooms (except for big rooms like the Rotunda and Center Stage) work the same online, so there are no surprises here (see Chapter 10 if you don't remember how chat works).

TITF: Tonight In The Forums

The next time you sign on to America Online, do this: use the Keyword TITF by the method appropriate to your computer. The Tonight In The Forums window appears. In this window, you'll be able to find out everything that's happening that night in the online forums: guest speakers, chats on particular topics, discussion groups, or whatever. Just double-click on the **Tonight in the PC/Mac Forums** entry in the list.

If you're interested in what's happening right now, double-click the **Check For Live Discussions** entry. This brings up a listing of all the active forum chat rooms, much like the list you used in Chapter 10 to change chat rooms. Just double-click on the one that strikes your fancy, and you'll be there.

TITF also gives you access to the Weekly Forum News specific to your model of computer. You can also get to the Rotunda, which is a huge online meeting area where hundreds of people can gather to see a guest speaker or play a group game. Double-click on the **Rotunda Entrance** item, and you'll get a second window, similar to the TITF window, with calendars of Rotunda events and a way to actually enter the Rotunda.

The Rotunda is like dozens of normal chat rooms linked together, only the "rooms" are called "rows." You can chat within your row, but not with other rows. To interact with the host or special guest, you need to submit your question or statement to the event host (who sorts out duplicate questions). Just so you're not completely lost, read the informational text about the Rotunda (or Center Stage, which works the same way) before you go in. It will save you a lot of confusion and let you enjoy the event.

Forum Events

In addition to the huge extravaganzas that happen in the Rotunda and other large meeting rooms online, individual forums often hold smaller events in their own chat rooms—which look and behave like the chat rooms in the People Connection. There is, however, one big difference between an "event" and a general chat in a forum. Very often, events are moderated by a host (usually part of the forum's staff) who introduces the guest(s). The guest has a few minutes to make any opening/introductory remarks (during which it is very rude to send any of your own chat). Then the floor is thrown open to questions and comments.

To avoid a general flood of confusing comments and questions, forum events are usually run under a protocol of some kind. If you have a question, instead of just blurting it out, you might be asked to send a question mark only, like this:

PIV: ?

If you have a comment, you send this message:

PIV: !

The forum host keeps track of the order in which members ask to speak. The host keeps things moving along by regularly interjecting comments on the order of:

FORUM HOST: PIV, your question? MS. DESMOND you're next. There are 6 people waiting in the queue.

When I see the host's statement above, I send my briefly worded question, and the guest answers. Meanwhile, MS. DESMOND types her comment so that when the host tells her to "go," all she has to do is press **Enter**. When the guest finishes answering a question, he lets the host know by typing "END" or "Next question?"

Using a protocol in an event room keeps things moving along, allows as many people as possible to ask questions, and keeps it from becoming totally chaotic, as it would if all 23 people talked at the same time. However, protocols aren't used all the time, nor are the same protocols used. The event host will explain the protocol du jour at the beginning of the event and then again before the question and answer period starts. If you come in late, you'll probably receive an Instant Message (IM) outlining the protocol as soon as you're in the room. When there is a protocol, please follow it. Protocols make life online in crowded event rooms so much more pleasant.

Conan the Librarian

Every forum has some sort of library that's maintained by the forum staff. Generally these contain software and/or text files related to the forum's theme or focus. You can access a forum's library by clicking on its Software Libraries button. The following figure shows the Windows Forum Software Libraries.

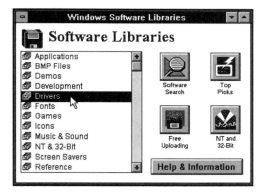

A software library—Sshhh!

Most libraries look about the same as this, with similar features. Some may only contain a scrolling list of the different libraries you can access; others may have highlight buttons like the ones shown here (Top Picks and NT and 32-bit). Just click on the button or double-click on the library name in the list box.

The next chapter has more information about looking for software and other files online, downloading them, using them, and sharing your own creations with others online.

Treading the (Message) Boards

One of the most popular uses for the forums on any online service is the chance it gives users to communicate with people who use the same computers, hardware, or software, or people with similar hobbies.

Not all online message boards are as heavily traveled as the Windows board. Some have only a few categories and fewer subcategories. In those cases, you might not get an introductory screen, but might go directly to the categories.

Members can post a question on a message board and get answers back from other members who may have conquered the same problem.

Think of a message board as a big filing cabinet. In the Windows message board, there are 16 categories. Therefore, it's like a filing cabinet with 16 drawers, each of which has a subject name on the front. Inside each drawer, there may be hundreds (really, hundreds) of file folders, each with labels related to the subject of the drawer. Inside each of those folders are the 81+ thousand messages.

Finding the Boards

To access the forum's message board, click on its **Message Board** button. You will see a window similar to the one shown here.

The Windows Forum message board.

The message board window above gives you lots of information and lots of options about what you can look at in the board area. The top of the window tells you there are 16 message categories and that in those categories there are more than 81,000 messages (yikes!). The latest message was posted 12/04/94. At the very bottom of the screen is the date you last visited the forum.

As you start your adventures online, you'll see a lot of the line "This area is new to you" (as shown in the figure). America Online keeps track of the forums you visit and the date and time of your visit—and it's a good thing, too. Here's why.

The record of the date and time of your last visit will help cut through all that underbrush so you can find what you want. Click on **Find New** to see only stuff that has been posted since the last time you visited. Click on **Find Since** to see only stuff that has been posted in the last 3 days, 7 days, or however many days you care to see at one clip. This can be a great timesaver.

You'll notice that there are four buttons on the message board window. The first one, List Categories, just shows you the sixteen broad categories on the board. Click on it to bring up a new window.

The categories window gives you the same sort of information at the top of the screen: the number of categories; the number of topics and postings in each category; and the date of the latest post in each category. You can scroll through the list of categories to see what information you're interested in browsing through.

To open a category, just double-click on it. It opens a window like the one coming right up, with all of the topics in the category you selected. Opening a category is like pulling open a drawer in that filing cabinet I mentioned.

Inside the category, you'll find subcategories (topics). Carrying the file cabinet metaphor through, the topics are like file folders in the cabinet drawer. They make it easier for you to narrow the search for the information you need. In this instance, I've selected Drivers as my topic.

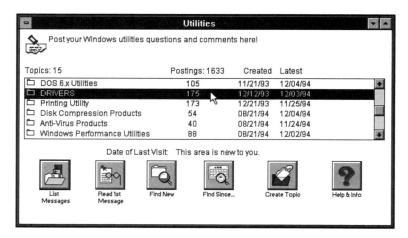

15 topics, no waiting...

If you read the information after the name, you see that the Drivers topic contains 175 messages. The topic was created on 12/12/93, and the latest message was added on 12/03/94. Double-click on the topic to open a list of all the individual message names (like the figure below).

A whole mess o' messages.

You can then scroll through the list looking for headings that seem to match the problem you're having or contain information you might need. You may have to click on the More button a few times to see them all. When you find a message you want to read, just double-click on it.

Adding a Message of Your Own

If you want to respond to a message you're reading or ask a related question, click the **Add Message** button. Clicking the Add Message button brings up a window that looks like an abridged email window. Instead of having To: and CC: boxes (it's already "addressed" to the message board), this window just has a Subject area box. The subject is automatically entered as "Re:" (for reply, or regarding) and the name of the message you're reading. You can change it if you care to. In the Enter Text area, type the message you want to post. When you're done composing the message, click on the **Post** button, and your message is added to that Topic area.

You can save money by composing your postings offline, using America Online's text editor. Create a new memo by selecting New from the File menu. Enter your text. Save the document by selecting **Save** from the File menu. When you find the area to which you want to post your message, open the saved file (using the **Open** command on the File menu). Click on the **Add Message** button. Then you can copy the message from your saved file, and paste it into the Add A Message window. Click on **Post**, and your message is on its way. This and other money/timesaving tips are in Chapter 22.

If you can't find a topic that suits your needs, you can create one of your own just as easily, and with only a few more steps. In the topic window (the one labeled Utilities in the earlier figure), click on the **Create Topic** button. You just need to enter a name for the category or topic, and a description. If you create a topic for (oh, say) Windows Games, your description might read: Tips and Tricks for Windows Gamesters!

Then you probably want to post the first message (it's pretty rude to just create topics for no reason). You should have a question or comment in mind before you create the topic. With that in mind, let's look at some posting tips.

Message Board Tips

I'm no Aunt Effie, but here are some tips that will help make posting, and answering other posts, a more enjoyable thing to do:

➤ When you're posting to a message board, try to keep your question as short and sweet as possible, while still providing all the information necessary to get an answer.

➤ As in email, when you reply to someone else's posting, it helps if you briefly quote the points of the message you're responding to. Offset the quote, like this:

>>The printer driver V4.1 HP DeskJet will not print Faxes<<

Then enter your reply. That saves everybody the trouble of having to find the original message to see what the question was. Don't reproduce the whole original message, though. That wastes everybody's time.

➤ If you find information you really want to have and to hold, you can print the contents of the message by selecting **P**rint from the File menu. You can also save the message as a text file by using the **S**ave or Save **A**s commands, also in the File menu. Both work the same as printing or saving a file in any application you've ever used.

Thread A group of messages on a related topic (also called a message thread). Just like a piece of sewing thread, you can follow the series of messages from start to finish. In order to save space on the message boards, old or inactive threads are turned into text files and stored in the forum library. These are called message or thread archives, and you can download them from most forum libraries.

➤ Try to avoid the dreaded "folder drift." Folder drift occurs when a message area starts out talking about, oh, Traveling with Pets, but the last message in the thread is somebody whining about how his nephew pulls his cat's tail. Stick to the subject at hand.

➤ Don't take stuff personally. If you post an opinion or view in a discussion area, you will get feedback. You may also get flamed (that's where someone, shall we say, questions your parentage, your IQ, or the size of your brain or other vital organs). Don't buy into it. Flaming wastes time and energy and tends to set off a chain reaction that gets everybody flaming.

Sure, disagree with someone. Sure, say *why* you disagree with him. You can even try to change the person's mind with logical arguments (but that rarely works). Posting a page of "You're such a stupid idiotic jerk for thinking that, I can't believe you can find your way home at night" doesn't do anyone any good. Think it, if you want, but don't post it.

If you get flamed, try not to take it personally. Don't respond. If you simply must answer, keep name-calling out of it.

The Least You Need to Know

This chapter taught you the basics about forums by using the Windows forum as an example. Remember these key points:

➤ You can look for forums related to your personal interests by starting with the main departments on the Main Menu.

➤ Once you find forums you like, you can go directly to them with the right Keyword.

➤ The Keyword: TITF will let you know what's happening "Tonight In The Forums," so you won't miss any really cool online events.

➤ Most forums have their own file/software library.

➤ Most forums have their own chat, conference, or event room, which works just like the chat rooms in the People Connection.

➤ Message boards are like big filing cabinets. The categories are like individual drawers; the topics are like file folders in the drawer; messages are like pieces of paper in the file folders.

➤ You can create new topics or messages with the click of an Add New button.

➤ Try not to flame. If for some reason you must, keep a fire extinguisher handy. People who flame often get burned.

Files for Days

I think I've teased you enough with my babble about uploading, downloading, and the wealth of software and information files available on America Online. Let's get to the point, cut to the chase, get to the heart of the matter. I'm out of clichés—let's just *do* it.

File Library Redux

In the last chapter we looked at forums, how they work, the things most forums have in common, and how to use them. However, I kind of skimmed over one thing: file libraries. We looked at them, but that was about it. Here's how the forum file libraries work. To access a forum's file library (let's use the Windows Forum again, okay?), click on the **Software Libraries** button in the forum's main window.

When you click on the library button, you'll see some variation of the following window.

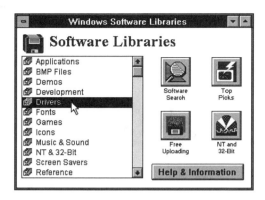

Déjà view: the Windows Forum software libraries.

Software Search (with Your Host Ed McMahon)

If you already know something about the software you want to find, you can search for software that meets your needs. It isn't 100% fool-proof (and I'm the fool that proved it), but it works more often than not. To begin, click the **Software Search** button on the right side of the Windows library screen. The Windows File Search window appears.

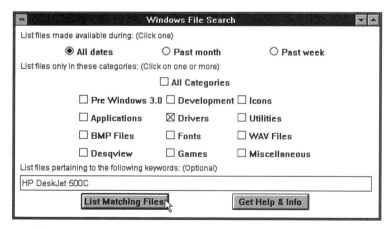

File searching.

There's no set order for entering this information, so I'm going to tell you the way I do it, and you can change the order however you like.

The first thing I usually do is click in the narrow text box at the bottom of the screen to put my cursor there. Then I type the word or phrase I want to use as my search string. In the figure, I'm looking for a printer driver for a Hewlett-Packard DeskJet 500C. That's pretty specific. I could also have entered just Hewlett-Packard, just DeskJet, or just 500C, but that probably would have netted me more files to look at. If you want, you can omit the search string altogether—but you'll get a *lot* of files to sort through.

Next I move up to the middle section, where all the forum's software categories are listed (these will vary from forum to forum). If I don't know where the file I want is located, I click in the **All Categories** check box. However, in this case I know I want a printer driver, so I'll click on the **Drivers** check box to narrow the search. Narrowing the search this way doesn't speed it up appreciably, but it keeps you from getting a lot of unrelated files.

Not all forum libraries are called Software Libraries. Some are called File Libraries, others are Information Libraries, and still others have clever or cute names that don't include "library" at all. The forum *Omni* Magazine Online calls its file library "OMNI Antimatter" to match the news-capsule section in the magazine. The point I'm trying to make is that just because you don't see the words "Software Libraries" in a forum, it doesn't mean that there isn't a file library there. It just may not leap out at you as obviously as some.

Then I move up to the three date choices. Normally I leave All Dates selected. Here's why: This date stuff has nothing to do with when the file/software was written, but with when it was *uploaded* to AOL. Yes, chances are good that brand new software has been uploaded recently; but chances are also good that a pile of old stuff has been uploaded recently, too. So, unless I know that the file is brand-spanking-new, I leave it set for All Dates.

When you have everything selected to your liking, click on **List Matching Files** at the bottom of the screen. AOL does its search and presents you with the results. Sometimes you'll get a little window that says something like "No files were found that matched the search criteria." Other times you'll get a list of files in the File Search Results window.

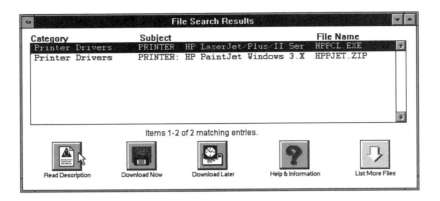

The search results are in!

I can't lie to you. I didn't find *anything* with the very specific HP DeskJet 500c search string, or even with the search string HP DeskJet. The results shown here turned up when I ran a search for just HP. But that's how file searching works sometimes.

If there are more titles than will fit in the window, you can scroll through the list looking for appropriate file names. You may need to click on the **List More Files** button, if there are a lot of files. You can tell if there are more because the Items count beneath the list of files will say something like "Items 1–20 of 140 matching entries," which means you're looking at only a fraction of the files that AOL found.

If you want more information about a file, you can double-click on its line entry and read a detailed description. A typical file description is shown in the next figure.

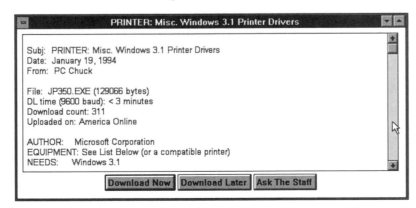

A typical file description. How typical.

138

The top of the description window shows some useful information, such as a general description of the type of file you're looking at (in the figure, that's Miscellaneous Windows 3.1 Printer Drivers), the date it was uploaded, and who uploaded it.

Below that, you see the file name and how large it is (in the figure, the file is called JP350.EXE, and it's 129066 bytes, which is about 129K). It will also tell you the *download time*, how long it will take to move this file from their computer to yours. This is a best guess. Depending on your computer and the amount of traffic online, it may take a little more, or it may take a little less. Next you'll see how many people have downloaded the file already. In the figure, it's 311, which sounds like a lot. However, there are some files online that tens of thousands of people have downloaded. Whoa.

Below *that*, you see the author of the software/file, followed by an Equipment line. The equipment information is of dubious value. Sometimes it lists what the author used to create the file, sometimes (as in the figure) it tells you what equipment *you* need to have, and other times it says something clever like "Nothing Special." Roughly translated, "Nothing Special" means that if you're reading this file on AOL, you must already have all the equipment you need to use this file. "Nothing Special" also turns up in the Needs entry, where the person uploading the file tells you what special software or hardware you must have to use the file. You'll also see a line saying whether the file is *freeware* or *shareware*. I'll explain what that means in a minute.

Below that (and out of sight in the figure) there is usually a longer description of what the file is and what it does. Simply scroll down the window to see this information. Often there are brief installation instructions, or information telling you which documentation file(s) show you how to install and/or use the file.

At the bottom of the window there are three buttons. To get the file immediately, click on the **Download Now** button. To add it to your download manager's list of files to get, click on **Download Later**. (We'll talk more about the download manager in a page or two.) The last button, Ask The Staff, enables you to send an email message to the forum's staff librarian should you want to ask about this or other files in the library (or any other question).

The file search we just did only searched through the file libraries of the Windows Forum. Any time you use the Search Libraries button in a forum, the search is restricted to that forum. If you want to search all of the software libraries in all of the computing forums, you need to use another searching method.

Widening the Search

If you want to find a file but don't know which computing forum(s) might have it, you can search all of them at once. The easiest way to do that is to select **Search Software Libraries** from the Go To menu. You can also use the Keyword: SOFTWARE to go to the Software Center (where all the Computing Forum libraries are collected for easy browsing), and then click on the **Search the Libraries** button.

Either method brings up a search dialog like the one you saw earlier. Instead of listing all of the different categories in one forum as shown earlier, you'll be able to choose from all the forums. Clicking on the All Categories check box tells AOL to search through every computing forum online.

Otherwise, this search works the same as the one you just saw. You enter your search string, select one or more categories, select a time period, and click **List Matching Files**.

Browsing for Software

If you don't have a particular bit of software in mind, or you'd just rather poke around in software libraries on your own, go right ahead. Here's how.

Since I seem to be obsessed with getting this printer problem solved, let's poke around in the Windows Forum libraries again. Go to the Windows Forum (Keyword: WINDOWS FORUM) and follow these steps:

1. Click on the **Software Libraries** button.

2. In the scroll box, double-click on the **Drivers** library. Another list of all the categories of drivers in the library appears.

3. Double-click on **Printer Driver** to open a list of the names of the individual files in the library.

4. Scroll through the list. You may have to click the **List More Files** button a few times to see all of them. When the More button appears dim, you've run out of files to look at.

5. Double-click on any interesting heading to read the file description.

I Want it NOW!

If you run into a file you'd like to have you can click on the **Download Now** button in the file description window or in the listing of files by name. This calls up a standard Save file dialog box, in which you can tell AOL where you want to store the file you're downloading. You might often want to use the very handy Download folder that's in your America Online folder; but it's completely up to you. When you've entered the necessary information in the Save dialog box, click **OK**. You see a little dialog box with a thermometer-type image that tells you how much of the file transfer is complete, and how much is left to do. It also gives you three options:

➤ You can tell it to sign off AOL when the transfer is complete. (This is very nice if you have something better to do than watch a file transfer—it's about as exciting as watching paint dry.)

➤ You can tell it to Finish Later. This adds the current file to your download manager (coming up next). You can then retrieve the file in a group with any other interesting files you've found. Be warned, if you click Finish Later while the Sign Off After Transfer option is checked, it will stop the transfer and sign you off of AOL. If you want to stay online, make sure the Sign Off After Transfer option isn't checked *before* you click Finish Later.

➤ You can click **Cancel** and tell your software to forget the whole thing. It will, too.

 Mac users don't have the Sign Off After Transfer option in the File Transfer display. If you want to automatically sign off after your transfer, click **Download Later** instead and use the down-load manager. You also don't have a Cancel button, but don't fret. You can use the universal Macintosh *Stop That!* command instead: ⌘-. (that's a period, by the way).

If you happen to be downloading a picture file in a compatible format (GIF or JPEG), and if you have your download preferences set to display image files on download, *and* if your computer is capable of doing it, watching files download is a little more interesting. As the file is transferred to your computer, you'll slowly be able to see the picture on your screen. This can come in handy because if you see a bit of the picture and you decide you don't like it, you can click **Cancel** and save yourself the download time. (We talked about setting preferences back in Chapter 6 if you need to brush up.)

After a few minutes (or however long it takes), the file transfer will be completed, you'll hear a voice say "File's done!," and you'll see a message saying the file has been transferred. Click **OK** or press **Enter** to continue on your merry, software-scrounging way (unless you selected Sign Off After Transfer, in which case you'll be disconnected).

The Download Manager

Personally, I rarely download a single file all by itself. I almost always click Download Later and let the download manager retrieve my files at the end of my session. Here's how it works. Instead of clicking Download Now, you click **Download Later**. When you do, AOL makes a note of the name and location of the file you want to download, and you get the message shown below.

This is what you see when you click Download Later.

If you want to look for more files, click **OK** and you can proceed. When you've scrounged up all the files you care to look for and you're ready to sign off, click **Download Manager** in that message box or select **Download Manager** from the File menu. (Or you can click on the **Download Manager** icon in the menu bar; it's the one with the clock and the floppy disk.) Regardless of which method you use, AOL displays the Download Manager shown here.

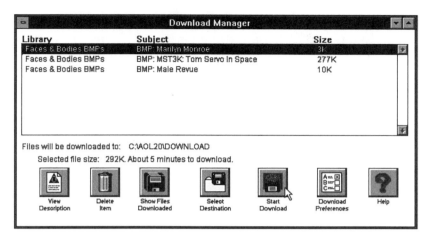

The Download Manager window, in all its glory.

As you can see above, the top part of the download manager lists all the files you told AOL to download later. (Just so you know, I carefully selected the files for the figure above, making sure I had a picture of a man, a woman, and a robot, just so no one would feel left out.) Below that you'll see information that tells you where the files will land when they are downloaded, how much space all the files will take up, and about how long it will take to transfer the files to your computer.

Across the bottom of the screen is a row of buttons. This is what they do:

➤ **View Description** opens the description of the file, like the one we looked at earlier. You can only look at the file description while online.

➤ **Delete Item** removes the selected item from the list; it will not be downloaded.

➤ **Show Files Downloaded** brings up a list of the last 20 or so files you've downloaded, including those you downloaded without the download manager. It's a good thing it keeps track because if you ask to download a file you've already downloaded, AOL reminds you that you've already got a copy and asks if you're sure you want to do it again. (You can change the number of files it lists with your download preferences.)

➤ **Select Destination** opens a standard Save dialog in which you can navigate to the disk, hard drive, or folder where you want all of your downloaded items stored.

➤ **Start Download** begins the process.

➤ **Download Preferences** lets you change your download preferences. You can do it while online or offline (offline doesn't cost you anything, though).

➤ **Help**... need I say more?

Mac users, when you click **Start Download**, you'll get a little dialog box that asks if you want to sign off when finished. If you do, click in the check box and then click **Continue**. If not, simply click **Continue**. Then you'll proceed as described here.

When you're ready, click **Start Download**. You get the same thermometer-type dialog box with the same options we saw earlier. If you want to sign off automatically after the transfer, remember to click in the **Sign Off After Transfer** check box. When the download is finished, you'll either be signed off or you'll stay online, depending on the option you selected.

If you ever forget to tell AOL to sign off after a transfer, and then you walk away and forget about it, don't panic. AOL monitors activity on all of the accounts that are signed on. If you don't do anything for an hour or so, AOL automatically signs you off. This keeps you from running up your online charges and phone bill unnecessarily. Note, however, that AOL doesn't ever keep track of what you're actually doing (that would be snooping); it only notes that you're interacting with the system somehow.

You can also fire up the download manager while offline. The only difference is that you can't view file descriptions. When you're signed off and click on **Start Download**, your software automatically connects to AOL to start the download. When it's done, you'll either remain online (if you didn't click on the Sign Off After Transfer check box) or sign off automatically.

Even cooler, if you're signed off and you have mail you want to receive or send, you can set your FlashSession preferences (covered in Chapter 9) to retrieve all the files in your download manager too. That way, you don't even have to be at home or awake for it to happen. It's all too cool and convenient.

A Word About Viruses

At the bottom of every file description online, you'll see a phrase like **File scanned with XYZ Utility and found to be virus free.** For every file that is uploaded to AOL, before it is placed in a forum library for distribution, it is tested to make sure there isn't a computer virus built-in.

You don't have to worry about viruses (or not much anyway) if you only download files from forum libraries. If, however, you accept files via email or download them from other online services or electronic bulletin boards, you should download or purchase a virus detection utility. There are a lot of these utilities available in freeware, shareware, and commercial varieties.

A **virus** is a bit of computer code hidden inside another file. When you use an infected file, the virus (like the viruses that cause colds and AIDS) can infect your computer. The virus may be relatively harmless and only flash an amusing message on your screen. On the other hand, it may be very harmful and destroy all the data on your hard drive (*ouch!*).

If you want to practice safe computing (and I know that you do), the very first file you download should be an antivirus program. Do a file search using "antivirus" as the search string. You'll sleep easier knowing all your valuable data is safe from viral infection.

Freeware, Shareware, and Demos

Generally all of the files available online for downloading fall into three categories: freeware, shareware, and demonstration versions (demos).

Freeware, as the name implies, is *free software*. You can download it, use it, or give copies to your friends, and never spend anything more for it than the cost of the phone call and online charges for downloading it. Freeware is great.

145

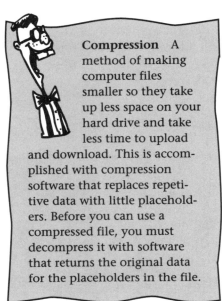

Compression A method of making computer files smaller so they take up less space on your hard drive and take less time to upload and download. This is accomplished with compression software that replaces repetitive data with little placeholders. Before you can use a compressed file, you must decompress it with software that returns the original data for the placeholders in the file.

Shareware, on the other hand, is not free. You do have to pay for it. However, you get to download it, install it on your computer, and try it out for a few days or weeks to see if you like it before you cough up the money. If you don't like it or don't use it, you can erase it from your hard drive and never give it another thought.

If you do like and use the shareware though, you're expected to send the program author the requested fee. Shareware fees generally range from $5–50 and are usually less than what you'd pay in a computer store. For your registration money, you usually get the latest version of the software, a manual, and some sort of registration number to short circuit the "This is an unregistered version of XYZ Application" messages that will pop up from time to time. Keeping and using shareware without sending in the requested fee is the epitome of tackiness. Aunt Effie will sic the Tackiness Police on you.

Demo software can fall into the category of either shareware or commercial (the stuff you buy in stores). Demos are copies of software that have one or two vital elements disabled so you can't use them. You might not be able to print a file or save a file to disk with it. If after using the demo you decide you want to own it, you must either go to a store and buy the real thing (for commercial products) or send the author a check (for shareware) for which she'll send you a fully functional copy of the program with manuals and so on. Demos are a very convenient way to try out software before you buy it, but they're not as cool as fully functional shareware.

Uploading Files

After you've been online a while, you may decide you want to share some of your own creations with the online community. To encourage people to share their creations, America Online doesn't charge you for the time you spend online uploading files.

When you have the file(s) that you want to upload together, consider *compressing* them so it takes less time for you to upload them and for other members to download them. Compression is covered in the next section.

When you're ready, sign on to AOL and navigate to the forum library to which you want to upload the file. Although you can download files from any library, there's usually only one place in each forum where you can upload. It's usually called New Files and Free Uploading in the smaller forums or *Something* Free Uploading (where *Something* is the name of the forum; Windows Free Uploading and such). The uploading area will look something like what's shown in the following figure.

The Windows Uploading area—it's free!

You can also identify an area to which you can upload by checking the Upload button. If it's grayed-out and clicking on it does nothing, you can't upload there.

To upload your file, click on the **Upload** button. An information screen appears. You need to enter some of the information about the file that we saw in the file descriptions earlier in this chapter. Just click once in the first box, and then you can Tab to the other boxes in order.

If you're uploading, say, a newsletter you created with Microsoft Works, you might type "Microsoft Works 4.0 Newsletter" as the subject. In the Author box, type your name (or the name of the person who created what you're uploading if it isn't your own work). For Equipment, list the equipment you used to create the file, specifically the computer type and application software. In the Needs box, enter any special requirements needed to use or view the file; for this example, you might put "MS Works 4.0" and a list of any unusual fonts you used. In the large text box at the bottom, you can write a brief description of the file: "A three column, 8.5" × 11" newsletter for our Church Civic Group with a 4-color banner" and whatever else you might like to say about it.

When you've entered all of the information, click on the **Select File** button. You'll get a standard Open file dialog box. Use it to locate the file you're uploading. Click on the file to select it, and then click **OK**. Your software begins to send the file to the AOL computers.

When it's done, you'll see a message that says "Your file has been submitted and will be reviewed." Just click **OK** to make that go away. All files sent to AOL are reviewed for content and tested for *viruses* before they actually appear in a library anywhere. That's the job of the forum librarians. Because they get a lot of files, yours might not show up for as much as a week or so.

Stuff Me? ZIP You!

As I mentioned earlier, many files you'll find online have been compressed so they take up less space and take less time to download. There are four standard compression methods accepted on AOL: ZIP, ARC, StuffIt, and self-extracting files.

ZIP and ARC are the compression standards for IBM-compatible computers. You can tell that a file has been "zipped" if its name ends with the three letter extension .zip. If it has been archived, it ends with .arc. StuffIt is the compression standard for Macintosh computers. When a file has been "stuffed," its name ends with the three letter extension .sit.

Many compression utilities can create self-extracting files. Their file names generally end with the extension .sea (for Self-Extracting Archive) or .EXE (for executable file). When you launch a file that's self-extracting, it decompresses itself. This type of file might also double as an installer, asking if you want to install the software on your computer.

Before you can use a compressed file, you must decompress it. Fortunately, America Online's software can decompress .sit and .zip files. In fact, you can set your downloading preferences (covered in Chapter 6) to automatically decompress files when you sign off. Unfortunately, you can't compress files with AOL. You need to download a shareware utility called PKZip (search for it by name). That will give you the ability to compress and decompress files whenever you want.

Now, don't be smug, but the Mac version of AOL does compress files. In the dialog box you get when attaching files to email or uploading to a file library, the bottom right corner of the screen has a check box that says Compress Files. When you click in the check box, you'll be asked where you want the compressed file saved. Navigate to the folder or disk, and click **OK**. Your original file remains unchanged.

If you want to compress files without going through AOL, do a file search online for "StuffIt Light." It's a shareware package from Aladdin Systems, the folks who make the commercial package called StuffIt Deluxe.

If you don't have your download preferences set to decompress files, you can decompress a file using the **Open** command in the **File** menu. Select the compressed file in the Open dialog and click **OK**. The AOL software should decompress the file, as long as it's a .zip, .sit, or .arc file.

The Least You Need to Know

That's about all there is to know about downloading and uploading files on AOL. As you begin to explore the various file libraries, keep these things in mind:

➤ If you know what kind of software or file you're looking for, you can save time by using the Search Library option, instead of doing it manually.

➤ The Search command in forum libraries only searches in that particular forum. To search all of the Computing Forum libraries, use the Keyword: QUICKFIND or select **Search Software Libraries** from the Go To menu.

➤ You can click **Download Now** to retrieve individual files immediately, or you can click **Download Later** and retrieve all your selected files with the download manager.

➤ When downloading, you can tell AOL to sign off automatically after a file has been transferred so you can walk away and get on with your life.

➤ Many files online are compressed. You have to decompress them before you can use them.

➤ File names that end with .zip, .sit, .arc, or .sea are definitely compressed. Some file names that end with .exe are also compressed (but they're self-extracting, so don't worry about it).

➤ Viruses can hurt your computer. Practice safe computing: download or purchase an antivirus utility, and use it. You don't need to be compulsive about it on AOL (everything in the file libraries is tested) unless you receive files by email, from friends, or through services that don't scan for viruses.

Information Please

I'm sure it has happened to you. You're going about your business when suddenly, out of the corner of your eye, you catch an interesting something on television or radio (I guess that would be "out of the corner of your ear"). Before you can get the whole picture, the news story is over, and you just have the idea that it was about something you'd be interested in. What do you do? (Suddenly I'm Dennis Hopper in *Speed*.) What *do* you do?

In homes that aren't online, you sit around and wait for the news again. Maybe you go channel surfing, looking for another news show or checking out CNN. In homes that are online, we fire up our modems and go information surfing.

On America Online you can track down hot stories of the day, technological news and information, or articles about your favorite passions.

Read All About It!

You may recall from your first venture online (way back in Chapter 5) that one of the regular features of AOL's welcoming In The Spotlight screen is a blurb about the top news story of the day. By clicking on the Top News Story of The Day button (at the bottom of the In The Spotlight screen), you can read the featured article and other stories detailing the latest fast-breaking news.

For folks who enjoy analysis and commentary, there's the online Newsstand, (shown here) where you can pick up hot-off-the-(digital)-press copies of your favorite newspapers and magazines. To get there, click on **The Newsstand** on the Main Menu or use the Keyword: NEWSSTAND.

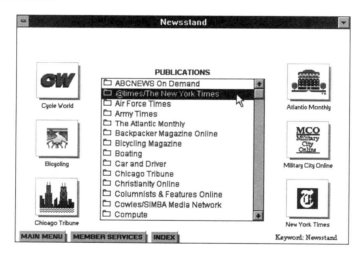

The Newsstand.

As you can see in the figure, the online Newsstand is like your neighborhood newsstand. You can choose your news from a wide variety of magazines and two major metropolitan newspapers. When you find a magazine that interests you, double-click its entry in the list box or click its button if it has one. (Don't rely on the buttons, though; they change almost weekly.)

Looking for News

Okay, let's say that news clip you heard was about your favorite actor's triumphant debut in a new Off Broadway show. You only heard the actor's name, but no details. How would you find out what's going on? This is what I'd do (if you're at your computer, you might want to play along):

1. Sign on to AOL and quickly go to the Main Menu.

2. From the Main Menu, click on **The Newsstand**.

3. At the Newsstand, click on the *New York Times* button (or double click on the **@times** listing in the scroll box. That takes you to the @times forum. The @times forum works like any other forum you may have explored online, with buttons for the various "sections" of the newspaper.

4. Since I'm looking for theater news, I click on the **Arts** button to display the Arts section of the Times.

5. In the Arts section, click on the **Theater** button to open the Theater section of *The Times*, shown here.

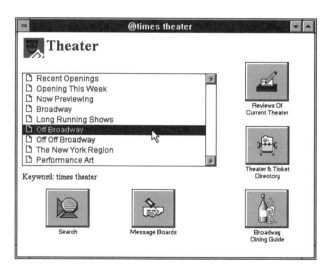

A life in the theater.

At this point, I have two options. I could click on the **Search** button and enter my favorite actor's name as the search string (that's covered in Chapters 12 and 14, if you've forgotten or are chapter surfing). The forum would list the names of every article in which the actor is mentioned. If you're a rabid Tom Cruise fan, say, that might be just the ticket.

On the other hand, I could just double-click on the **Off Broadway** listing to bring up a list of all the currently running Off Broadway shows. That listing gives me the same suite of information that appears in the *Times'* summary of shows playing on and Off Broadway: the name of the play, playwright, principal actors, director, theater name and address, and so on. Now all I need to do is skim through the listing until I see my star's name.

If you want more information, click the Reviews of Current Theater button in the Theater window to see if the play has been reviewed and what the *Times'* drama critic thought of it. You could even find out how to order tickets (click the **Theater & Ticket Directory** button) and pick a restaurant to dine in before or after the show (click the **Broadway Dining Guide** button). Sardi's perhaps?

You can print any information you turn up here (or in any of the forums, of course) and/or save it to your hard drive in a text file so you can take the information with you on your jaunt to the Big Apple. After you see the show, you may want to return to @times and post a message in the message board area (especially if the critic blasted the play and you really enjoyed it). Just click on the **Message Boards** button and post your own review.

This scenario works in any information gathering situation. If there's something you need to know that's in the news, go to the Newsstand (Keyword: NEWSSTAND). Find a magazine or newspaper that's likely to have the coverage you're after. Then you can either manually sift through the whole list of articles or use the forum's Search function to do the looking for you.

Many of the Newsstand's forums also have file libraries from which you can download supplemental information, such as the photographs that go with a news story, or copies of older news stories. You can even keep up to date with computing news through several online computer magazines: (including *Compute, Home Office Computing,* and *Mac Home Journal* among others).

IC: Industry Connection

Computer magazines are fine for general information, but if you need detailed information about a particular product, you can get help straight from the horse's mouth in the Industry Connection. AOL's Industry Connection groups together hundreds and hundreds of software and hardware manufacturers in one easy-to-access area.

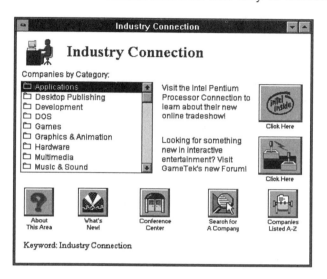

Connecting with industry leaders.

As a "for instance," I've been checking out the Industry Connection a *lot* lately, looking for software upgrades for my Mac. Since Apple released the Mac OS version 7.5 with QuickDraw GX, I've been looking for GX-compatible drivers for my fax modem and my label printer.

Here's how I access the Industry Connection:

1. I sign on to AOL.

2. I use the Keyword: INDUSTRY CONNECTION (actually, just "IC" works fine).

3. I use the alphabetical listing of companies to find the modem's manufacturer (Global Village Communications).

4. When I find it, I double-click on the name and *poof!* I'm at the Global Village Communication area.

After you find a manufacturer in the Industry Connection for the first time, you can use a Keyword to go right to their area again, without having to search through the Industry Connection's main screen. To get to Global Village's area, I use the Keyword: GLOBAL VILLAGE. If you're up to performing an experiment, randomly pick a company's name and try using it as a Keyword. If the company has a forum on AOL, chances are you will go right to their area in the Industry Connection. Just see if that's not true.

Once at Global Village's area, I can read their company news (by double-clicking on the Company News listing) for new product and upgrade announcements. I can see what other products they make by double-clicking on the Product Information listing. What I've been doing most often, though, is double-clicking on their Software Library so I can poke around in their file library for a new GX-compatible driver. No luck yet.

Actually, Global Village is one of the few companies that doesn't routinely answer questions in their message area. If you want online technical support from Global Village, send them email addressed to GlobalVill, and they'll reply by email.

When I'm done in the library, and feeling all sullen and cranky about not being able to use QuickDraw GX, I usually pop into the Let's Discuss message board (by double-clicking its listing) to see who else is ticked off at the lack of a driver. When I see that lots of people are upset about it, too, I don't feel so bad. Of course, you can scan the topics in the message area to see if anyone else has had a problem like yours, read the advice they've been given, and try it yourself. I've fixed a number of computer troubles that way.

If you can't find a solution to your problem, you can always post a message of your own (Chapter 11 tells you how; Chapter 22 tells you how to do it for less money). Most of the companies that have areas in the Industry Connection have customer service people who regularly patrol the message boards to read and respond to your questions.

One-Time-Only Features

When disaster strikes—earthquake, flood, riots, or anything that threatens a large area—America Online is usually right on top of it. They set up special areas and chat rooms where you can collect the latest news, offer help, and track down friends and family members who live in or near the affected area.

I remember that during the last big earthquake in Los Angeles, people were getting more reliable information online than they were through the news media. Local newspapers were actually quoting people they interviewed online, since they couldn't get through to Los Angeles by phone. People were able to track down family members, contact them directly, or get in touch through other online members, and find out what exactly was going on.

 America Online users can get through to a disaster area because members use *local* access numbers, and don't have to rely on long distance connections to get through. As long as the local phones are working in the affected area, information can be sent and received through America Online. Pretty cool.

God forbid that AOL should need to set up another such temporary area. But you can rest assured that if the need arises, AOL will be there to keep the information flowing.

The Least You Need to Know

Although this chapter looked at only a few examples of the information resources available online, the general principles will work in any of the areas on AOL:

➤ The Newsstand (Keyword: NEWSSTAND) is your source for online newspapers and magazines. You can find the latest news of the world, plus coverage of your favorite leisure and hobby activities.

➤ In most Newsstand forums, you can browse title listings for articles that catch your interest, or you can use the search function to find articles on particular topics.

➤ Many Newsstand forums have software libraries that include photographs and yesterday's news.

➤ The Industry Connection gives you late-breaking news of another sort. You can find press releases, product announcements, software upgrades, and helpful information from thousands of hardware and software companies.

➤ Most Industry Connection message boards are patrolled by customer service representatives so you can get answers to your questions—straight from the horse's mouth.

➤ When disaster strikes, you can often find special information areas and chat rooms set up to keep you informed and in touch with family and friends in the affected area.

Chapter 14

Educational Programming

In This Chapter

➤ Help with homework

➤ Looking stuff up

➤ Higher education, digital-style

Like most grandmothers, mine had a fleet of sayings about learning, education, and, of course, the state of kids today. Most of her messages stuck, at least the ones about education. To keep her happy (and to let you know that America Online is not only about fun), here's a little chapter devoted to the educational resources you can find online. You get at them by clicking the Education icon on the Main Menu. Here you will find resources for students of all ages, and even an online university.

Teachers on Duty

One of my education traumas was settling down to do my homework and realizing that I didn't have a clue what the teacher had been talking about. I only wish America Online had been around back then—I would have signed on and run, not walked, to the Education department and the Academic Assistance Center (or AAC) crying for help.

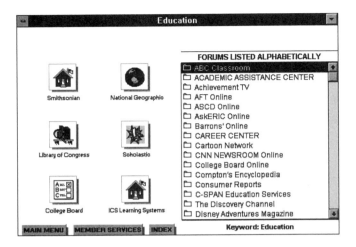

The Education department.

To get to the AAC (see the next figure), double-click the **Academic Assistance Center** listing in the Education department window, or use the Keyword: HOMEWORK.

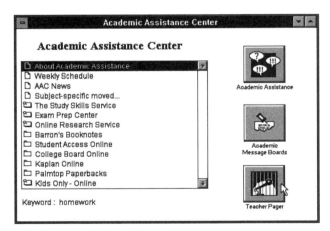

The Academic Assistance Center—they're ready to assist you.

The AAC is designed to help students with their homework (hence the Keyword), reinforce newly learned concepts, and help work rusty academic skills back into shape with brain aerobics. One of the main features is the actual Academic Assistance area (click the **Academic Assistance** button to enter), which contains three chat rooms, each devoted to a specific topic area and hosted by a teacher.

160

Rooms may cover a range of topics. On a typical day the topics from 6–7 PM were Math for grades 1–8, History, and Writing. Students can pop in, ask their questions or get other assistance, and then get back to their homework with a minimum of fuss. If there isn't a room scheduled for a topic you need help with, pop in anyhow. There may be a teacher with knowledge of your subject around, and you might still be able to get help.

The schedule is posted one week at a time, Sunday through Friday. No official topics are scheduled on Saturdays, but you can often find a teacher hanging out in the room to help. Specific topics are scheduled from about 10 AM until Midnight, eastern time. Most are for an hour, with a few (like Auto Repair) scheduled for only half an hour. You can read the schedule by double-clicking on the Weekly Schedule item in the AAC list box. Of course, it might be more convenient to print it out (with the Print command in your File menu) or save it to your hard disk (with the Save command in your File menu) for future reference.

Teachers on Call

If, for some reason, you have a question that flummoxes even the teacher on duty in one of the chat rooms, you can ask for additional help. Click on the **Teacher Pager** button on the AAC forum to bring up a pre-addressed email form that students can fill out and send. That message is directed to the appropriate staff member, and you are promised an answer by email within 48 hours (though you may only wait 6–12 hours).

When asking a question using Teacher Pager, keep a couple of things in mind:

Ask a specific question. Saying "I'm having trouble with history" isn't a question. "Can you explain Lafayette's role in the Revolutionary War to me?" *is* a question. Say what you need to know, and be *specific*.

Provide as much information as you can. Your specific question(s), your grade level, and the course/subject will help the teachers better answer your question.

Keep it short. You can provide all of that information and ask a question very briefly: "Hi, I'm a 6th grade student. We're studying the Revolutionary War in American History class. Can you explain Lafayette's role in the war to me? I don't get it. Thank you."

Asking specific questions, providing enough information, and keeping it short makes sure that the teacher knows exactly what you want to know, answers your question, and doesn't get bogged down with a lot of extra words. Saying "please" and "thank you" is always a good idea.

Academic Messages

In addition to the chat rooms and the Teacher Pager, there's also a message area (click on the **Academic Message Boards** button) where you can post your questions in a number of subject areas. Messages posted here are open for general discussion by students and teachers alike. Questions that get asked a lot (what we byte-heads call FAQs, or Frequently Asked Questions) are forwarded to the teaching staff. Don't be surprised if you get an email response to a message you posted on the boards.

Additional Study Stuff

The Academic Research Service (the Online Research Service in the AAC scroll list) provides help to students in high school through graduate school who are writing research-type papers. Just double-click on the list entry to access the area. You post messages in the appropriate topic area, and the service points you in the right research direction.

Follow the guidelines for asking questions from the Teacher Pager section for best results. You will get leads (you might find information in "such and such" a book), basic information ("The Llama is a quadruped"), and research strategies to save you time in the library stacks. You will not get completed papers, text files of quotable material, or copies of reference books. The Research Service provides help, but it doesn't do the work for you.

Although the Academic Research Service won't send you a book by email, you can download electronic versions of books in the form of text files you can read with your word processor or books you can read on your Newton MessagePad or other PDA (Personal Digital Assistant) device. They're located in the Palmtop Paperbacks section. Double-click on its entry in the list box. See Chapter 12 for how to find and download files.

Look It Up Yourself

In addition to those educational resources aimed specifically at students, there is a pile of other learning opportunities. You can learn on your own, just for the fun of it, or on an I-need-to-know basis for work or school.

Compton's Encyclopedia Online

If you know you need information on a particular subject, you can always look it up yourself in Compton's Encyclopedia online. Compton's lets you enter a search string to find articles that have the specified word or phrase in the title or in the text.

To access Compton's Encyclopedia, double-click on the **Compton's Encyclopedia** listing in the Education department's list box. If you prefer, you can use the Reference Desk; it will open the window shown here.

Compton's Online.

The scroll box in the Compton's window contains mostly information on how to best use the encyclopedia. You should read some of this before you try to do actual research. The tips are invaluable and will save you time and money online. There's also information on how to save and print articles and on the correct way to cite (with a footnote or endnote) Compton's material you use in a paper or report. Remember: if you didn't cite it, you stole it.

To search the encyclopedia, click on either the **Search on Titles** or **Search on Full Text** button. If you select Search on Titles, AOL only looks through the names of all the articles. If you select Search on Full

Text, AOL looks through every word in every article in the encyclopedia; therefore, this takes much longer. You might want to search titles first, and then search the full text only if you don't turn up enough information in your first few tries. Clicking on either search button brings up a dialog like the one shown here. I chose to search through titles only to start. Because I've become such a fan of *The X-Files*, I entered "UFOs" as my search string. I then clicked on List Articles.

Enter words to
search for here.

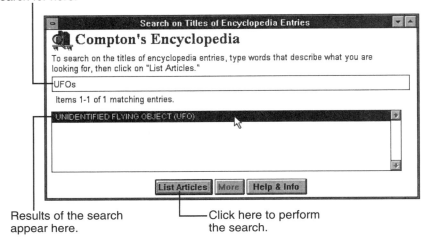

Results of the search
appear here.

Click here to perform
the search.

Searching for signs of intelligent life in the universe...

If you care about such geeky details, the searching method AOL uses is called a Boolean search. With Boolean searches, you can include "and" or "not" between two search words. For example, if you wanted information about uncommon roses, you might enter the string "roses not red." The encyclopedia would first find all the articles that covered roses in general, and then eliminate the articles that were about red roses only.

Alternatively, you could enter a string on the order of "Roses and rare," which would only give you articles about rare roses. Of course, it could also turn up articles about common roses and rare steaks—which is why I suggest you carefully read the tips on searching before you try it yourself.

There was only one article with UFO in the title (which smacks of a government cover-up, if you ask me). If you have a more productive search, you may need to click on **More** a few times to see all of the titles listed in the results window. However, to read my one lonely article, I simply double-clicked its title.

With the article on my screen, I could read it, copy and paste the bits I wanted to use into my research paper (with appropriate citations), and save or print the whole article for future reference. Compton's Encyclopedia online can save you from having to *shlep* to the library to finish a report.

Other Resources

I don't want you to think there's only information like what they're always trying to make you read in school. You can find diverse resources, such as the following forums:

ABC Classroom (the TV Network, not the alphabet)

CNN Newsroom

The Discovery Channel

Disney Adventures Magazine

ICS Learning Systems (without Sally Struthers asking "Would you like to earn more money?")

The Learning Channel

Library of Congress Online

National Geographic Online

Scientific American

Smithsonian Online

There are more resources for students and still more for teachers too. I think it would be well worth anyone's time to spend an hour or so poking around all the interesting information available in the Education Department. Used in conjunction with the news resources covered in Chapter 13, you should have all the information you need right at your fingertips.

Continuing Education

Grade school and high school students aren't the only ones who can benefit from the educational resources on AOL. With the Electronic University Network (Keyword: EUN), you can complete your Bachelor's degree or go for a Ph.D. or Master's degree online.

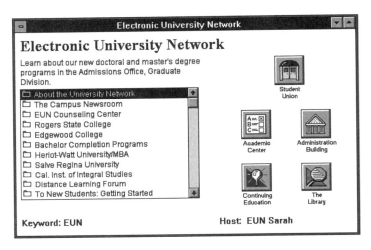

Taking home-study to new heights.

Although it's a shameless plug, high school students considering college may also want to check out *The Complete Idiot's Guide to Getting into College*. Now, if only there was a *Complete Idiot's Guide to Life in the '90s*, we'd be in business.

The Electronic University Network works with several academic institutions to offer degree programs to digital students around the world. Each offers courses in what it does best, such as Heriot-Watt's MBA program.

Like any college campus, there's a Library (of files), a Student Union (a chat area—still under construction at this writing), and an Administration Building. You can attend EUN as an undergraduate, graduate, or continuing education student. EUN offers a variety of courses, from programming in C+ to methods for working toward world peace, for a variety of fees.

Speaking of fees, courses cost about the same per credit as your average college courses (after all, they *are* college courses). The benefits are being able to attend classes from home, thereby saving yourself the expenses of transportation, housing, and (maybe) baby-sitters and such. If you think you might be interested in signing up, explore the area and read all of the course descriptions and information about costs and financing. You'll find most of the nitty-gritty details in the Administration Building.

From time to time, EUN offers a free mini-course (called Distance Learning 101) that introduces you to the experience of studying online. You may want to check it out. EUN undergraduate credits are accepted by over 2,500 colleges in the United States, in case you later decide you want the full college treatment.

The Least You Need to Know

For any students reading this, I don't want the stuff from the top of the chapter to give you the idea that education isn't fun. That was mainly for the parental-types. I've always had a blast in school, and even managed to learn a thing or two in the process. Just don't tell anyone.

➤ You get to the Education Department by clicking on Education on AOL's Main Menu or by using the Keyword: EDUCATION.

➤ You'll find many more educational resources here than I had space to cover in this chapter, including stuff as cool as National Public Radio (NPR Outreach) and a digital version of the Smithsonian Institute.

➤ The Academic Assistance Center (Keyword: HOMEWORK) offers all kinds of help to students who need concepts reinforced or questions answered.

➤ You can get academic assistance three ways: in live chat (use the **Academic Assistance** button), through email (send your questions with the **Teacher Pager**), and with the discussions posted to the message area (click the **Academic Message Boards** button).

➤ For the "do-it-yourself" crowd, you can do everyday research with Compton's Encyclopedia (Keyword: ENCYCLOPEDIA).

➤ College-bound students can start or finish their degrees with the Electronic University Network (Keyword: EUN) and learn from the privacy of their own homes.

Chapter 15

Fun Stuff

In This Chapter

➤ Fun stuff for everybody

➤ Fun teen-type stuff

➤ Fun kid stuff

➤ And we'll have fun, fun, fun 'til our daddy takes the modem away

This chapter looks at only a few of the many fun things you can do online—the things most users seem to enjoy a lot. They may be right up your alley, they may not. If they aren't, explore. Find or create your own fun. This chapter also looks at fun places for teens and kids to visit.

Fun Rooms

Much of the fun online comes from interacting with other users in chat rooms: getting together in a social setting, letting your hair down, and just relaxing with pleasant and amusing company. Two such rooms that pop up regularly are the Romance Connection and La Pub.

Romancin'

One of the most popular things to do online is flirt shamelessly. I guess the stress of modern working and living, the need to stick close to home, and general shyness make it difficult for many individuals to meet new people. Online flirting makes it easier. Things you feel self-conscious about in public (your looks, weight, appalling fashion sense, that scar) don't apply online because people can't see you. There are no bad hair days online. And there's none of that "I'm too tired to go out" excuse because you don't "go" anywhere. You just log on, flirt, log off, and fall right into bed for a good night's sleep.

You'll find Romance Connection rooms in The People Connection with all the other chat rooms (see Chapter 10 for details). I've seen them at all hours—even as early as 9 a.m. (If you aren't looking for romance *per se*, but do want to flirt, look for rooms called The Flirts Nook. They may be more your speed.)

Don't confuse Romance Connection chat rooms with the Romance Connection. (The Romance Connection is in the PC Studio; just click on the **PC Studio** button in any chat room.) The Romance Connection in the PC Studio is like the personal ads section of your newspaper. You can post a description of yourself, or read descriptions of others.

Romance Connection rooms are much the same as other chat rooms online, with all the same features and functions. The only difference is that, as a rule, the topics of conversation rarely get heavy. It's mostly friendly chat, harmless flirting, and the occasional case of what we called "goo-goo eyes" when I was a kid.

Does that mean you can't meet special people online? No. Does it mean relationships don't get serious? No. As a matter of fact, you can see talk shows (*Geraldo*, for instance) on the topic of "Married people who met online."

Very often, the people you meet online are from all over the country, but once in awhile you'll meet someone who lives down the street or at least near your home (it has happened to me). Often folks meet online and then pick up the flirting in person. If you think you might like to meet an online friend, there are some tips coming up a little later.

Where Everybody Knows Your Name

La Pub is a digital pub. You'll find it in The People Connection with all the other chat rooms (see Chapter 10 for details). Just as you would in a regular pub, you can hang out, knock back a frosty beverage, and chat with those around you. You can even shoot a game of darts if you like.

The nice thing about La Pub is that it has all the ambiance of a night of pub-crawling, without the loud music, cigarette smoke, and hangover. The beverages are all digital unless you provide your own. It's a nice place to just kick back and chat. After a few visits, you'll notice that there's a crowd of regulars who pop in (just like at your own favorite hang out), and you'll get to know each other pretty well.

Before you try a Romance Connection chat room, you may want to read through Chapter 7 for some of the finer points of online etiquette. Flirting is pretty free-form, but some rules *do* apply. Before you let your pre-teen and teen-aged children pop in, you may want to check it out for yourself, too. The flirting can get a little "adult" in nature.

Meeting and Greeting

Say you meet someone online and decide you want to meet face to face. Should you? Why not? As long as you keep a few things in mind when you set up your meeting, you should be fine. Some of these are just practical tips; others come from personal experience.

➤ Don't offer to meet right away. Give yourself a chance to get to know the person better online first.

➤ If distant travel is involved, don't make the trip just to meet. You may not care for each other in person and might wind up wasting a pile of money or frequent flyer miles. If you happen to be in the other's city for another reason, then sure, you should meet. You'll still have other things to do if your meeting turns out other than you expected.

➤ Meet in a public place: a restaurant, bookstore, coffee house, or someplace where there are other people. Don't go to either person's home. That's awkward and potentially dangerous. Face it, you don't really *know* this person. Who knows what ulterior motives they may have? Play it very safe for the first few meetings.

➤ Describe yourselves accurately so you both know what the other person really looks like. If you, shall we say, stretch the truth a little, you might not be able to find each other in a crowded public place. You might also set yourselves up for serious disappointment if this is a flirty sort of thing.

➤ Don't believe that picture in your head. Talking to someone online is like listening to a voice on the radio: you build up an image in your head that, more often than not, is completely wrong. Don't pay attention to it.

➤ It's generally a bad idea to go into these meetings with any expectations. Even though you feel like you know this person, you're really meeting for the very first time.

➤ Don't let a bad first meeting spoil your online relationship. There must be something about the person you like, otherwise you wouldn't have wanted to meet in the first place. Even if a flirty-thing doesn't turn into a romance-thing, or even a friendship-thing, you can still *talk*.

Fun and Games

There are two kinds of games you can play online: games held in game rooms in the People Connection and other online games like RabbitJack's Casino. This section explains them both.

Game Rooms

Game rooms are usually hosted by two people who are part of America Online's staff. One acts as host, and the other acts as scorekeeper. Both try to keep the game moving and entertaining. You can find Trivia games, "Name That Tune" sort of games, and some games that defy description. Generally, games are played in the evenings, when there are more folks online.

You'll find that game rooms, like some chat rooms, attract a hearty band of regulars who can be as entertaining as the game itself. Game rooms are easy to spot—look for names like these:

Acronyms	Alphabet Soup
Blankety Blanks	Borderlines
Charades	Comic Lines
Compass Clues	Crypto Puzzles
Danglers	Dictionary
Ditto	Double Dare
DrawKcab	Fender Benders
Harmony	Hinky Pinky
InCommon	Initials
QUIK GuessMe Game	QUIK Harmony Game
QUIK InCommon Game	QUIK Name It Game
QUIK Who Am I Game	

Game room schedules are posted in the PC Studio. You can find them listed by day or week. Just click the **PC Studio** button in any chat room and look for the Game Parlor.

RabbitJack's Casino, and Others

As a real casino junkie (the Las Vegas type), I'm sorry to report that RabbitJack's Casino is only available to DOS and Windows users of AOL. Sorry Mac people.

To get to the Casino, use the Keyword: CASINO. As you can see in the following figure, it looks much the same as any other forum online. In the scroll box on the left, there are lots of informational files (including lists of the top winners). Your first time in, you should check out The Beginner's Corner for advice, tips, and rules of play. Below the casino files, you'll also find information about other games you can play online (such as a role-playing game called AD&D Neverwinter Nights and an educational game called MasterWord).

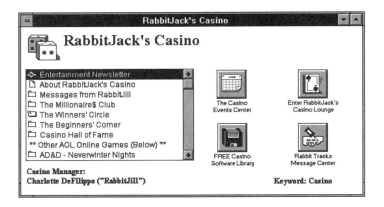

Make or lose a million in play money in the Casino.

The right side of the window has the usual assortment of buttons.

➤ **The Casino Events Calendar** brings up a list of what's happening in the Casino and when.

➤ **Enter RabbitJack's Casino Lounge** takes you into a chat room where you can hang out and chat with all the other high rollers. From the lounge, you can enter the Casino.

➤ **FREE Casino Software Library** contains the software you need to actually gamble in the Casino, plus instructions for installing it. You *cannot* play without the software appropriate to your computer (there are DOS and Windows versions). Fortunately, the online time it takes to download those files is free.

The Casino Software Library.

➤ **Rabbit Tracks Message Center** takes you to the Casino's message area, where you can post questions and compare strategies with other players.

After you download and install the Casino software, you can enter the Casino (it looks just like a regular chat room). When you do, you wind up at one of several gaming tables, you're given a wad of money to gamble with, and you play. If you win, you can bank extra cash for later use. If you lose it all, you're done until the next day when you can get more money. (If you lose all that fake money in one day, keep your *real* money away from a *real* casino. Please.) It takes some time to learn and get used to the Casino, but the forum is dripping with helpful information files and staff members, so don't be afraid to try. You might like it.

All the games in RabbitJack's Casino are played in parlors, most of which are numbered from 1 to 999 (the high rollers play in parlors 900–999). The games are played much like their regular casino versions (Bingo, Blackjack, Poker, Slot Machines).

You play either by selecting menu items or by using shortcut keys (I recommend the shortcuts because they're faster—if you can remember them). Like most DOS and Windows shortcuts, Casino shortcuts require you to press the Alt key and a letter at the same time. The following list gives you all of the Casino shortcuts. You may want to copy this list and keep it by your computer for handy reference.

These shortcuts work in all RabbitJack's Casino games:

Alt+G	=	Go To
Alt+H	=	Help
Alt+L	=	List Player and Table/Parlor/Row Number
Alt+Q	=	Quit
Alt+T	=	List active Tables, Parlors, or Rows for the game you are currently playing
Alt+X	=	Toggle Sound On/Off

These shortcuts work when you're playing Blackjack:

Alt+B	=	Send Bet
Alt+C	=	Take Card (Hit)

Alt+D	=	Decrease Bet/Double Down (when appropriate)
Alt+I	=	Increase Bet
Alt+S	=	Stand
Alt+Z	=	Maximum Bet

Use these shortcuts in the Poker parlors:

Alt+A	=	Ante
Alt+B	=	Bet
Alt+C	=	Check (Pass) or Call (if there is a bet)
Alt+D	=	Decrease Bet
Alt+F	=	Fold
Alt+I	=	Increase Bet
Alt+P	=	Peek at Hole Card
Alt+R	=	Raise
Alt+S	=	Send Bet
Alt+Z	=	Bet or Raise Maximum

The Slot Machines use these shortcuts:

Alt+I	=	Insert Chip
Alt+P	=	Pull Handle
Alt+Z	=	Play All Rows

These are the Bingo shortcuts:

Alt+B	=	Call "Bingo!"
Alt+C	=	Cover Card
Alt+N	=	New Card
Alt+R	=	Register Card
Alt+S	=	Show Bankroll

By the time you read this, the Casino will have a new game called WordWorks. It will be a cross between Bingo and a word-making game. Watch for it.

Fun for Teens

Most of the areas and rooms I've discussed are appropriate for teen-aged folks; however, often when teens and older people mix, both sets end up annoyed. Teens might think the older folks are too dull and uptight; older adults may think teens are too rambunctious and uncontrolled. Both may be right. If you're a teen and are not interested in mingling with older AOL members, there are often "Teens only" rooms available in the People Connection.

To find something specifically for teens, click the **Rooms** button from any Lobby. Scroll through the list of rooms (you may have to use the **More** button to see them all) looking for rooms with the word "Teen" in them. You'll find rooms like Teen Chat, Teen Game Parlor, and similar rooms where teens can hang out together online.

Kid Space

If you think teens and adults sometimes clash, imagine what can happen when you mix adults, teens, and kids. Talk about conflicting needs. That's why there's a whole department devoted to kids only. Oddly enough, it's called Kids Only. As you can see in the following figure, Kids Only is a full-fledged forum that offers many kid-sized versions of forums and areas from around America Online.

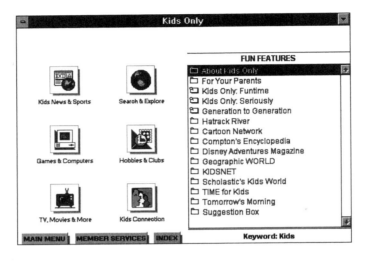

KOOL: Kids Only OnLine.

You may want to add Kids Only to your list of Favorite Places in your Go To menu. Doing so will save time and make it easier for a younger child to find the area. Chapter 22 explains how.

Even if you block your children's access to some adult chat rooms or forums with the Parental Controls (covered in Chapter 6), they can still use similar Kids Only versions here. Access Kids Only by clicking the Kids Only button on the Main Menu or by using the Keyword: KIDS. That takes you to the forum shown above, which works like any other forum you've seen.

I won't even try to tell you what's good for your children. However, I will suggest three things:

➤ Before you let your child use Kids Only, go through it by yourself. Read the About Kids Only and For Your Parents files. Poke your nose into all the connecting areas and satisfy your curiosity about the area.

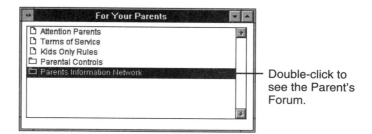

Double-click to see the Parent's Forum.

FYP: For Your Parents.

➤ The first few times your kid signs on to use Kids Only, work with him or her. Show your kid how things work and where things are. Then stand back and only help out when asked.

➤ Stay involved. Kids Only is great, but it's only a forum. Use the Parents Information Network Forum available under the For Your Parents menu item. It keeps you informed of online events and activities, new services, and kid-related news so you can be better informed. It also helps you stay involved, which might keep your child interested and engaged in the online activities.

For your peace of mind, Kids Only is staffed at all times. Information and text is written for kids, not *down* to kids. Although parents may pop into kid chat and event rooms to observe, they may not participate. In that respect, the only adults allowed are staff members. I think it's just great that kids have a place of their own online. Watch the area and your kids grow together.

The Least You Need to Know

All work and no play makes Jack a dull geek, so remember these tidbits about how to have fun on America Online:

➤ People Connection chat rooms offer tons of fun. Check out Romance Connection, Flirts Nook, La Pub, and other fun-sounding rooms. Don't forget to look for similar rooms with "Teen" in the name, if you're a teenager.

➤ You'll find live games (like Quik Harmony and the rest) in the People Connection, listed with the other rooms. Just double-click to enter the room and have fun.

➤ Game room schedules are posted in the PC Studio. Click on the **PC Studio** button in any chat room, or use the Keyword: PC STUDIO. In the PC Studio, double-click the **Games Parlor** entry in the list box, and then double-click the calendar you want to read, print, or save to disk.

➤ If, someday, you decide you want to meet one of your online friends in person, go for it—but do it cautiously. Meet in a public place: a restaurant, bookstore, coffee house, or somewhere where other people are around. Don't go to either person's home. That's awkward and potentially dangerous.

➤ RabbitJack's Casino is great fun, but you must download and install the proper software for your DOS or Windows computer before you can play. Using keyboard shortcuts speeds the games along.

➤ Kids Only is a forum with many kid-sized versions of popular AOL features (including chat rooms). Parents should explore it first, and then help their kids find their way around.

Chapter 16

Shopping!

In This Chapter

➤ This little piggy went 2Market

➤ This little piggy bought an AOL T-shirt

➤ This little piggy flew to San Francisco

➤ And this little piggy went *"Yikes!"* when he saw his credit card bill

Generally, I enjoy shopping. I really do. But there's something about the intensity and mania of shopping from Thanksgiving to New Year's that sets my teeth on edge. I prefer to get in, get what I need, and get out. What a perfect time to explore and use the shopping opportunities on America Online!

The Marketplace: Home of The AOL Store and More

In the Marketplace, you can find vendors peddling computer equipment, office supplies, books, automotive services, and lots more. Think of the Marketplace as a huge mall. As in a mall, I'm sure more stores will be added regularly, so keep your eyes peeled. To get to the Marketplace, click on the **Marketplace** button on the Main Menu.

To teach you the ins and outs of shopping in the Marketplace, let's take a trek to the AOL store. Just as the Disney Store sells Disney stuff, and Warner Brothers Stores sell Warner stuff, the AOL store sells AOL stuff (and it's the only place to get this stuff). One of the cool things about wearing something with the AOL logo on it is that people will stop me on the street and ask, "What's your screen name?" Sometimes you'll even get e-mail from them a couple of days later. That *never* happens when you wear a Mickey Mouse shirt.

To get to the AOL store, double-click on the **America Online Store** entry in the Marketplace's list box. Or you can just use the Keyword: AMERICA ONLINE STORE. However you get there, the store looks like the figure shown below. But because products are being added all the time, it may look a little different.

The AOL store.

As usual with any department or forum online, the first item you see in the store's list box is a text file that will tell you about the store. You might want to read it first because, just like a regular store, the AOL store is changing all the time.

Below that, you'll see folders for the products available online. The America Online Tour Guide is for a book that you don't need since you have this one. The Internet Publications is a group of books about the

Internet (discussed in Chapter 17). The Apparel and Mug, Gym Bag & Umbrella listings are for those particular items imprinted with the AOL logo (we'll be coming back to them in a second).

Below those are entries for the Motley Fool Investment Primer and AD&D Neverwinter Nights Software. These are products related to two online forums. The Motley Fool (Keyword: FOOL) is in the Personal Finance department. You might want to check out the forum before you check out the related products. AD&D Neverwinter Nights (Keyword: AD&D) is an online version of Advanced Dungeons and Dragons, a role playing game. You can play it online but you need special software, and you can order it here. Check out the forum. If you're into gaming, it's a real hoot.

> You can Sign on a Friend, free of online charges, by going to Member Services (see Chapter 20) or by using the Keyword: FRIEND. You're doing AOL a favor, so let them pay for the time.

The America Online Product Photos listing is a library of (what a surprise) photos of the products you can buy online. We'll peek in there in a moment, too.

In the suggestion box, you can drop off your ideas, comments, and questions about the AOL Store and its products. Sign on a Friend is a special deal in which, if you ask AOL to send your friend a free AOL starter kit and your friend signs on and stays online for a while, you get free hours as a thank-you gift.

Okay, let's say you want an AOL T-shirt. Here's how you'd find one:

1. Since we're looking for clothing, double-click on the **Apparel** entry in the list box. That gives you a list of the various clothes you can buy online.

2. Browse for whatever you want. I'm interested in the AOL 6-color white T-shirt. When you find what you want, double-click on it to view a description like the one shown on the following page.

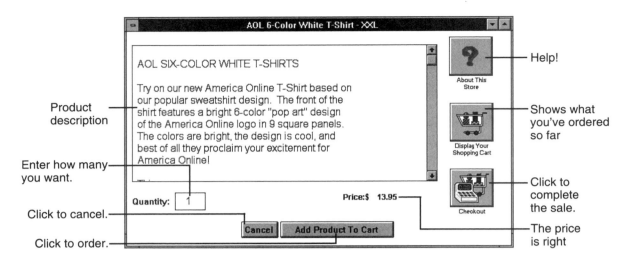

The product description and order blank.

In the AOL store, the product description is also the order form. Since AOL already has your name, address, and valid credit card information (from when you signed up), all you have to do to purchase a product is click on the Add Product to Cart button. (You'll still have a chance to change your mind.) But don't click that button yet. Maybe you're having a tough time imagining a "bright 6-color 'pop art' design of the America Online logo in 9 square panels." I know I am! You can take a look at the actual T-shirt design before you buy it. Here's how.

1. While the description window is still open, click on the Window menu and select **America Online Store** from the list of open windows at the bottom of the menu. That will bring the main store window (what, are we window shopping?) to the front of your screen.

2. Double-click on the **America Online Product Photos** entry in the list box to open a list of all the photos available.

3. Scroll through the list until you find the photo.

4. Double-click the photo's name. In this example, it's the one called 6-color T-shirt Photo.

Sit back in stunned amazement while AOL displays a lovely photograph of the T-shirt. When you decide whether or not to buy, use the Window menu to go back to the product description window, and then click **Cancel** or **Add Product to Shopping Cart**. Shop around, selecting whatever you care to buy. When you're done, click **Display Your Shopping Cart** to review your choices. At this point, you can delete any items from your list, cancel the whole deal, or click on **Checkout**.

To delete an item from your shopping cart, just click on it to select it and click **Remove Item From Cart**. To cancel an entire set of purchases, repeat the process for each item. When the last has been removed from your cart, you'll get a message saying **Your Shopping Cart is Empty**. You can then go back into the store or go on your merry way online.

If you still want to purchase an item in your cart, when you click Checkout, you'll get a series of windows confirming your order. For the AOL Store, you don't need to provide any credit card or shipping information; it's billed the same way you pay your AOL charges, and it's sent to the address you provided as your mailing address.

When you click Checkout, AOL totals your purchase(s), bills the same credit card you use to pay for AOL, and tells you approximately how long it will be before your package(s) arrive.

2Market, 2Market...

2Market (Keyword: 2MARKET) is a whole 'nother shopping forum within the Marketplace, which means it has the full assortment of forum features (online help, a message area, and an auditorium/chat room, but no file library). You can see it in the following figure.

2Market is a whole shopping forum.

The CD-ROM Offer button, shown in the figure, will only benefit users who have a CD-ROM drive attached to their computers. It's an offer for the CD-based version of the 2Market catalog. CD-ROM catalogs are the new hot techno-geeky way of shopping and are very convenient. And when you're done with the CD or get the next issue, you can turn the old CDs into lovely Christmas ornaments.

It was pre-Christmas crazy-time when I visited, so 2Market was decked out with lots of holiday gift suggestions. Clicking on the Gift Shopping button brought up several collections of gifts from all the 2Market vendors, grouped in convenient categories, such as Gifts for Him, Gifts for Her, Business Gifts, and the ever-popular Gifts Under $35.

The Events and Promotions button brought up information about special attractions (guest speakers and such) and holiday contests. The Product Spotlights featured an assortment of popular items from all of the 2Market vendors. I skipped all that in favor of the Collections button so I could get at everything all at once. It brings up the collections screen shown here.

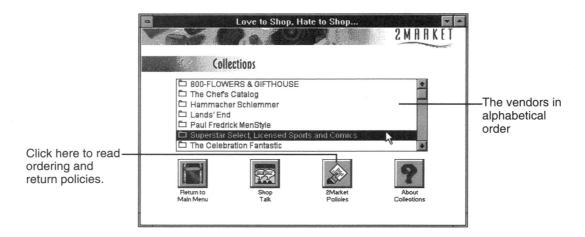

The 2Market Collection—easy pickin's.

Since I have a godson who's quite the comic book connoisseur, I started by double-clicking the vendor **Superstar Select, Licensed Sports and Comics.** Double-clicking on a vendor name brings up a list

186

of all the products they have available online. If a product catches your eye, double-click its entry in the list box to see a product description like the one in the next figure. You'll notice that in 2Market, you don't have to look at product photos in a separate library; when available, they're displayed right with the product description.

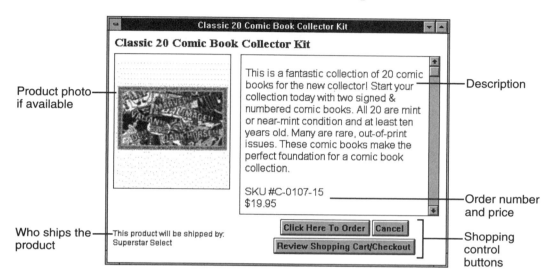

2Market's product descriptions include photos.

The shopping buttons at the bottom of the window work just like the ones in the AOL Store:

➤ When you click **Click Here To Order**, you will be asked to select a size and/or color, if it's appropriate to the item. You'll also be asked to select a method of shipping (UPS, Federal Express, or plain ol' U.S. mail). Then the item is added to your shopping cart.

➤ **Cancel** cancels the order and returns you to the product listing (as does simply closing the description window).

➤ **Review Shopping Cart/Checkout** displays a list of everything you've ordered so far and lets you delete individual items, cancel the whole sale, or finish up the order. It's shown in the following figure.

187

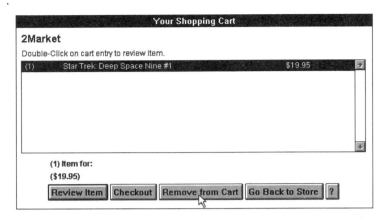

My shopping cart.

If you click on an item (to select it) and click Review Item, you'll see the product description and photo (if available) again. Just like in the AOL store, discussed earlier, you can remove any or all items from your cart by clicking on the item to select it and clicking Remove from Cart. Repeat the process as often as you need.

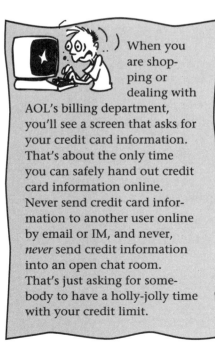 When you are shopping or dealing with AOL's billing department, you'll see a screen that asks for your credit card information. That's about the only time you can safely hand out credit card information online. Never send credit card information to another user online by email or IM, and never, *never* send credit information into an open chat room. That's just asking for somebody to have a holly-jolly time with your credit limit.

Clicking on Go Back to Store closes the Shopping Cart window so you may continue shopping. When you click Checkout, you're asked to provide credit card information to pay for your purchase.

Unlike in the AOL store, when you order a product in 2Market, the purchase is not billed to the credit card with which you pay for AOL. Because you need to provide credit card information, you can use the same card or a different card. Type the information carefully, and double-check it before you click **Continue**. If you enter your credit card number incorrectly, it will delay your merchandise.

After you provide the credit card information, you'll be shown your home billing address—the one you provided when you first joined AOL. If it's correct (check the phone number especially—mine was wrong), you can just click **Continue**.

188

If you want it sent to your address, click on **Copy from BILLING**, and (oddly enough) it copies your address from the Billing Address screen you just reviewed. If you want the merchandise shipped to another address (as a gift, say), you need to type in the shipping address and phone number. When you're done, click **Place Order**.

AOL records your purchase and presents you with a little window that says **Thank You, Order #123456789 Has Been Entered. Please note for future reference.** Write down the order number (in case you need to check on your order) and click **OK**. Your order is on its way.

Note that when you're shopping online, wherever applicable, you will have to pay sales tax. Shipping charges are also additional. They start at approximately $5 for UPS Ground Service shipping and go up to a minimum of $15 for Federal Express delivery. Heavier items costs more to ship, of course.

But Wait! There's More!

The AOL Store and 2Market aren't the only shopping opportunities that exist in the Marketplace. You can:

➤ Order flowers from 1-800-FLOWERS

➤ Get computer hardware and software from Computer Express and the Comp-u-store gateway.

➤ Get books and even CD-ROM titles from the Online Bookstore.

➤ Buy movie-related merchandise from the Hollywood Online Store.

And even more. Just double-click on the store's listing in the Marketplace scroll box or click on a button (these buttons change weekly, almost daily). All the other stores online work much the same as 2Market, so you won't be puzzled (or you can click the Help button if you are). Have your credit card handy, because you never know when the urge to shop will overtake you.

Got Me a Ticket for an Aero-Plane...

...ain't got time to take a fast train. Sorry. '60s flashback. One of the cooler opportunities for shopping isn't even in the Marketplace. It's EAAsy Sabre, and it's in the Travel department.

EAAsy Sabre is American Airlines' flight reservation system, the same one that many travel agents use. You can use it yourself to book your own flights, make hotel reservations, and even reserve a rental car at your destination. To get to EAAsy Sabre, click on the **Travel** button in the Main Menu, and then click on the **EAAsy Sabre** button in the Travel window.

EAAsy Sabre isn't actually part of AOL. It's a service of its own. AOL offers access to EAAsy Sabre by way of a gateway. There are a couple of areas online that are gateways to other services; most notable of these is the Internet Connection (see Chapter 17). A *gateway*, as the word implies, is a connection between two different computer services that enables you to access information from one service without disconnecting from the host service (in this case, AOL).

For Windows and DOS AOL users, EAAsy Sabre is a text-based system in which you enter the city you'd like to leave from, the city you're going to, and the date(s) and time(s) you want to travel. EAAsy Sabre searches through its database of flight information and presents you with several options that meet your needs.

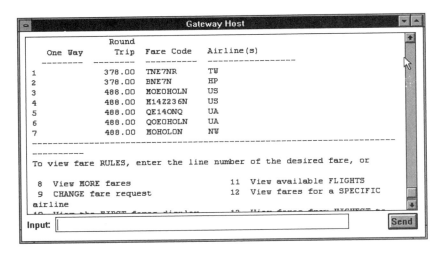

EAAsy Sabre with WAOL.

You'll notice that the EAAsy Sabre window looks a lot like a chat room. Instead of entering chat in the Input text box, you enter the number of the command you want to use (8 to view more fares, for example) and press **Enter**. It isn't exactly easy (it helps if you know those obscure airline and airport codes they use, like PHL for Philadelphia), so take your time and read the instructions. Many of the travel codes are explained in a text file called (duh) "Travel Codes." Just double-click on it to read, print, or save a copy to your hard drive.

Mac users have a slightly easier way to go. It still helps to know what SFO and all that means, but the Mac EAAsy Sabre is more Mac-like (see the figure below), so you can click on buttons instead of typing command numbers.

The Macintosh version of EAAsy Sabre.

If you want, you can just visit EAAsy Sabre, fool around with fantasy vacations, and then cancel everything before you leave. In order to actually reserve tickets, you need to be a member. Membership is free, and it gets you a member number and password you need to remember (so no one can book flights in your name without your knowing it). It also stores a profile for you that includes your seating preference and other information.

To become an EAAsy Sabre member, enter EAAsy Sabre by clicking on its button on the Travel screen. Select option 5 by typing **5** in the text box and pressing **Enter**. You'll be asked a series of questions (name, address, what password you would like to use, credit card information for payment, and so on). Just follow the instructions on screen. When the system asks for your AAdvantage membership number (that's American Airlines' frequent flyer program), you can enter it if you're a member or just press **Enter**. That's all there is to it, and membership is free.

How It Works

When you enter EAAsy Sabre, you move through its features by entering the numbers next to the items in the text display (in the WAOL figure earlier, that would be 8 to see more fares, 9 to change your fare request, and so on).

When you're searching for flight information, EAAsy Sabre asks you for the following information it needs:

➤ Departure point (the city or airport you're leaving from)

➤ Destination (the city or airport you're going to)

➤ Date you're leaving

➤ Time of day you prefer to fly

If you're booking a round-trip flight, it also asks for the day and time of your return trip. Your destination and departure information can be entered as a city name or as airline codes for the airports (if you know them). You can get a list of codes by selecting About The System from the Main Menu and selecting Travel Codes.

Once you enter your information, EAAsy Sabre returns with a list of flights that meet your needs. You can get more information about each, check the fares and restrictions, and actually book the flight.

Fare codes are pure gobbledygook (TNE7NR is very helpful, isn't it?). To get more information on the codes, enter the line number of the flight you want more information about, and that mess will be translated for you. Restrictions can include advance purchase requirements, time of day for flying, specific days of the week to fly (such as a stay over Saturday requirement), length of stay, and cancellation penalties.

Be sure to read the rules for each fare before you book a flight. If you can't figure it out, call American Airlines (they're in the phone book) or your travel agent, and ask for a better translation. You don't want to get stuck with tickets you can't use.

Finally, after you select your flight and return flight, you'll be asked to confirm your selection. You can cancel at any point up to and including the confirmation screen (cancellation methods vary from screen to screen, so be sure you read the on-screen directions carefully before you enter anything). Once you confirm, however, your flight is booked, and your tickets will arrive in the mail in a few days.

EAAsy Sabre Tips

Like any online search routine, there are good ways and bad ways to approach searching through EAAsy Sabre's database of flight information. Here are a few tips:

➤ Be flexible. You may be able to find a better price if you leave or return a day earlier/later.

➤ Explore all of your options. Try entering your data a few times in a few different ways. You may get a better deal leaving from a smaller airport if you have more than one nearby.

➤ It may be less expensive to book two flights to get to your destination. For example, look for a flight from Philadelphia to Las Vegas and then a flight from Las Vegas to San Francisco, instead of Philadelphia to San Francisco. Do the same thing for the return flight.

➤ Check the restrictions: you can save money on cut-rate flights. But if your plans change, you may be stuck with useless tickets.

The first time you try to use EAAsy Sabre, put a travel agent or travel-wise friend on the job so you have something to compare your results with. If you have a friend who also happens to be a travel agent, that's all the better. See if you can shmooze a list of all the airline and airport codes out of her. Ask if you can watch while she uses EAAsy Sabre from her computer. Both would be very handy indeed. Before you leave on your trip, you might want to explore the rest of the Travel Forum for tips, tricks, and things to do. Happy trails!

The Least You Need to Know

There's nothing like shopping from the comfort of your own home. America Online has gathered an assortment of vendors to meet many of your shopping needs.

➤ Most of your shopping opportunities are located in the Marketplace on the Main Menu (except for EAAsy Sabre, which is in the Travel department).

➤ The AOL store is where you'll find stuff that's imprinted with the AOL logo.

➤ 2Market (Keyword: 2Market) is a collection of online vendors selling a wide variety of goods, including everything from pots and pans to comic books and collectibles.

➤ You can cancel your order anytime up to the very last second, when you click Check Me Out or Place Order (depending on the store you're in).

➤ Anyone can browse through EAAsy Sabre, but you have to be a registered member in order to actually book a flight. Check the About EAAsy Sabre information online for details and instructions.

AHOY!

Chapter 17

Internet, Ahoy!

In This Chapter

➤ What *is* an Internet, exactly?

➤ AOL's Internet Connection

➤ Emailing the world

➤ Gophers and Webs and WAIS (*oh, my!*)

Volumes (and I mean *volumes*) have been written about the Internet, and don't forget all the hype surrounding the "Information Superhighway." America Online lets you tap into that highway *now*, without the wait.

What's an Internet?

The Internet is an *inter*national *net*work of computers that makes possible the transfer of information around the world. For the most part, these computers are on college campuses and in government and corporate offices. However, plain folks like you and me can (and do) access the Internet in a number of ways—one of which is through America Online.

If you find the Internet bug biting you, and you want more (or more direct) access than AOL currently offers, I strongly suggest you pick up a good book about using the Internet and your particular type of computer system. At best, Internet jargon can be confusing; at worst, it's a muddy, muddled mess. A good book will help you immensely, as will some experimentation with the less expensive access AOL gives you. PC users may want to take a look at Peter Kent's *The Complete Idiot's Guide to the Internet*, available from Alpha Books.

Generally speaking, the Internet is the way many scientists, academics, and students communicate, share information, and confer around the world. You can also download all kinds of files, get juicy bits of gossip, and find some pretty twisted humor.

News travels fast on the Net (as some call it). The story of the math problem that plagues many of Intel's Pentium processor chips first appeared on the Net. It was then quickly followed up by pages and pages of sarcastic humor (like "The Top 10.2675 Reasons to Upgrade to a Pentium"). If people talk about it, think about it, love it, or hate it, there's probably a newsgroup devoted to it on the Net.

At the moment, AOL offers basic access to features of the Net. In the near future, there will be more. Not too long after that (probably in 1996), AOL will offer full Internet access. I can't wait.

Before we plunge headlong into this heady stuff, be warned: the Internet is complex (actually, more like controlled chaos) and habit-forming. If you read this and find yourself interested in checking out the Net, experiment a little, and then come back and read this again. It will make more sense and stay with you better the second time around. I promise.

The Internet Connection

All of AOL's Internet access is available in one convenient location: the Internet Connection (Keyword: INTERNET). As you can see in the following figure, the Internet Connection *looks* like just about every other forum online—but it gives you a connection to the whole wide world.

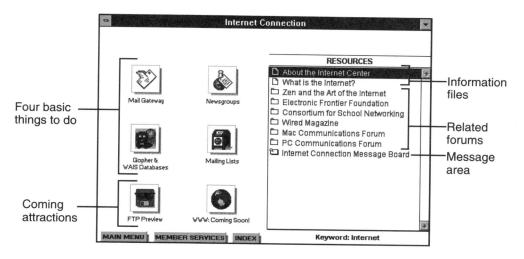

Four basic things to do
Coming attractions

Information files
Related forums
Message area

The Internet Connection: Welcome to the World.

In the Resources scroll box, you'll find general information about the Net (what it is, why it is, and such), plus specific information on how to use it. You should read as much of it as you can because it's the best source for the latest in how-to information and the level of access changes often.

While researching and writing this, I kept having to go back and take new screenshots because AOL kept adding stuff to the Internet Connection. First it was the FTP preview (coming up), then it was WWW access (also coming up), and then it was more informational files. Well, you get the idea. Read the online information files in all the Internet areas you frequent. This stuff changes too fast for me (or this book) to keep up with it. Remember the Keyword: NEW keeps you up to date.

Below the informational resources, there is access to other forums online that deal (somehow) with the Internet. For example, the Mac and PC Communications forums provide tips, information, and software for connecting to the Net (and other bulletin board systems). The Electronic Frontier Foundation is a non-profit group interested in

197

Cyberspace is a word coined by science fiction author William Gibson in his novel *Neuromancer* (a "must read" for true geek wannabes). When computer users on opposite sides of the country meet and talk in real-time, the ethereal, computer-generated place they meet is cyberspace.

keeping *cyberspace* open, free, and available to all. Their forum keeps you up-to-date and in-the-know. It keeps me paranoid.

There's also access to the Internet Connection's message area, where you can post questions you have about using the various features or look for interesting things to do.

On the other side of the Internet Connection window is a collection of buttons that give you the main features of the forum: Mail Gateway, Newsgroups, Mailing Lists, and Gopher & WAIS Databases. We'll look at each of these, plus take a peek at some of the features (like the FTP Preview) that are under construction.

Internet Mail Gateway

If you read the chapter on shopping (Chapter 16), you may recall that a gateway provides you with a connection from one online service to another. AOL has a gateway that allows you to send mail from your AOL account to anyone that is in any way accessible to the Internet.

Clicking on the Internet Mail Gateway button gives you a window with a scrollable list of information resources and tips on composing and sending mail. You might or might not want to read these files (most of the important information is here in this chapter). You can also compose mail, but that's only a convenience; you can send mail to and through the Internet from anywhere online that you can compose mail, not just from the Internet Connection.

You could, for example, send email to a friend who uses CompuServe (another online service) just by using the right email address. The mail would then leave AOL's computers, be zapped through the Internet, and be delivered to the CompuServe computers via their Internet gateway. An Internet address looks like this (don't panic):

70713.3554@compuserve.com.

This is what it means:

➤ **70713.3554** is my own personal membership number on Compu-Serve (if you use this address, I'll get the mail, so only send it if you mean it, thanks).

➤ **@** indicates the end of the person's email address and the beginning of the address for the online service or host computer. The @ is an old-fashioned abbreviation for "at."

➤ **compuserve** is, of course, the name of the service where the person's account is. It could just as easily be the name of any other online service with Internet access (**aol**, **eworld**, **genie**, **prodigy**, and so on).

➤ **.com** is an extension that tells what kind of service or organization is involved. CompuServe is a *com*mercial, money-making organization. Educational addresses end with **.edu**, government addresses with **.gov**, and military addresses with **.mil**.

If you wanted to write to me on CompuServe from your AOL account, you'd address the letter by typing **70713.3554@compuserve.com** in the TO: box. Then you simply compose the rest of the mail as usual (see Chapter 9 for details). When I have received and read your mail on Compu-Serve, I would reply with email addressed to: **yourscreename@aol.com**.

Despite the wild and wacky looking addresses, email sent to the Internet works the same as email sent to any AOL account, *except* for the following:

➤ You can't use the Attach File option. If you want to send a short text file (6–8 pages) to someone, just copy and paste it into the body of your message. If you want to send an application, you need to consult the Communications Forum appropriate to your computer (Keyword: TELECOM) for a file utility that

When you want to reply to mail you receive from the Internet, don't hurt yourself retyping the address. If you click on the Reply button, AOL automatically addresses your reply. If you think you'll be writing to someone via Internet on a regular basis, add the correct address to your Address Book (see Chapter 9) and save yourself the hassle of typing and remembering where all the @'s and periods go.

will convert the program code into text you can send in a letter. The recipient must then convert it back to code. Such utilities are called "Encoding/decoding" utilities.

The file utilities that convert application files into mailable text are the stuff of real techno-nerds and are way beyond the scope of this book. If you're interested, do a file search for **MPACK/UNPACK** (for DOS and Windows users) or **BINHEX** (for Mac users), read the documentation, and check in the communications forums. I've been online for 10 years, and I've only used an encoder/decoder maybe five times in total. Don't feel like you need to rush right out and get one.

➤ You can't check the status of mail you've sent. Once your mail leaves AOL, there's no way of telling when or if it was received. AOL will only tell you when you sent it, or say "Not applicable."

➤ Mail coming in from the Internet is not reformatted, so it may look a little odd when you read it.

➤ Incoming mail that's really big (1MB or more in size) will be split into several smaller messages and numbered so you can tell what order to read them.

➤ Outgoing messages can't be larger than about 32K (6–8 pages of text). If you need to send more, split the message into several smaller mailings.

➤ Any special characters (such as "é" or "ç") will be turned into blank spaces during the sending process. Avoid using them.

➤ Internet mail leaves an address trail to tell you where and how the mail was sent. The address trail appears at the beginning and end of the message, and looks something like this:

```
———————————— Headers ————————————
From juliet@metaxis.com Sat Dec 24 06:55:11 1994
Received: metaxis.com by mailgate.prod.aol.net with ESMTP
(1.37.109.11/16.2) id AA047050111; Sat, 24 Dec 1994 06:55:11 -0500
Return-Path: <juliet@metaxis.com>
Received: from unix3.metaxis.com (juliet@unix3.metaxis.com
[198.69.186.5]) by metaxis.com (8.6.9/8.6.9) with ESMTP id
```

```
GAA06112; Sat, 24 Dec 1994 06:56:19 -0500
(lots of gibberish cut out)
Date: Sat, 24 Dec 1994 06:56:17 -0500 (EST)
X-Mailer: ELM [version 2.4 PL24]
Content-Type: text
Content-Length: 8383
```

If you know what you're doing (and if someone like me doesn't cut out half of it), you can figure out which scenic route your email took to get to you. If not, it will give you a headache. One or the other is always true, and sometimes both.

Other than those few oddities, email sent to the Internet behaves just the same as mail sent to another member on AOL.

Newsgroup Groupies

An Internet newsgroup is like the message boards you'll find all over AOL. It's a collection of messages posted back and forth from members of the same newsgroup. Groups are devoted to particular topics (and you should try to stay on the subject when posting to them). To get at the newsgroups, click on the **Newsgroups** button in the Internet Connection window or use the Keyword: NEWSGROUPS. Either method gives you the window shown below. On the left side of the window, you'll find the typical list of informational files. You should read them since the Internet areas seem to change on a daily basis.

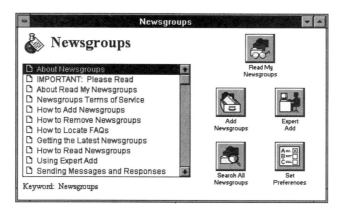

Get your newsgroups here!

On the right side of the screen are the buttons for newsgroup functions. The following list describes those buttons in order of appearance.

➤ **Read My Newsgroups** brings up a list of all your newsgroups (you have a standard set even if you've never visited here before). The newsgroups work like any other message area online. You double-click on the Newsgroups that interest you, and then you can read individual messages or the whole thread. You can also remove unwanted newsgroups from the list.

To reply to a message you've read, click on the **Reply** button below the message and type in your reply. (You *really* have done all this before, but some of the button names have changed, that's all.)

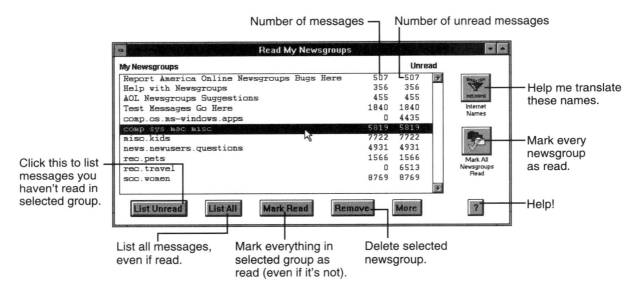

Number of messages — Number of unread messages

Help me translate these names.

Mark every newsgroup as read.

Click this to list messages you haven't read in selected group.

Help!

List all messages, even if read.

Mark everything in selected group as read (even if it's not).

Delete selected newsgroup.

Newsgroups for days.

➤ **Add Newsgroups** gives you a list of all the newsgroups available, so you can pick and choose which ones you want to see when you select Read My Newsgroups. It's very simple: just double-click on the newsgroup(s) you want added to your list.

➤ **Expert Add** works the same as the Add Newsgroups button, but it assumes you know what you're doing, so it doesn't hold your hand. I wouldn't try it until you're confident of your Netting skills.

➤ **Search All Newsgroups** accesses a standard search dialog box—you've seen it before. You enter a word or phrase, and AOL searches through all of the available newsgroup names for those that match your search string. It could save you lots of browsing time.

➤ **Set Preferences** opens a window in which you can tell AOL how to display the information from your newsgroup. You can have all that header information (similar to what you saw in the email section) displayed at the top or bottom of messages or removed entirely. You can sort messages by date (oldest or newest first) or alphabetically by name. AOL translates the newsgroup names into something like English, or you can have abridged Internet-style names. You can also add a Signature statement that will appear at the bottom of every single message you post. After you set your preferences, your newsgroup messages will be displayed accordingly.

In simplest terms, here's how to browse, add, and/or delete a newsgroup from your list. First, get to the Internet Connection (use the Keyword: INTERNET).

To read your newsgroups, click on the **Read My Newsgroups** button. Find the group you want to read and double-click on its listing in the scroll box. Browse, read, and enjoy. When you're done, close that window and browse through another group if you care to.

If you're disappointed with a newsgroup, you can delete it from your list. If the window is closed, click the **Read My Newsgroups** button to open the list of your newsgroups. Click on the listing for the group you want to delete. That selects it. Then click the **Remove** button. Poof! It's gone from your list.

To add a new newsgroup, click on the **Add Newsgroups** button. Scroll through the list of newsgroups, and double-click any

If you use a signature, keep it simple: your name, your Internet address, maybe a brief statement about yourself, a quote you like, or your credentials or degrees. You might use something like this:

> **John Pivovarnick, Complete Idiot. piv@aol.com**
>
> **I think, therefore ... I forget the rest.**

People who pay big bucks (up to thousands of dollars per month) for Internet access get justly annoyed by long, silly, and pointless signatures that they have to pay to read. Keep it *very* short and very sweet.

name you find interesting and about which you want to see more information (if it's available). If the group strikes your fancy, click on the **Add** button. The next time you select Read My Newsgroups, the new group will be in your list.

Gopher & WAIS Databases

Gopher is a way of browsing through tons of information quickly on the Internet. Member organizations and individuals set up Gopher servers that contain nothing but menus of items. Double-clicking on a menu item retrieves that item: sometimes it's a text file, sometimes it's another set of menus. It's called Gopher because it will "go-pher" the information you want *and* because it was developed by the University of Minnesota—and their school mascot is the Golden Gopher.

AOL's version of Gopher is more structured than what you'll find on the Internet, making it a little more stable and easier to browse. Just double-click on the category you're interested in, and you'll be presented with a list of all the Gophers that fall under it (in some categories, you'll need to click the **More** button to see them all). Then you can browse and click 'til you're blue in the face.

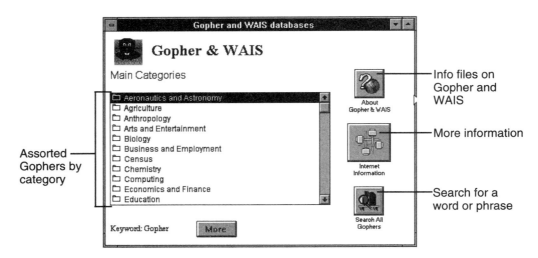

Speedy browsing.

A folder icon in front of a listing means that you can double-click that entry to bring up another list of menus. If you click on a listing marked with a file icon (the dog-eared sheet of paper), you will get a text file you can read, print, or save. An open book icon indicates that you can do a search.

By clicking on the Search All Gophers button (at the bottom right corner of the screen), you can use a standard search dialog box to look in all the Gopher listings for the word or phrase that interests you. Most of the searches in the Gopher & WAIS area use WAIS databases—which would explain the name of the area. WAIS (pronounced "ways") stands for Wide Area Information Server, and it's a method for quickly searching through tons of information originally developed for use on huge supercomputers.

Mailing Lists

Mailing lists are discussion groups that, like newsgroups, cover a particular subject area. Unlike newsgroups, mailing list discussions are conducted by email.

Clicking on the Mailing Lists button brings up the window shown below. Information files are in the scroll box (need I remind you to read them?). To find a list you'd like to join, click **Search Mailing Lists** (to the right of the window, as shown below). You'll get the standard search dialog box. Enter a word or phrase that matches your interest. The search returns a list of database entries that match your search phrase.

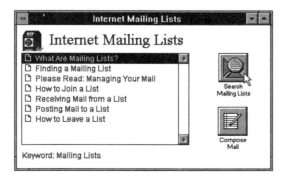

Put me on your mailing list.

Double-click on the entry that you want to read, and you'll get information about the list, information on how to join, and sometimes tips on finding other mailing lists about your particular interest. The details vary from list to list, but generally speaking, membership requires that you drop somebody a note with your email address and other information (that's why there's a Compose Mail button in the main window). You'll then be added to that list, and you'll start getting *tons* of email.

I mean it—tons of mail. Your AOL mailbox can only handle 550 pieces of mail at a time. If you don't read your mail regularly, a mailing list can push you right over the top, and things will start to be deleted. Trust me, you don't want that to happen. To help you manage your mail, here are five tips you should read before you subscribe to any mailing lists:

➤ Read the mailing list description completely before you join. Joining and then quitting a list in short order is pretty rude and wastes all the participants' time.

➤ Don't join if you don't mean it. If you're only curious, try other information sources (a newsgroup, maybe) before you join a mailing list.

➤ If you do join, sign on regularly to read your mail, "Ignore" it, or do a FlashSession a few times a week just to keep it clear. If the system starts deleting mail you haven't read, you might lose some that you really want.

➤ When you subscribe to a mailing list, keep a copy of the information from the database (the one that told you how to join). It also tells you how to quit the list, in case you lose interest or it isn't what you expected.

➤ If you quit a mailing list, be nice about it. You may have been disappointed by a lot of mail you weren't interested in, but the person in charge of subscriptions has had a pile of work dumped on his or her desk just adding and removing your name from the list of subscribers.

Coming Attractions: FTP and WWW

FTP is *not* that fellow with wings on his feet who delivers flowers; it's the way files (both text and applications) are sent and received via the Internet. It stands for *file transfer protocol*. It also is the name of the application you use to move those files. Right now, AOL's take on FTP is only being previewed online. That means you can look it over and try it out (if you're the brave sort), but it's by no means complete.

By the time you read this, it will be in place and fully operational (or close to it). Make sure you read any informational files in the area before you try your hand at it. Nothing is set yet, so I won't lumber you with what could turn out to be bogus instructions.

There's also advance hype about WWW access. WWW stands for World Wide Web, a hypertext-based system (like HyperCard or HyperPad) where you click on a word (like rhinoceros) or picture on a page to go to another page with information about that word or picture. It's very cool and very convenient, but right now WWW is strictly at the "Watch This Space" level. To check its current status, pop into the Internet Connection.

However, both new features are evidence of AOL's commitment to bringing full Internet access to its members in as fast and simple (two items that don't always go hand in hand) a manner as they can manage. Be prepared.

The Least You Need to Know

➤ There are a lot of these bulleted lists in this chapter.

➤ The Internet is an *inter*national *net*work of computers that enables the transfer of information around the world.

➤ AOL access is limited but is growing quickly. Use the Keyword: INTERNET.

➤ Email can be sent to anyone, anywhere as long as they have an Internet address or use an online service with Internet access.

➤ In spite of some name changes on a few buttons, newsgroups look and behave very much like all of the other message areas on AOL.

➤ Mailing lists, like newsgroups, are discussion groups; but mailing lists correspond via email instead of a message area.

➤ Gopher is a speedy way to browse through huge amounts of information online.

Part 3
Assorted Advice and How-To Stuff

In this third part of the book, you'll find some information you may need right away—and some you may never need. You'll find stuff about taking America Online with you when you travel, reviews of some of my favorite areas and files online, tips on troubleshooting and saving money, a glossary, and instructions on how to use the disk that's glued inside the back cover. Since the disk is only for Windows users, Chapter 24, "About That Disk…," also has instructions for Mac and DOS users on how to build their own utility disks.

You might want to read a chapter or two, skim through it all, or save reading things here until you need them online. I leave it up to you.

Chapter 18

On the Road with AOL

In This Chapter

➤ Finding local access numbers

➤ Creating location files

➤ Travel tips

Sometimes, in the course of human events, it becomes necessary to hit the road, Jack. You're finally taking a vacation. You need to attend a conference, convention, or other work-related event; you're moving to another city; or maybe you just need to be somewhere else for a bit. When it happens, you might want to be able to keep up with your email, friends, and other online adventures. You can.

First Things First

If you're moving or your everyday computer is portable, you can skip ahead. If you're traveling with a laptop that you don't use regularly (for example, one that you borrowed or rented for the occasion), you might need this section.

Before you can access America Online from the road, you need to be sure the computer you're going to be using is up to the job. That means it must meet these three criteria:

➤ It has the AOL software installed on its hard drive.

➤ It's equipped with a working modem (internal or external) that is connected properly.

➤ Wherever you'll be, there will be a phone line handy.

If your traveling computer doesn't have the AOL software installed, install it from your original disk, following exactly the same process discussed in Chapter 3. When the software is installed, make sure the modem works and is connected to the working phone line.

You set up the software just like you did in Chapter 4, but with one *big* difference. Because you're already a member of AOL, when you go through the registration process (also covered in Chapter 4), instead of entering the registration number and password from the certificate that came with your software, you'll enter your screen name (any of them) and its password. When you do that, AOL updates the software on your computer so that it has all of your screen names, passwords, and other account information.

Finding Local Access Numbers

When you travel to another city, you don't want to access AOL through your hometown local access number. That would probably be a long distance call of the highest order. Instead, you can find a local access number for the city you'll be visiting. There are three (count 'em *three*) ways to find local access numbers.

Look Online Before You Travel

Before you leave on your trip, sign on to AOL. Use the Keyword: ACCESS to go to the free Member Services area (discussed in Chapter 20). You'll see the Local Access Numbers dialog box.

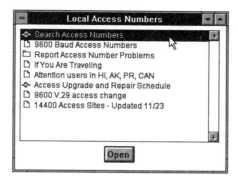

Searching for access numbers online.

Double-click on the **Search Access Numbers** line. The Search Access Numbers window appears. It's a standard search screen like you've used online before (if you've been following the examples in this book, anyhow).

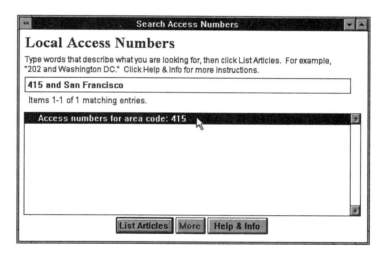

Paydirt!

In the text box at the top of the screen, enter the name of the city you'll be visiting and its area code. Then click the **List Articles** button at the bottom of the screen.

In the figure, I've entered *415 and San Francisco* (don't forget the "and" between search words) because I visited there in January for the annual MacWorld convention. When I ran the search, AOL turned up one set of access numbers that applied to San Francisco and area code 415. To read the list of numbers, double-click on the entry. The report will look something like the one shown here.

```
┌──────────────────────────────────────────────────────────────┐
│          Access numbers for area code: 415                     │
├──────────────────────────────────────────────────────────────┤
│ Access numbers for area code: 415                              │
│                                                                │
│ Updated: 94-12-06                                              │
│                                                                │
│ PALO ALTO          CA 9600    (415)856-4854    Sprint          │
│ SAN CARLOS         CA 9600    (415)591-8578    Sprint          │
│ SAN FRANCISCO      CA 9600    (415)247-9976    Sprint          │
│ SAN RAFAEL         CA 9600    (415)499-1629    Sprint          │
│ CONCORD            CA 2400    (510)674-0127    Sprint          │
│ FREMONT            CA 2400    (510)490-2050    Sprint          │
│ HAYWARD            CA 2400    (510)727-1708    Sprint          │
│ OAKLAND            CA 2400    (510)834-3194    Sprint          │
│ PALO ALTO          CA 2400    (415)856-0484    Sprint          │
│ PINOLE/VALLEJO     CA 2400    (510)724-2225    Sprint          │
│ SACRAMENTO         CA 2400    (916)443-7434    Sprint          │
│ SAN CARLOS         CA 2400    (415)595-8870    Sprint          │
└──────────────────────────────────────────────────────────────┘
```

Access numbers galore.

At this point, you can scroll through the list and jot down the number(s) you think you'll want to use (you should select at least two). If you want to really be prepared, like the good Boy or Girl Scout that you are, you can print a copy of the list (or save a copy as a text file) to take with you. Now you're set—you just need to create a new location file for your software. If you want to know how to do that, skip ahead to the section called "Let Your Software Do the Work."

Pick Up the Phone

If you don't get a local access number before you go, you're doomed. You'll never get on AOL now. Never, never, NEVER! (Mwah-hah-hah!)

Just kidding—don't be so paranoid! When you get to your destination, you can get a local access number by just picking up a telephone. Sprint, the company that runs SprintNet (one of the networks that lets you sign on to America Online through a local access number), runs a toll-free 800-number through which you can get access number information.

It's one of those "If you have a touch-tone phone press 1" systems, so call from a touch-tone telephone. However, before you call you need to have the following stuff handy:

➤ Paper and a pencil to write things down.

➤ The telephone number you will be calling America Online *from*. You might want to check into your hotel room, or wherever, before you call—just so you know.

➤ The speed (from 300 to 14,400 baud) of the modem you will be using.

When you have all that together, dial 1-800-473-7983, and a pleasant recorded voice talks you through the process. Have your pen and paper handy, and get two access numbers—just in case. When you've got them, you'll need to set up another location file. That's coming right up.

Let Your Software Do the Work

The process of creating a location file as described here is similar to what you'll go through with a Mac, but there's one *major* difference. To create a new location file, you begin by clicking on your **File** menu. Drag your cursor down to **New**. Select **Locality** from the submenu.

There won't be a text box to enter the location name in. Instead, when you save the file, you'll be asked to name the location file. Give the name of the city (or whatever) you're setting it up for.

If you don't care to tinker with AOL yourself, you can let the software do the work for you. This procedure works whether you are at home or have reached your destination. Before you can get the software to look for access numbers though, you have to create a location file for your destination. Even if you already have the access numbers you need (you've used one of the methods described earlier in the chapter), you still need to create a location file.

To create a location file, first launch your AOL software. When you see the Welcome/Sign On screen, do the following:

1. Click on the **Set Up** button. AOL displays the Network & Modem Setup dialog box.

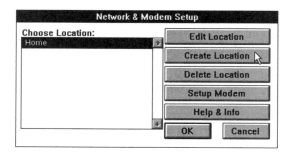

Setting up.

2. Click **Create Location.** A Network Setup dialog box (similar to the one here) appears. (You saw one much like this back in Chapter 6.)

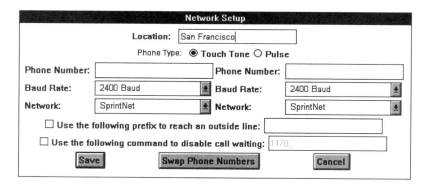

Enter location information.

3. In the Location box at the top of the Network Setup dialog, enter the name of the city you're visiting.

4. Leave the Phone Number boxes alone (unless you've already gotten access numbers by another method; then just type them in), but do select the appropriate modem speed in each Baud Rate box.

5. Click **Save**, and AOL saves the new location file. The software returns you to the Welcome/Sign On screen. Where the screen indicates your Current Location, it will tell the name of the city you just entered in the Location file (in this case, San Francisco).

A new current location.

If you need to get a set of local access numbers for your new location file, follow these steps:

1. Select **New Local#** from the pop-up list of Screen Names (it's the last item).

2. Click **Sign On**, and your software calls up the toll-free number you used to get your first access numbers way back in Chapter 4.

3. You'll be asked to enter the area code from which you'll be calling. Enter it, and AOL searches for the access numbers within that area code.

4. Select your first access number from the list and click **OK**.

5. Select your second access number from the list and click **OK**.

You'll be asked to confirm your selections. Make any changes you care to (like deleting the area code from the number,

When you actually arrive at your destination, you may need to fiddle with the setup. If you're staying in a hotel, you may need to enter a 9 or some other digit(s) to get an outside line from your room. If you're staying with friends or family, they may have call waiting, which you'll want to disable. Both of these topics are covered in Chapter 6 if you need a refresher.

You might also want to check and make sure the local access number(s) you've chosen are actually local. You don't want to saddle a friend or yourself (on your hotel bill) with hours of long distance calls.

perhaps), and then click **OK** again. AOL records the access numbers for your new location in the Network Setup box. You're all set.

To return to your home setup, click on the **Setup** button and double click on the **Home** location. You'll be set up to access AOL from home again (home again, home again, jiggedy-jig).

The steps previously outlined for creating a location file and getting local access numbers will work for any location file you need to create. You may want to have a location file for your home, your office, and any place you visit regularly. I have one set up for my home (which *is* my office), one for when I visit my family, and one for when I go to New York City (which isn't as often as I'd like).

I also keep a miscellaneous location file for places I don't go to often—that way I'm not cluttering up my hard drive with location files for every place I've ever been with my laptop. All I have to do is enter the new local access numbers and fiddle with the dialing prefixes.

If you do wind up with a pile of extraneous location files, it's simple to get rid of them. Click once on the location name in the Network & Modem Setup box to select it. Then click **Delete Location**. Poof! It's gone.

Travel Tips

Whether it's for business, for pleasure, or out of necessity, traveling can be traumatic enough without computer glitches giving you grief, too. Here are some tips to make traveling with your computer less stressful.

If you're staying at a hotel, call and make sure that you can connect your modem to the phone line in your room. You need to check two things in particular:

➤ Make sure there's a phone jack you can plug into (either that there's a spare, or that the phone can be unplugged). If you simply cannot get a room with a phone jack you can plug into, either you'll go into AOL withdrawal, or you'll need to buy one of those modem adapters (where you put the telephone's handset on the modem and everything goes through the ear and mouth pieces, instead of directly into the phone line). You can call your modem's manufacturer for details.

➤ Make sure that the hotel doesn't use a PBX phone system. Most modems, especially fax modems, don't work with PBX phone systems. They're digital and much more powerful than standard phone lines, and using them can damage your modem. Ask before you plug into the phone line. You can sidestep the PBX problem with an adapter, which should also be available from your modem's manufacturer or your favorite computer store.

If you need or want to use your computer during your flight, ask when you are making your reservations if it's allowed, or call the airline before you make your reservations. Airlines have gotten pretty weird about passengers using electronic equipment in-flight. They claim the electronics can interfere with their navigational systems. Unfortunately, none of the airlines seem to agree on which electronics cause the problem.

Finally, if you've traveled with a computer before, you know enough to do the following:

➤ Take a spare battery or two, especially if the flight will last longer than one battery is likely to last.

➤ Take your power cord and/or battery charger so you can plug in and recharge whenever possible.

➤ Carry your equipment in a padded bag, and take it on the plane with you. Even if you don't want to work, *never* check your delicate electronics unless you have indestructible stainless steel luggage.

➤ Contrary to popular opinion, you can send your computer, disks, and such through the X-ray machine. It won't harm your stuff—I've done it. I was scared to death the first time, but I did it.

➤ DO NOT pass any of your computer equipment through the metal detector (that doorway shaped thing you walk through). That is dangerous to your equipment because it uses magnets to detect metal. Magnets will scramble every bit of data on your hard drive and floppy disks. Don't do it.

➤ Be prepared to turn your computer on to prove to security that it is a computer and not a device for international terrorism.

➤ Never leave your computer in the trunk of a car for more than a few minutes. Car trunks get too hot and too cold. Plastic will melt, or freeze and crack.

➤ If your computer does get too hot or cold, let it sit long enough to come back to room temperature before you use it again. It may take an hour or two. Read a magazine.

➤ Make sure you have a game or two loaded on your laptop—you can't work all of the time.

➤ Have fun and send me a post card.

The Least You Need to Know

Taking your AOL friends with you when you travel can be enjoyable and can keep you from getting too homesick while on the road. It's very easy and only takes a little planning.

➤ You can get local access numbers in any of three ways: online (Keyword: ACCESS), by calling Sprint (1-800-472-7983), or by letting your software call and configure a new location setup.

➤ Location files prepared in advance will spare you a lot of pressure on the road—and who needs the pressure? The most you'll need to do is tinker with the pre-dial stuff for outside lines and to disable call waiting.

➤ Before you leave, make sure that the place you'll be staying is equipped to deal with your computer: a phone jack you can plug into and no PBX phone system.

These Are a Few of My Favorite Things

This chapter is all about the things I like, use, and/or recommend to folks who might be interested or have need of them. Check it out.

Features I Use a Lot

These are the AOL features that I use almost every time I sign onto AOL. I'll tell you how they work (or point you to the chapter that explains how) and why I use them.

Online Clock

On more than one occasion, I have lost all track of time while online and wound up spending hours longer than I intended to. To avoid running up my phone bills and online charges, I've programmed myself to check the online clock regularly. The online clock tells you what time it is (in military time) and how long you've been online.

You can call up the online clock in three ways:

➤ Click on the alarm clock icon in the Windows toolbar.

➤ Select **Online Clock** from your **G**o To menu.

➤ Use the Keyword: CLOCK.

I usually try to keep my online sessions to about an hour (not counting download time). So at the 44-minute mark, I start to wrap things up; I make sure I've found all the files I want, visited forums where I've posted messages, and so on. It's a good habit to get into and you can adjust the time limit to suit your own needs and pocketbook.

FlashSessions and Download Manager

I'm an email and file junkie. I correspond on a regular basis with a lot of people on America Online, other services (CompuServe and eWorld), and the Internet. (AOL's Internet access is another favorite feature of mine. It's covered in Chapter 17, so I won't belabor the point here.)

Whenever I sign onto AOL, I tend to ignore any mail that might be waiting for me so I can do a sweep of the computing forums. I look for all the files and information that make a toy-brain like me happy. I slap them into my download manager and sign off.

Later on, I use the download manager to retrieve my files in the middle of the night. I wait until the wee-small hours for two reasons. First, because of my work schedule, I don't like to tie up my computer with a long download session when I should be working. Second, in the middle of the night, online time is generally less expensive (in terms of the phone bill), and AOL is less populated. And when AOL isn't busy, downloads usually take less time, which also saves money.

If I know I have a wad of email waiting for me or if I have a pile of my own all ready to send, instead of using the Download Manager, I use a FlashSession. FlashSessions can retrieve your new mail, send your outgoing mail, *and* collect any files you have listed in your download manager. FlashSessions are covered in Chapter 9; the download manager is covered in Chapter 12. Both are pretty painless and very useful.

Keywords!

I rarely use a menu or forum button to go *anywhere* online. I use Keywords. "But, John," you say, "how can you remember all of those Keywords?" It isn't difficult. Most Keywords on AOL are fairly obvious: like the Keyword for the Computing Forum is COMPUTING. If you know where you want to go, you probably can guess the right Keyword. And, the more you use Keywords, the easier they are to remember and use. Chapter 23 is nothing but Keywords.

Picture This, If You Will

In addition to being a toy brain, I also like to shop—usually for toys (go figure). The newest versions of the America Online software (for Windows and Mac) have incorporated multimedia features that make shopping online less of a guessing game.

In the figure below, not only can you read the description of the Bugs Bunny and friends T-shirt, but you can see the shirt on your monitor. No more trying to figure out what the shirt (or whatever) looks like from a 20-words-or-less description.

No more guessing what T-shirts in the online store look like.

To see these pictures online, you need to set your Multimedia Preferences to display them. That's covered in Chapter 6. Shopping in general is covered in Chapter 16. If you're interested in the T-shirt shown above, I found it in 2Market in the Holiday Central area (more on that in a second).

Forums I Visit a Lot

Right up front I'll tell you that I visit the Software Center at *least* once a week to see what's new in all of the forum libraries. I'll talk about all the fun and fabulous files you can find there in a little bit. However, because you may not be the byte-head that I am, I'll tell you about the noncomputing forums that I visit regularly, too.

Holiday Central

Holiday Central (Keyword; HOLIDAY) is a seasonal area that gathers files related to upcoming holidays in one convenient forum. In the following figure, it's geared toward Christmas and Hanukkah. In September and October, it's for Halloween. In January and February, it will be all about Valentine's Day.

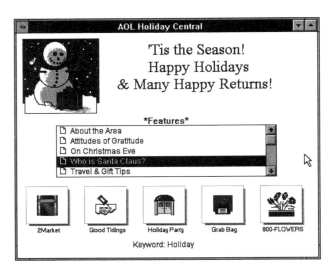

Ho-ho-ho-Holiday Central.

Holiday Central works like most forums online. It has a message area (Good Tidings), chat room (Holiday Party), and file library (Grab Bag), plus it has opportunities to shop (2Market and 800-Flowers). The button names may change to suit the holiday, but the features remain the same.

I found the Bugs Bunny T-shirt you saw earlier in the online Warner Bros. Store, which is part of 2Market. 800-Flowers, a featured vendor right now, is an online florist that had a special offer on fresh-cut Christmas trees and a $10-off coupon for first-time buyers.

The file library contains all sorts of seasonal goodies: graphic files in a variety of formats, animation files, sounds, holiday fonts, and other things to help spice up your own holiday creations. This Christmas, I used some of the fonts and graphics to make my own slightly twisted holiday cards, send letters from Santa to kids in the family, and create all kinds of other holiday items (banners, decorations, and so on). You can use a page layout program, one of the "Works" packages (Microsoft Works or ClarisWorks, for example), or even a stand-alone card-making application (such as The Print Shop) to put these Holiday Central goodies to use.

Of course, by the time you read this, Christmas Present will have turned into Christmas Past, and another holiday will have taken the spotlight. Whatever the occasion, Holiday Central can save you time, energy, and effort during already hectic holiday seasons.

DC Comics Online

I have several friends who are heavily into comic books (or *graphic novels*, if you want to be politically correct). I enjoy them, but I'm not quite a fanatic. I regularly visit the DC Comics Online area to download graphics for a godson who's starting to collect comic books. (That's not "collect" as in he has a lot of them, but "Collect" as in *Put on these gloves before you touch that, Uncle John*. He's serious about it.) I like to make cards for him featuring his favorite characters, create custom startup screens for his Macintosh, and keep myself apprised of comic book conventions, sales, and such for gifts he'll appreciate.

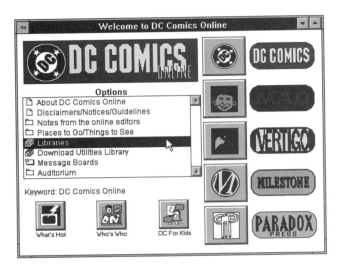

A comic maven's dream.

DC Comics' forum is a standard forum with individual departments for the various imprints (publishing companies they own). In the figure above, you can see the buttons for them on the right side of the screen: classic DC Comics (*Superman, Batman*); *MAD Magazine* (What, me worry?); Vertigo (*Sandman*); Milestone (I'm not sure what they publish, *Vamps*, I think—I'm not that big a fan); and Paradox Press (graphic novels with book-quality bindings). From these departments, you can access the features of the main forum (the chat room, file libraries, and so on) or you can get individual information files about the magazines and books of each imprint.

Science Fiction and Science Fact

Being the science fiction/fact fan that I am, I often check in at two forums just to see what's happening.

In *OMNI* Magazine Online (Keyword: OMNI), I like to look for weird science: photos of the "face" on Mars, reports of UFO sightings, and other bizarre and quirky factoids that *OMNI* is known for. They often have interesting guest speakers and information you just wouldn't find anywhere else. A few months ago, I found a copy of the *Roswell Declaration*, which is part of a mail-in campaign to get the government to declassify and release their files related to the UFO (or weather balloon, depending on your level of belief) that crashed in Roswell, New Mexico back in the 1940s.

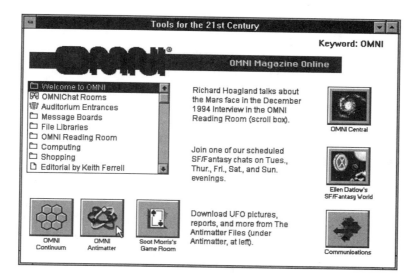

OMNI Magazine Online.

With the Sci-Fi Channel forum (Keyword: SCIFI CHANNEL), I like to keep up with the latest buzz about science fiction television—including *Sci-Fi Buzz*, the channel's weekly news magazine for fans of SF in all its variations. Author Harlan Ellison is a weekly commentator, and you can't find more hard-core SF than that.

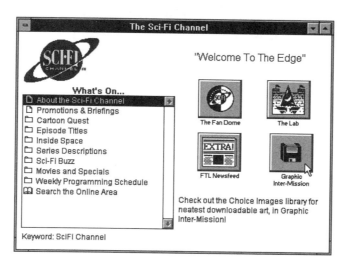

The Sci-Fi Channel.

My favorite thing about the Sci-Fi Channel forum is that I can keep up to date with their *FTL Newsfeeds*, which (if you haven't seen them) are short "film at eleven" sort of news clips with a science fiction edge. They're like 30-second soap operas. I got addicted to the story line last year, but now I don't get to watch very often; so I keep up through the forum.

DeskTop Publishing Resource Center and Designs Online

Although I enjoy and use the DeskTop Publishing Resource Center (Keyword: DTP), my favorite part is the Designs Online area (Keyword: DESIGNS ONLINE). In the Designs Online area, lots and lots of people have uploaded their own designs to share with the world. Trying to figure out how to create a greeting card with your software? Check here—someone probably figured it out already.

Ideas you can borrow and adapt to your own DTP projects.

You can find templates for all of the common desktop publishing chores: flyers, brochures, newsletters, and more. If I have a new project, one that I haven't tackled before, I often browse through the template library (by clicking on the Templates button) to see what others have done before. Even if I don't use a template, they often give me an idea of what I want (and don't want) my project to look like when it's finished. Looking at others' work gives me a creative kick in the pants.

Special Needs Areas

I firmly believe that computers and online services are marvelous tools to help people help themselves. I don't care what the difficulty is: shyness, low self-image, physical or emotional challenges, geographic isolation—anything.

Online services eliminate barriers to communication, as well as many social impediments (like superficial judgments based on appearances). Online, you're judged by what you think and do instead of by where you live and what you look like. It offers many people a chance to socialize who might not otherwise have the opportunity or the cooperation of other people. Nowhere is this more apparent than in three specific areas online: the disABILITIES forum, the HIV Support Group, and the SeniorNet forum.

Template A fill-in-the-blanks version of a particular type of publishing file. Instead of finding graphics and text, you'll find place-holders that tell you where to put your graphics and text (they actually say "Insert your graphic here"). This really speeds up the design process because you don't have to start from scratch.

disABILITIES

You can tell by the capitalization of the word how the folks in the disABILITIES forum (Keyword: DISABILITIES) view themselves. They aren't disabled, they're just enabled differently than most.

The disABILITIES forum contains text files, software, and resource information for people who don't have the standard allotment of limbs, fingers, senses, motor skills, or whatever. It enables them to harness the power of computing and put it to work *for* them, instead of against them. There are scheduled chats, self-help sessions, and other online events. Information about assistive technologies (such as alternative keyboards and input devices) abounds, and the software libraries are full of add-ins to make computers easier to deal with.

Before you download any templates from the Designs Online area, make sure you know the name and version number of the application you're using. Templates are generally designed to be used with specific applications.

The same goes for graphic files. The easiest way to get the format you need is to see which formats your application(s) can handle. You don't want to spend time and money downloading a template you can't use.

Use of the resources in this forum also opens up the rest of the online world. Imagine being able to chat with people who, in face-to-face conversation, might not be able to get past your wheelchair, leg brace, missing arm, or whatever. The resources work, most of the software is freeware, and there's no reason not to try them if you or someone you know can't deal with a standard computer setup.

A friend of mine, a confirmed AOL addict, was unable to use the service after he developed serious eye trouble. He couldn't see well enough to use a keyboard, much less find an icon to point at and click on. One visit to the disABILITIES software library (and about 15 minutes worth of download time) was enough to get him back online and enjoying himself—and able to use his computer again in general.

HIV/AIDS Support Group

Like anyone with a life-threatening illness, AIDS patients tend to suffer alone. Family and friends can't really understand what it feels like to have the disease, even though they try to be sympathetic. Add to that the emotional battering that can come with even *admitting* you're infected with this stigmatized virus, and you might begin to understand the patients' need to talk to others with the same condition.

When their health is reasonably good, many patients are able to travel to a live support meeting (if there is one nearby), where they can share their experiences and get help and advice. In remote areas, in bad weather, or when health fails, travel may be difficult if not impossible.

Most forums have a Suggestion Box available; it's usually a line entry in the forums scroll box. Just double-click on **Suggestion Box**. The suggestion boxes work like the Ask the Staff buttons in the file libraries, automatically addressing and sending your comment(s) to the Forum Leader as email. Piece of cake.

Under the auspices of the Gay and Lesbian Community Forum on AOL (Keyword: GLCF), there is a weekly support group where patients can meet online in a private room. Don't feel like you can't attend if you're heterosexual. The meetings are open to *anyone* infected with the virus. Anonymity is respected. You can find more information about this by double-clicking on the **Conference Schedule** in the forum and scrolling through the calendar of events.

You can also find information about other online support groups (such as Alcoholics Anonymous, among others) throughout Clubs and Interests, accessible through the Main Menu. Whatever your condition or needs, even if you live alone, you don't have to go it alone. If there isn't a support group that meets your needs, don't be shy. Drop a suggestion in the Suggestion Box of the forum that seems to be a likely host and ask if they can start one or help you try to start one. If you don't ask for it, you don't get it—that's my motto.

SeniorNet

I first became aware of SeniorNet when I was working on a book called *The Home Computer Companion*, and I think it's a fantastic resource for folks over 55. SeniorNet started out as a research project in 1986. Mary Furlong, EdD, Professor of Education at the University of San Francisco, wanted to see if computers and telecommunications could enhance the lives of older adults. They can, and they do. Since then, SeniorNet has grown into an organization with over 5,000 members nationwide, with Learning Centers (classrooms where members can learn about computers and computing) in more than 50 U.S. cities.

Some of the perks of being a member include a special member's rate on AOL, and the opportunity to meet, chat with, and share experiences with other members from across the nation. The SeniorNet Online area is the base of operations. The Community Center is the chat room, and it's usually hopping with activity. Members of SeniorNet (or *Netters* as they call themselves) are a lively and outspoken crew who love the opportunity SeniorNet has given them.

If you or someone you know is 55 or older and has an interest in computing, check out the SeniorNet area online (Keyword: SENIORNET). It's fun, affordable, and informative.

Fun and Fabulous Files (and Where to Find Them)

For both beginners and old-timers alike, the easiest and fastest way to find the files that are fun, practical, and hot (the ones that *everybody's* downloading) is to go to the Software Center (Keyword: SOFTWARE) and check out the top downloads.

I like to check the Top Downloads (double-click **Top Software Downloads** in the list box) each month. Here's why: Computer-geeks like to talk shop and swap tips. When one geek finds a great bit of software, word tends to spread—fast. Others download it and talk about it, and then more download it. It spirals out of control until everybody has that file or software. The reverse is also true. If the geeks-that-be don't like something, or it has only limited appeal, the file's download counter won't break 100.

Once a month, some brave soul goes through all the forum librar-ies to see what files were downloaded the most. They're all gathered together in one spot so you can easily peruse the files, amuse yourself, and have fun, fun, fun downloading stuff 'til your daddy takes your modem away. If you want a fast, easy way to cruise through a smorgas-bord of software from all the computing forums, this is the place to start. You might want to check out the details on browsing and down-loading files back in Chapter 12 before you start. Otherwise, go nuts.

The Least You Need to Know

There are only a few things you need to remember from this chapter:

➤ The features I use a lot may not be ones you'll use a lot. These are simply examples of what I use and why. It isn't set in stone. You'll develop your own habits online.

➤ The great thing about advice is that you don't have to take it.

➤ There are hundreds of forums online that aren't related to computing. You don't have to be a geek like me to enjoy cruising the forums.

➤ While AOL is all about fun, there are some serious areas, too. Don't be afraid to explore them—they won't bite you.

Chapter 20

Member Services

In This Chapter

➤ Getting there

➤ Billing information

➤ Securing yourself

➤ Help me! Help me!

We've pretty much glossed over a few of the main departments on America Online (such as Sports, Entertainment, and Personal Finance), mainly because I feel it's more fun to *explore* than it is to have someone say "Do this, go there" for every single department. You're not sheep, right? You'll find what you like. However, I do feel that it's important to show you one last area online: Member Services. That's because if you're ever in a jam, it's there to help you, online or off, and it's free of all online charges.

All Forums Lead to Member Services

You'll notice during your explorations online that there's a little rectangle at the bottom of most department and forum main screens that says "Member Services." Click on it, and it will take you right to the Member Services area. You can also select **Member Services** from your **Go To** menu or use the Keyword: HELP.

However you do it, the first thing you'll see is a little dialog box asking if you really, really want to enter the free area. Here's why: since Member Services is free of online charges, all the windows (chat rooms, forums, libraries, and such) that are open on your screen will disappear when you enter Member Services. If you aren't in the middle of some juicy chat or any other "I can't bear to leave" stuff, click on **Yes**. Otherwise, click **No**. When you click Yes, the Member Services screen appears.

Inside Member Services

The Member Services screen features ten buttons that let you do a number of helpful things. Two of the most used buttons are right at the top: Billing Information and Account Security.

Member Services—it's FREE!

Bill Me, Baby!

One click on the Billing Information button brings up the Billing Information screen. With it, you can change your name and address (if you get married, move, or enter the Witness Protection Program), change your method of payment, get an explanation of billing terms, and get a detailed bill. You can also change your password, add and delete screen names, create or edit your member profile, ask billing questions, or cancel your account. Just double-click on a list item to open it.

Since we talked about passwords, screen names, and member profiles back in Chapter 6, I won't go over them again here. Instead, let's look at a billing summary. To call up your account charges so far, double-click **Current Month's Billing Summary** or use the Keyword: BILLING. AOL will think about it for a moment and then display the Current Bill Summary dialog box.

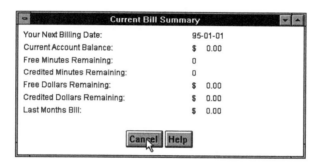

A sample bill. (I won't show my real one—it would scare you.)

Your current billing summary gives you seven bits of information.

➤ **Your Next Billing Date** That's the next time AOL will charge your credit card for the month's online charges.

➤ **Current Account Balance** What you owe so far. Generally, this will only show your basic $9.95 membership fee until you use up your free hours.

➤ **Free Minutes Remaining** How many of your free monthly hours you have left (in minutes). Five free hours would be shown as 300 minutes (for the math squeamish).

➤ **Credited Minutes Remaining** If you receive a time credit on your account (maybe as a prize in a game room—it happens), this will show how many of them you have left.

➤ **Free Dollars Remaining** Did you know you can give gift certificates for AOL time? You can buy them in the AOL Store (discussed in Chapter 16). The dollar value of the gift certificate goes here, and the amount ticks down as you use it.

 Why does AOL *talk* about billing in hours, but actually bill in minutes? One is psychological: if you hear you're charged almost six cents per minute, it *sounds* more expensive than saying $3.50 an hour, even though it works out the same. The other reason is fairness. If they billed in hours and you were online for 48 minutes, you'd be charged for 12 minutes you didn't use. Billing in minutes is much fairer, and it's hard to get worked up over 12 seconds.

➤ **Credited Dollars Remaining** Same as Credited Minutes Remaining, but with dollars instead of minutes.

➤ **Last Month's Bill** Total you were charged for your online usage last month. It helps you keep to your budget.

For your first few months online, it may help if you pop in here once or twice a month until you get an idea of how much the service will cost based on the way you and your family use it.

Account Security

Clicking on the Account Security button brings up the Account Security screen. Basically, it's a scrolling text box with account security tips and information. Read it. It's very helpful and—hey—it's free.

Beside the text box there are three buttons: Change Password, Parental Control, and Terms of Service. We talked about the importance of changing your password and how to do it in Chapter 6. We also talked about how to use Parental Control to keep your kids out of certain areas online (like chat rooms) in Chapter 6, too. You should have read the Terms of Service (TOS) when you first signed on as a member (way back in Chapter 4). If you didn't, do it now.

Help and Support

The bottom of the Member Services main screen has eight buttons that offer a plethora of help, either online or off. Online help is composed of a Members' Online Support Forum that offers all manner of specific help for common problems online. It also offers easy access to other Member Services features (such as changing your password) and a list of local access numbers if you need to travel (see Chapter 18 for more information).

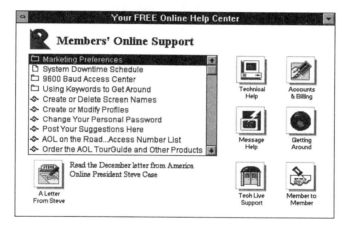

It's so supportive!

The Members' Online Support Forum offers all the features of any other forum online, including a message area (Member to Member) where you can post questions you haven't been able to find answers to. Other members will help you out.

The other main feature of the Online Help part of Member Services is Tech Live Support. Tech Live is an online auditorium like the Rotunda (Chapter 10) where you can ask real live technical people real live technical questions about America Online. However, you should try to find the answers in the other Member Services areas first. Save Tech Live for real "*Geesh*, I've tried everything and just can't figure it out" kinds of questions.

Offline help consists of four buttons that bring up information screens telling you how to get help when you can't connect to AOL. However, if you can't connect to AOL, you can't get at these screens, so read each one *now* (and maybe print or save a copy of each for future reference).

Both online and offline help are covered in a little more detail in Chapter 21, which is coming right up.

So Long, and Thanks for All the Help

When you're done in Member Services, just select **Exit Free Area** from your Go To menu. You'll get a dialog box asking if you really, really want to exit the free area. Click **Yes**, and you'll return to the regular pay-as-you-go areas online.

The Least You Need to Know

This is a short little chapter, but it's an important resource for free, helpful stuff you can do online.

➤ If you ever need help online, just use the Keyword: HELP to go to Member Services, a veritable banquet of help.

➤ The Keyword: BILLING takes you right to the Billing Information area, where you can fiddle with everything related to your account (password, screen names, member profile, and so on) and look at a summary of your current charges.

➤ Practice safe computing: change your password regularly.

➤ Members' Online Support is a full-fledged forum where members help each other out with stuff online.

Chapter 21

Troubleshooting America Online

In This Chapter

➤ Easy solutions to common problems

➤ Sources of help when you aren't connected to AOL

➤ Sources of help when you *are* connected

In my experience, once your America Online software is installed and configured and you've used it successfully, things rarely go wrong. The most trouble I've had has been using new versions of the software. But that's *my* experience; your experiences may differ.

To help you over the rough spots, here's a bunch of advice culled from other places in the book, plus some additional information on how to figure out what's wrong, why it's wrong, and how to fix it.

Generally Speaking

Generally speaking, there's nothing that can go *so* wrong with America Online that your computer will explode or anything—so don't panic. Also generally speaking, there are only four sources of things that can go wrong when you're trying to do something with AOL: your hardware, your software, the local connection (or *node*), or AOL's computers in Virginia.

When something goes wrong, and *what* goes wrong, can give you an indication of *where* something is boogered up (*boogered up*, now that's a highly technical term; use it to impress your friends). For example: if you're trying to start up AOL and get connected, but nothing is happening, the problem is with your hardware and/or software. It has to be, because you haven't called out and attempted to connect.

On the other hand, if AOL starts up fine and dials out fine, but you run into trouble trying to connect to your local access number, the troublemaker is probably your software or your local node. It isn't likely to be your hardware because you wouldn't have gotten as far as you did if your modem was broken. (That's not to say it *can't* be your hardware, just that it's low on the list.)

On the other hand (which would give you three hands—and make you a wicked touch-typist), if the problem occurred once you were connected to America Online, it's probably being caused by their computers. Depending on what happened, it could also be your local node or your computer.

Get the idea? It's kind of like the food chain. In the food chain, the smaller and weaker you are the more things there are that can eat you. With the connection chain, the further along you go, the more things there are that can mess up your computer.

AOL Software Won't Launch

If you're having trouble getting your America Online software up and running, the software may have been installed incorrectly or incompletely, or may have been damaged by some unknown mishap. It happens. Reinstall and reconfigure your software following the instructions in Chapters 3 and 4.

Modem Woes

Your software starts fine, but when you try to get it to use your modem, all sorts of craziness happens. You get an error message saying **AOL can't initialize your modem** or the modem **won't accept commands**. Your first step is to check the obvious:

➤ Is the modem connected properly? Cables tight? Correct port?

➤ Plugged in?

➤ Turned on?

➤ Any necessary driver software installed? (This is mostly for Macs, but it wouldn't hurt to check your modem manual.)

If that all seems to be fine, try turning off your modem. Wait about 30 seconds, turn it back on, and try again.

If that doesn't fix it, you may want to try using your modem with the plain communications software that came in the box with it (or that's installed on your hard drive) or try signing on to another online service (maybe CompuServe, PRODIGY, or eWorld if you're a member). If you've got Microsoft Works or a similar "Works" package, most have a communications module. You might want to test with that. Check your software manual for details.

Naturally, if you have an internal modem (one installed inside your computer), things work a little differently. Instead of checking cables, you should pop the hood of your computer and make sure the modem card is seated fully in the slot (check your manual for proper installation instructions). Also, make sure the phone line is connected. If you want to try turning your internal modem off, you have to shut down your computer. Wait 30 seconds or so and turn it back on.

If your modem works with the other software, your AOL setup is probably the culprit. Check to make sure that all the information you've entered in your setup is correct for your modem (see Chapters 4 and 6 for details). If your modem is connected properly and doesn't respond to any communications software, there's something wrong with the modem. Check the manual and/or call the manufacturer's technical support number.

Can't Connect to Local Access Number

You launch AOL fine, it initializes your modem, and it dials the local access number. But for some reason, it won't connect to your local node. There are a couple of things that might cause this to happen.

No Dial Tone

When you try to dial your local access number, if your modem doesn't hear a dial tone, you'll get a message that says (duh) **No Dial Tone**. Chances are, your modem isn't connected to your phone line (check to make sure); it isn't connected *correctly* (many modems have two jacks: one for the phone line, and one for a telephone; make sure each is plugged into the proper jack); or your phone line isn't working.

If you have a phone connected to the same line, pick up the receiver and listen. If you don't hear a dial tone, press the cutoff button a few times. That may get you a dial tone again. If not, you may want to have a friend or neighbor call that number and/or report the line trouble to your phone company. Of course, you can do that yourself if you have a second phone line that's working.

When you do hear a dial tone, hang up the phone and try your modem again. If it still won't work, it's possible that the modem is set up wrong or is defective. Check the modem manual for installation, setup, and configuration information.

Access Number Is Busy

It happens. That's why you have two local access numbers. If both are busy, try the numbers several times, waiting 5–10 minutes between attempts. If they're *still* busy, try getting another set of access numbers, as described in Chapter 18.

Before you go changing anything in your AOL setup, write down all the information on your setup screen the way it is now. If you go into a frenzy of info-swapping, you might forget what it looked like before you started—and you may want to change it back.

It also wouldn't hurt to make sure you've got the correct phone information entered in the setup box. You entered the phone number correctly. The touch-tone vs. rotary selection is correct. You've entered the correct number (like "9") to get an outside line (if necessary). And you've disabled call-waiting if you have it. If you make any changes, save the new settings (just click on **Save**), and then try again. Chapters 4 and 6 have details.

No Answer at Local Access Number

Same deal as "Access Number is Busy." Try a few times, waiting a few minutes between tries. While you're waiting, double-check the phone number(s) and other phone information settings in the setup screen. If you make any changes, save the new settings (click on **Save**), and then try again. Chapters 4 and 6 have the set up details. If it still doesn't answer, try to get another access number, as described in Chapter 18.

No Carrier Signal

Your modem dials the number, the number answers, but you don't get that digital "Hi, how you doin'?" squeal from the modem at your local access number. Try the solutions described in "Access Number Is Busy" and "No Answer at Local Access Number."

Final Connection to AOL Didn't Happen

Sometimes you call up your local access number and connect with no problem, but then something goes wonky (another technical term) when the local node tries to connect you to America Online. What happens to me is that I'll sit there while the sign on screen says **Requesting Network Access** or **Checking Password**. Then I'll get a polite error message saying I am no longer connected to America Online. I didn't know I was connected in the first place.

Remember the old saying "If at first you don't succeed, try, try, again." Before you fool around with any of your hardware or software, try a few more times, waiting a few minutes between attempts. The problem, most likely, is with your local node or America Online. Don't panic. If it takes too long, if you get impatient, or if it happens often, check out Chapter 18 for advice on getting new local access numbers.

It may seem like a *really* obvious point, but if you don't have call waiting, don't click in the check box labeled "disable call waiting." It confuses your phone line, and you won't be able to connect to AOL.

Problems After You've Connected to AOL

Sometimes stuff happens after you sign on to America Online, and you have no idea why. The following scenarios are typical; read my typical solutions.

Everything Is Sooooo Sssslooooowwww

If you're in a chat room or downloading a file and it seems to be taking forever to get anything done, the problem is that there's a lot of traffic on AOL or on your local access node. Remember that there are *thousands* of people using this service, and they're all trying to do the same things. This can slow things down and, since it takes you longer to do what you want to do, it runs up your phone bill and online charges. Here are a few things you can try to help alleviate the problem.

➤ Sign off and connect again. That often solves the problem if the source is your local node.

➤ Try another local access number—preferably one that's less active. Unfortunately, the only way to tell if it is less active is to try it.

➤ Stop downloading files. Use the download manager (Chapter 12) or a FlashSession (Chapter 9) to retrieve them in the middle of the night when things should be perkier.

➤ Sign off, wait awhile, and try again later.

You Have Been Disconnected from AOL

Suddenly being knocked offline is known as "being punted." For no apparent reason, you're treated like a football and drop-kicked off the service. It happens from time to time and for a number of reasons you don't really need to know. The only thing to do about it is to pick yourself up, dust yourself off, and start all over again.

If it happens regularly, make sure your call waiting (if you have it) is disabled in your current setup. (Chapter 6 tells you how.) The clicking sound an incoming call makes on your phone can disrupt the flow of information to your computer, making AOL's computer think you've hung up. You could also try another set of local access numbers.

Trouble Downloading Files

When you download files, whether one at a time or in a bunch with the download manager, you can't seem to get AOL to finish the job. You get disconnected or otherwise interrupted. The first thing to do is try again. The problem may be a slow-down or a "punt" situation like that just described. There may just be too many people trying to download files at the same time.

If the problem happens all the time, there may be another difficulty. Check the following:

➤ If you have call waiting, make sure you've checked the Disable Call Waiting check box in your setup screen. See Chapter 6 for instructions.

➤ If you use a screen saver (the one built into Windows or one from After Dark), turn it off before you start a long download. Most screen savers kick in if there isn't any keyboard or mouse activity for a few minutes. During a download, there isn't any activity like that, but your computer is still busy. If the screen saver starts up in the middle of a download, it can booger up the process or even damage the files as they're being downloaded. Check your screen saver manual for instructions on how to temporarily turn it off.

 If you have trouble downloading a file, you can receive a *download credit* for the time you spent doing the bogus download. Go to the free Member Services area (Keyword: MEMBER SERVICES) and click on the **Billing** button. Then double-click on **Request Download Credit** in the list box. Chapter 20 is all about Member Services.

Computer Peculiarities

The problems discussed so far were in the most general of terms and were the most common problems. Other problems and solutions are peculiar to the kind of computer you're using.

Macintosh

The biggest bug-bear with Macs is the dreaded INIT or Extension Conflict. That's where two or more of the extensions in your Extension folder are squabbling like spoiled brats and won't let you get anything done. Extension conflicts can cause all kinds of strange and bizarre behavior with your Mac—usually, right when you're starting it up, but at other times as well.

To see if your problem is an extension conflict, restart your Mac (using the **Restart** command on the **Special** menu). When the little Mac icon appears on your screen, press and hold the **Shift** key until the Welcome to Macintosh screen appears. That will disable all of your extensions. If that fixes the problem, you've got an extension conflict that needs to be resolved—a Mac without at least a few extensions won't do much.

Check your Macintosh manual or a good Mac book (like *The Complete Idiot's Guide to the Mac*) for instructions on resolving an extension conflict and other Mac-specific problems. For AOL-specific problems, you might want to use one of the online or offline help resources discussed in a few pages.

IBM-Compatible

Because there are so many manufacturers of IBM-compatible computers, and they come in so many different configurations (especially the number of serial or COM ports—where you'd connect your modem), it is close to impossible to anticipate all possible configuration problems.

It seems to me that the most common problem, however, would be telling your AOL software your modem is plugged into one COM port (say, COM1) when it is actually plugged into another (COM2). The result? Your software would be unable to talk to your modem because it doesn't know where it is. There are two ways to resolve this:

➤ Look at the back of your PC and note which port your modem is plugged into. Check your computer or I/O card manual to see what port it is. Change your AOL setup to the proper port and try again.

➤ If you can't figure it out by looking and checking the manual, try the process of elimination. Change the port selection in your setup to each available port, one at a time. Try connecting to AOL with each port. The one that works is the one that's right.

Chapter 6 talks about changing your setup in detail. For other PC-specific problems, you might want to use one of the online or offline help resources discussed later in the chapter.

Modem Peculiarities

If you're using a high speed modem (say 9600 baud and higher) and you want to use that extra speed with America Online, check your modem's manual for configuration tips. Some modems require that AOL's software be set for "Hardware Handshaking." Others require different settings for X-On/X-Off and/or "flow control."

You don't really need to know what all that means (they're just buzzwords applied to how modems connect to each other and regulate the flow of junk back and forth). However, you *do* need to know how

246

you should set those options in your AOL setup. If your modem's manual doesn't explain it clearly, you might want to call the modem manufacturer's technical support line, or call AOL's toll-free support number (that's coming up soon).

Offline Help

If you're having trouble connecting to AOL at all, naturally you'll need to use the offline help resources. One resource is the information from America Online's Help menu. Just select **Help** from the Help menu. You'll get a help screen that can answer a number of the most common questions. If you don't know how to use Help, there's even help on help: select **How to Use Help** from the Help menu.

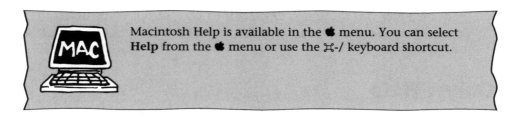

Macintosh Help is available in the ⌘ menu. You can select **Help** from the ⌘ menu or use the ⌘-/ keyboard shortcut.

Help by Fax

If you have access to a fax machine (or a modem that can receive faxes), you can get printed help instructions by calling America Online's automated FAXLink Service. Call 1-800-827-5551 from a touch-tone phone and follow the recorded instructions. You'll be faxed a list of all the available faxes. You can choose what you need from the list, call the 800 number again, and key in the item numbers of the fax(es) you want.

Technical Support

America Online also maintains a toll-free technical support line that you can call with your questions. Live people take your questions from 9 AM until 2 AM Monday through Friday, and from Noon to 1 AM on weekends (that's Eastern time, by the way). Prerecorded answers to commonly asked questions are available at the same number 24 hours a day, 7 days a week. Call 1-800-827-3338.

Technical Support Bulletin Board

Most folks who are new to the world of computers and modems may not want to try this, but if you're feeling experimental, AOL offers an electronic bulletin board service (BBS) full of technical information, including access numbers, connecting, and troubleshooting information.

The BBS is open 24 hours a day. You can access it with your modem and any generic telecommunications software (*not* the America Online software). Of course, if the problem is that your modem won't work, you won't be able to try this.

Your communication software should be set to use the standard 8 data bits, 1 stop bit, and no parity. The toll-free number is 1-800-827-5808. When you log onto the BBS, you'll be asked if you can display ANSI graphics. For most PCs, that will be a "Yes." For most Macs, that will be a "No." If all that is gibberish to you, check your modem manual or the documentation that came with your communications software.

Online Help

There are almost as many ways of getting help with a problem online as there are offline.

Trouble Doing Something

Most windows you'll encounter online have a Help button. If you don't know or forget how something works, click on the **Help** button.

Ask in a Chat Room

If you're having trouble, you can always pop into a Chat Room and ask a Guide or another user for help. Guides are a great resource; if they don't know the answer to your question, they will at least be able to point you in the right direction. You can usually find a Guide in a lobby. Select **Go To Lobby** from your Go To menu.

Other users are also a good source of help. A lot of folks online (like myself) have been using the service for years and know the ins and outs pretty well.

Ask in a Help Room

During peak hours, you'll often see rooms named WAOL HELP, PCAOL Help, and MAC HELP in the People Connection. These rooms are staffed by Guides who know their stuff. Pop into the room specific to your computer and version of AOL. The Guide will greet you and let you know when to ask your question (it's on a first-come first-served basis).

To find a help room:

1. Select **Go To Lobby** from your Go To menu.

2. Once you're in the lobby, click on the **Rooms** button.

3. Scroll through the list of rooms until you find the help room you need, and then double-click on it.

If it's very busy, you may have to click on the **More** button several times to see all of the rooms. If there isn't a help room available, don't panic. There is another option.

Tech Live

Tech Live (Keyword: TECH LIVE) is a huge online auditorium staffed by technical support people. As in a help room, when you enter, you are greeted by the staffer on duty and told how many people are ahead of you (if any). Wait your turn. When asked, explain your problem briefly but completely. Help will happen.

Tech Live is *only* for questions about using America Online, though, so if you have other technical questions, you'll need to take them to the appropriate computing forum. Tech Live is staffed Monday–Friday 9 AM to 2 AM Eastern and Saturday–Sunday Noon to 1 AM Eastern.

The Least You Need to Know

With all of these helpful resources around, you should never encounter a problem so bizarre that no one can help you out of it. (Life should be so fully explained.)

➤ When trouble happens, don't panic.

➤ The problems that crop up can be tracked to one of four sources: your hardware, your software, the local access node, or America Online. Knowing when the problem happened and what happened can help you figure out where it happened.

➤ You can get help offline with your Help menu and through toll-free numbers.

➤ You can get help online from Help buttons, Guides, other members, help rooms, and Tech Live.

Chapter 22

Saving Time and Money

In This Chapter

➤ How to avoid hassles with multiple members at home

➤ Stuff you can do offline

➤ Tips for saving time online

With this chapter more than any other, I've really had to think about why and how I do things online, because a lot of this is second nature to me now. It will happen to you, too, soon enough. Practice makes perfect. You'll be amazed when your online floundering becomes the graceful and elegant use of your online time.

Who's on First?

Technically, this isn't a "Time Is Money" type of timesaving tip, but it will (I hope) save you time arguing over whose turn it is to sign on to AOL. It's aimed at homes with multiple AOL members scrambling for online time. If you live alone or with people who don't use AOL, you may skip blithely along—although you might want to do some of the budget-type stuff.

Do the Math

Before you even begin discussing "Who's on first?", you need to figure out a budget. How much money are you willing to invest in AOL each month?

The person who pays the bills and balances the budget should take it upon him- or herself to set a financially practical dollar limit for the house. Figure out what that means in hours, and then divide the hours among the users in the home. For example, say you decide that your family can spend a maximum of $40 a month on America Online. Subtract the basic $9.95 a month membership fee, and you have $30.05 to spend. The $9.95 gets you 5 hours of use, and if you divide $30.05 by the $2.95 per hour rate for additional hours, you'll find you can use another 10 hours (and about 11 minutes) online. That gives you a total of 15 hours a month. You then need to divide that 15 hours among the users in your home.

This strategy is for a family situation in which children won't be expected to pay for their own online charges. In a house where everyone pays their own, it should be up to each person to set their own time/money budget. If there are youngsters in the home and you want to teach them about money and bills, you can ask them to pay for their own usage (either a percentage or the whole thing, depending on the situation). Alternatively, in an all-adult household, you may just have to put one person in charge of checking the bill (use the Keyword: BILLING) to figure out what each person needs to ante up when the bill comes due.

Don't forget to figure in the local calling charges from your phone bill, too. Also, when paying the AOL bill with a credit card, I've found it helpful to send the card company the amount I'd normally pay *plus* the amount of last month's charges. It keeps me from maxing out the card. Just a thought.

Whatever the method or reasoning, you should have some guidelines covering how much time each member can spend online.

Post a Schedule

Once you have an idea of how many dollars/hours your household can spend online each month, you need to divvy up that time so that everyone gets a fair share. I didn't say *equal* share (though it could be an even split), but fair.

A child who uses the educational resources online (like those discussed in Chapter 14) may need a little more time than a child who only frequents chat rooms. Although this might encourage the other child to use the educational resources, it might just cause a fight.

You may want to post a schedule that says when each person can sign on and for how long. The AOL schedule should fit in with the schedule you've set up for sharing the computer in general. You should enforce the schedule, but be flexible so that you can accommodate special projects, homework, or research needs even if it isn't that user's turn.

By the way, *The Home Computer Companion* (Alpha Books, 1994) has an excellent section on kids and computers. It includes other scheduling tips and lots of ideas for other things you can do with your computer. Check it out.

Keep Track of the Time

It's easy to lose all sense of time online (I'd swear to it in court), so you might want to use a kitchen timer or an alarm clock to keep everyone on schedule. Start the timer when someone signs on. When the bell sounds, they need to sign off. If they sign off before the time's elapsed, they get to keep those remaining minutes and use them later.

With kids, you may want to print up "time checks," AOL play money created with a word processor or page layout program. You'd probably need to do several denominations: some for 1 hour and others in 1-, 5-, 10-, and 15-minute increments. That way you could make "change" in minutes. Everybody gets vouchers for their time allotment each month. As they spend time online, they turn in the appropriate number of time checks. When they're out of checks, they're out of time.

You could also print up reward vouchers: similar coupons that say "You did such a good job with (fill in the blank: cleaning your room, doing the dishes, or whatever), you're being rewarded with X minutes on America Online." The kids could then use the vouchers for extra online activities. The basic idea is this: set a dollar or time limit for your usage each month so you don't ruin your budget. Then come up with a way to stick to that limit that's as fair as you can make it for all participants.

Saving Money

These tips are all given elsewhere in this book, but I thought it might be a good idea to pull them all together in one place for easy reference.

Work Offline Whenever Possible

Anything you type online (email, forum posts, even chat or IMs) can be composed offline.

You can write and address email (covered in Chapter 9) offline and save it for later delivery by just clicking on the **Send Later** button. You can also read your mail offline by using FlashSessions to retrieve it. (More FlashSession tips in a moment.)

You can also write any text you want to post in a message area while offline. Here's how:

1. Select **New** from AOL's File menu. That opens an untitled text file like the one shown below.

Composing a message for later posting.

2. Type your message.

3. Save your message by selecting **Save** from the File menu. You'll be asked to name the file and tell AOL where to save it. Name it something that will remind you of its contents.

When you've written and saved as many messages as you care to post, then sign on to AOL. Navigate to the first message area and find the appropriate category and the appropriate topic. Then follow these steps:

1. Click on the **Add Message** button. The Add A Message window appears.

2. Select **Open** from your File menu and select the saved message file you want to post. The file will open on top of the Add A Message window (see the figure below).

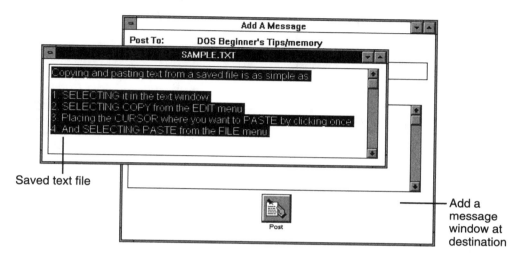

Saved text file

Add a message window at destination

Copying and pasting your saved message.

3. Select all the text for this message by clicking and dragging over it.

4. Select **Copy** from the Edit menu.

5. Click on the **Add A Message** window to bring it to the front. If the cursor isn't in the text box, click in the location where you want to place it.

6. Select **Paste** from the Edit menu. Your text appears in the text box.

7. Type a name/subject in the Subject box.

8. Click the **Post** button.

Your message is posted, and you didn't waste a lot of time online scratching your head over the right thing to say. Repeat the process until all of your saved messages have been posted. There's more on message areas in Chapter 11.

If you have something you say all of the time in chat rooms or in Instant Messages (like I'm always explaining what "Piv" stands for), you can save that as a text file, too. Just follow the instructions above, and then copy and paste it a sentence or two at a time into the box where you'd normally type your side of a conversation or IM.

If you *do* find yourself using a lot of prepared chat room phrases, you might want to look for a macro program online. A macro program replaces a complicated keyboard sequence (like typing a line of chat) with a key combination. The key combination tells the program "Type that phrase (whatever) now." And it does. Macros have many uses offline, too (like typing your name and address for you whenever you need it).

Curious PC users may want to search for "GhostWriter." Mac users may want to search for "TypeIt4Me." Both are macro programs available in many file libraries online. There are also commercial macro programs available (such as QuicKeys for the Mac). Check in your favorite software store or mail order catalog.

Use FlashSessions

When you log on to America Online and see that you've got mail, if you can't resist, go ahead and click on the Read New Mail button. Look at your list of new mail. You may be able to tell from the sender's name or the subject line whether or not you want/need to read it. Read the things you want to read. If the email doesn't need any further reply and you don't need to save it, don't do anything else with it.

If you need to save the piece of mail (because it needs an answer, it is too long to read online, or you need to keep the information), follow the steps below. (You can do this after you read each letter, or you can wait until you've looked at all of your mail.)

1. Close any open mail. That will put you back at the New Mail window, which lists your new mail by name.

2. Click on the mail you want to save to select it.

3. While it's selected, click on the **Keep As New** button. That tells AOL to pretend that you didn't read it. You'll hear the "You've got mail!" sound again, but it will just be that piece of mail bouncing back into your mailbox.

4. Repeat the process for each piece of mail you want to keep.

5. Go on about your online business.

6. When you're ready to sign off, select **Activate FlashSession Now** from your **M**ail menu. You'll see a dialog box with your FlashSession options.

7. Click in the **Sign Off When Done** check box.

8. Click **Begin**.

America Online saves all of your newly unread mail as FlashMail that you can read offline and disconnects you from the service. You can then read and reply to the mail at your leisure and send your replies with a FlashSession the next time you sign on or at a scheduled day and time. Chapter 9 has all the details on FlashSessions.

Don't Download Files Attached to Mail

When you're setting up your FlashSessions (as described in Chapter 9), *don't* click in the check box labeled "...and attached files" (see the following figure).

FlashSession preferences.

When that box is checked, FlashSessions automatically retrieve any attached file, no matter how silly or how long it takes. Instead, let FlashSessions get the mail. Read the mail, and if the file attached to the mail sounds interesting, click on the **Download Later** button. That adds the file to your download manager. The file is retrieved the next time you do a FlashSession, as long as the Download selected files option is checked. Using this strategy, you only spend time downloading files that you really want—or at least that you *think* you want.

You can always tell when email has a file attached to it. When you're looking at the mail in the New Mail window or your Incoming FlashMail window, there is a small picture of a floppy disk in front of the listing of any mail that has a file attached. When you read mail that has a file attached, AOL displays Download Now and Download Later buttons at the bottom of the screen. That's the only time you'll see those buttons in mail windows.

Use Keywords

The next chapter has a list of all the Keywords you can use on America Online (current as of the time of this writing). They save you a lot of time and money. Check it out.

Customize Your Go To Menu

When you first install America Online, your Go To menu has 10 pre-defined "Favorite Places" that you can zip to just by selecting one from the menu. However, they aren't *your* favorites; you didn't pick them.

When you start to visit a forum regularly, you can add it to your Favorite Places list, and then that will really be a list of *your* favorites. Here's how. To start, select **Edit Favorite Places** from the Go To menu, as shown above. The Favorite Places dialog box appears.

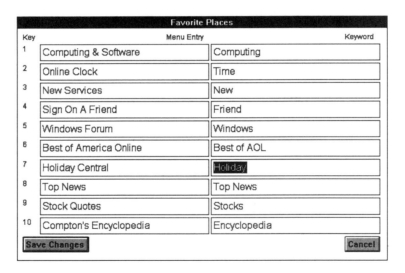

Make Favorite Places your real favorites.

In the Favorite Places dialog box, select a menu entry by click-dragging over it and type in the name of the department or forum (anything you can get to with a Keyword) with which you want to replace it. That replaces the old entry with your new one. Then select the Keyword for the old entry, and type the Keyword for your new favorite place. (Did I mention that the next chapter is completely about Keywords? I thought so.)

If you care to, you can move things around so that the forums you visit most are at the top of the list and your lesser favorites are in the bottom slots. Or, you can use whatever arrangement seems most convenient to you. Items appear in the same order in your Go To menu as they do in the editing dialog box. Just type yours where you want them, or copy and paste old entries into their new positions.

When you're done, click **Save Changes**. The dialog box closes, and your Go To menu magically contains your new favorite places. Now all you have to do is select a place from the list, and bada-bing, bada-boom—you're there.

Learn Your Keyboard Shortcuts

If you look back at the picture of the Go To menu in the last section (or at any AOL menu on your screen), you'll notice that many menu commands have keyboard shortcuts. For example, holding down the Ctrl key and pressing the letter D (Ctrl+D for short) is the same as selecting Main Menu from the Go To menu. Try it: pressing Ctrl+D while online brings AOL's Main Menu right to the top of your screen.

 Mac menus have keyboard shortcuts, too. Instead of pressing the Control key first, Mac shortcuts use the ⌘ key with the clover leaf symbol on it. It's also known as the Command key.

All of your favorite places entries have keyboard shortcuts (Ctrl+0 through Ctrl+9) so you can press two keys to take you to your favorite place instead of having to select an item from a menu. If you can remember them (it takes a little practice) and make an effort to use them, they'll save you snips of time here and there. Although they won't save you tons of time, even fractions of a second can add up when you're paying by the minute.

The Least You Need to Know

When you're paying for the use of a service like America Online, it helps if you develop a time-efficient way of dealing with everyday things you do. Here's a summary.

➤ Email is one of the most time-consuming things to deal with online. Use FlashSessions so you can deal with it offline instead.

➤ Compose any message area postings you care to write offline. Then Copy and Paste them into the Add A Message window online, in the appropriate message board.

➤ FlashSessions are a way of saving lots of time and money. Use them.

➤ Learn and use the Keywords for your favorite areas online; they'll get you there in a flash.

➤ If you can remember them (and you can, with practice), using keyboard shortcuts for often used commands (like pressing Ctrl+D to bring the Main Menu forward) will also save you lots of mousing around time online.

➤ If you come up with any more time- or money-saving ideas, send them to me, PIV, on AOL. I'm as cheap as they come.

Keywords for Days

As you know, Keywords are one of the fastest methods for getting around America Online. Like the radio station that plays "Love songs, nothing but love songs," this chapter is "Keywords, nothing but Keywords."

Refresher Course: Keywords 101

You'll find these little marvels all over AOL: at the bottom of most area screens, in instructions, and in informational text, and Guides hand them out like lollipops. All Keywords are presented online in a standard format:

Keyword: ACCESS

The actual Keyword is presented in all capital letters so it can easily be picked out of the surrounding text. However, you don't have to enter it in all capitals or in all lowercase. It doesn't matter.

Most Keywords are fairly obvious—that's what makes them *key* words. In the format example, the ACCESS keyword takes you to the listing of local access numbers online. If you know the name of the area you want to go to but don't know the "correct" Keyword, try an obvious choice: it will work more often than not.

To use a Keyword, you have to tell AOL that you want to use one by entering a keyboard shortcut (Ctrl+K on an IBM-compatible, ⌘-K on a Mac), by selecting the Keyword item from the Go To menu, or by clicking the Keyword icon on the Windows menu bar. When the Keyword dialog appears, type the Keyword you want to use in the text box and press **Enter**. Bada-bing, bada-boom. You're at wherever the Keyword takes you.

About the Keyword List

Right now, there are about 1700 Keywords you can use on America Online—so start memorizing. There will be a quiz at the end of the chapter. (Just kidding.)

Actually, there are usually a few variations of a Keyword that will work online. For example, the Keywords DOS, DOS5, DOSFORUM, and 5.0 will all take you to the DOS Forum online. For the sake of space, I've tried to eliminate as much duplication as possible from the list—but that still leaves about a thousand of them (yikes!).

This Keyword listing is alphabetical by Keyword and follows the format:

KEYWORD—Area or forum name.

Area or forum names followed by a * symbol are located in the free Member Services area, which means it doesn't add to your online charges to access these services. However, you also won't be able to do any chatting, downloading, or other of the usual online stuff while you're in the free area.

Entries followed by [M/PC] are computer-specific areas. If you use a PC, you'll go to the PC version of that area. Macs go to the Mac version. However, you can usually access either once you get there.

Entries that appear in **boldface** are areas that I found worthy of note for one reason or another. For example, the Beginner's Forum appears in bold because it will help you continue learning about AOL;

the Gay and Lesbian Community Forum appears in bold because most online services aren't open-minded enough to devote a whole forum to politically or emotionally charged topics. They may interest you, they may not; I just wanted to point them out.

As always, this list is pretty up-to-date at the moment I'm typing it, but it will be old news by the time you read it because new stuff is added to AOL all the time. Use the Keyword: NEW to find new areas. To find the latest Keyword list(s), use SURF or KEYWORDS as a software search string (Chapter 12 has details on doing a search). Okay, here we go.

Numbers and Symbols

@TIMES—@times/*The New York Times* Online

3D—3D Resource Center

3DSIG—3D Interest Group

5THGENERATION—Fifth Generation

9600—9600 Baud Access Center *

A

AAII—AAII Online

AARP—American Association of Retired People

AATRIX—Aatrix Software, Inc.

ABBATEVIDEO—Abbate Video

ABC—ABC Online

ABCCLASSROOM—The ABC Classroom

ABCDAYTIME—ABC Daytime/ Soapline

ABCNEWS—ABC News-On-Demand

ABCPRIMETIME—ABC Prime Time

ABCRADIO—ABC Radio

ABCSPORTS—ABC Sports

ABF—Beginners' Forum

ABM—Adventures by Mail

ACADEMY—Starfleet Academy

ACCESS—Local access numbers *

ACCOLADE—Accolade, Inc.

ACER—Acer America Corporation

ACHIEVEMENTTV—Achievement TV

ACOT—Apple Classrooms of Tomorrow

ACT—Kaplan Online/SAT, ACT, College

ACTIVISION—Activision

AD&D—AD&D Neverwinter Nights

ADOPTION—Adoption Forum

ADS—auto_des_sys, Inc.

ADSIG—Advertising Special Interest Group

ADVANCED—Advanced Software, Inc.

ADVANCEDGRAVIS—Advanced Gravis

ADVENTURE—Games Forum [M/PC]

ADVICE—Advice & Tips

AECSIG—Architects, Engineers, and Construction Special Interest Group

AFFINITY—Affinity Microsystems

AFRICANAMERICAN—The Exchange

AFT—American Federation of Teachers

AFTERWARDS—Afterwards Coffeehouse

ALADDIN—Aladdin Systems, Inc.

ALDUS—Aldus Corporation

ALTSYS—Altsys Corporation

ALYSIS—Alysis Software

AMATEURRADIO—Ham Radio Club

AMBROSIA—Ambrosia Software

AMERICANHISTORY—National Museum of American History

AMERICANINDIAN—The Exchange

ANIMATEDSOFTWARE—Animated Software

ANOTHERCO—Another Company

AOLSTORE—America Online Store

APDA—Apple Professional Developer's Association

APOGEE—Apogee Software

APPLESCRIPT—AppleScript interest group

APPMAKER—Bowers Development

APPS—Applications/Business Forum [M/PC]

ARES—Ares Microdevelopment, Inc.

ARGOSY—Argosy

ARIEL—Ariel Publishing

ART—Graphics Forum [M/PC]

ARTEMIS—Artemis Software

ARTICULATE—Articulate Systems

ARTIFICE—Artifice, Inc.

ASCD—Association for Supervisor and Curriculum Development

ASCTECH—Alpha Software Corporation

ASI—Articulate Systems

ASIAN—The Exchange

ASKAOL—Member Services *

ASKERIC—AskERIC

ASTRONOMY—Astronomy Club

ASYMETRIX—Asymetrix Corporation

ATLANTIC—*The Atlantic Monthly* Online

ATTICUS—Atticus Software

AUDIO—*Stereo Review* Online magazine

AUDIO/VIDEO—Dolby Audio/Video Forum

AUDITORIUM—Center Stage

AUTO—AutoVantage

AUTOCAD—CAD Resource Center

AUTOEXEC—Tune Up Your PC

AVIATION—Aviation Club

AVID—Avid DTV Group

AVOCAT—Avocat Systems

B

B&B—Bed & Breakfast U.S.A.

BABYBOOMERS—Baby Boomers area

BACKPACKER—*Backpacker* Magazine

BARRONS—Barrons Booknotes

BASEBALL—Sports department

BASELINE—Baseline Publishing

BASEVIEW—Baseview Products, Inc.

BASKETBALL—Sports department

BBS—BBS Corner

BCS—Boston Computer Society

BEER—Wine & Dine Online

BEGINNER—Beginners' Forum

BERKELEY—Berkeley Systems

BEST—Best Products

BESTOFAOL—Best of America Online showcase

BETHESDA—Bethesda Softworks, Inc.

BEYOND—Beyond, Inc.

BIKENET—The Bicycle Network

BILLING—Account and Billing *

BIOSCAN—OPTIMAS Corporation

BITJUGGLERS—Bit Jugglers

BLIND—DisABILITIES Forum

BMUG—Berkley Macintosh Users Group

BOARDWATCH—*Boardwatch* Magazine

BOAT—Boating Online

BOATS—The Exchange

BOATING—Boating menu

BOOKS—Book Bestsellers area

BOOKSTORE—Online Bookstore

BOWERS—Bowers Development

BOXING—Sports department

BRAINSTORM—Brainstorm Products

BRODERBUND—Broderbund Software

BUDDHISM—Religion & Ethics Forum

BULLMOOSE—Bull Moose Tavern

BULLSANDBEARS—Bulls and Bears Game

BUNGIE—Bungie Software

BUSINESS—Business News area

BUSINESSCENTER—Microsoft Small Business Center

BUSINESSSCHOOL—Kaplan Online/GMAT, Business School

BUSINESSSENSE—Business Sense

BUSINESSSTRATEGIES—Business Strategies

BYTE—ByteWorks

BYTEBYBYTE—Byte By Byte Corporation

C

CAERE—Caere Corporation

CALLISTO—Callisto Corporation

CAMERAS—Popular Photography Online

CAMPUS—Interactive Education Services

CAMPUSLIFE—Campus Life

CANCEL—Cancel Account *

CAPITAL—Capital Connection

CARANDDRIVER—*Car and Driver* Magazine

CARDINAL—Cardinal Technologies, Inc.

CAREER—Career Center

CAREERNEWS—*USA Today* "Industry Watch" section

CAREERS—Career Center

CARTOONNETWORK—Cartoon Network

CARTOONS—Cartoon collection

CARUSO—Inside Technology

CASABLANCA—Casa Blanca

CASADY—Casady & Greene

CASINO—RabbitJack's Casino

CBD—Commerce Business Daily

CELEBRITYCOOKBOOK— Celebrity Cookbook

CENTERSTAGE—Center Stage auditorium

CENTRALPOINT—Central Point Software

CESOFTWARE—CE Software

CHARTER—Charter Schools Forum

CHECKFREE—CheckFree

CHESS—Play-By-Mail & Strategy Gaming Forum

CHICAGO—Chicago Online

CHICO—California State University

CHRIST—Christianity Online

CHRISTIAN—Religion & Ethics Forum

CHRISTIANCOMPUTING— Christian Computing

CHRISTIANHISTORY—Christian History

CHRISTIANITY—Christianity Online

CLARIS—Claris

CLASSES—Interactive Education Services

CLASSIFIED—Classifieds Online

CLINTON—White House Forum

CLOCK—Time of day and length of time online

CLUBPERFORMA—Apple Club Performa

CMC—Creative Musician's Coalition

CMT—Coda Music Tech

CNN—CNN Newsroom Online

CODA—Coda Music Tech

COINS—The Exchange

COLCHAT—Chicago Online Chat

COLEDUCATION—Chicago Online Education

COLLIFESTYLES—Chicago Online Lifestyles

COLMARKETPLACE—Chicago Online Marketplace

COLNEWS—Chicago Online News, Business & Weather

COLPLANNER—Chicago Online Planner

COLSPORTS—Chicago Online Sports

COLLECTING—The Exchange

COLLEGE—College Board

COLUMNS—Columnists & Features Online

COMMANDO—Kim Komando's Komputer Clinic

COMMUNICATIONS—Comm/
Telecom/Networking Forum
[M/PC]

COMPANY—Hoover's Hand-
book of Company Profiles

COMPAQ—Compaq

COMPOSERS—Composer's
Coffeehouse

COMPTONS—Encyclopedia

COMPUSTORE—Comp-u-Store
Gateway

COMPUTE—Compute

COMPUTERAMERICA—Craig
Crossman's Computer
America

COMPUTEREXPRESS—Com-
puter Express

COMPUTERLAW—CyberLaw,
Cyberlex

**COMPUTERTERMS—Dictio-
nary of Computer Terms**

COMPUTING—Computing
department [M/PC]

COMPUTOON—CompuToon
area

CONFERENCE—Weekly calen-
dar of forum activity

CONFIG—Tune Up Your PC

CONNECTIX—Connectix

**CONSUMER—Consumer
Reports**

CONTACTS—Employer
Contacts

COOPER—JLCooper Electronics

COREL—CorelDRAW Resource
Center

COSA—Company of Science
and Art

COSN—Consortium for School
Networking

COSTAR—CoStar

COURSES—Interactive Education Services

COURTTV—Court TV

COWLES—Cowles/SIMBA
Media Information Network

CPI—Computer Peripherals,
Inc.

**CRC—Computing Resource
Center**

CREDIT—Credit for connect
problems *

CRITICS—Critic's Choice

CSLIVE—Tech Help Live *

CSPAN—C-SPAN

CSPANCLASSROOM—C-SPAN
Educational Services

CSUC—California State University

CT—*Christianity Today*

CURRICULUM—Assoc. for
Supervisor & Curriculum
Development

CUSTOMERSERVICE—Member
Services *

D

DACEASY—DacEasy, Inc.

DANCINGRABBIT—Dancing Rabbit Creations

DATABASE—Database Support SPECIAL INTEREST GROUP

DATAPAK—DataPak Software

DATATIMES—DataTimes Sport Reports

DATAWATCH—Datawatch

DATING—Romance Connection message boards

DAVIDSON—Davidson & Associates

DAYNA—Dayna Communications

DAYSTAR—Daystar Digital

DCCOMICS—DC Comics Online

DEAD—Grateful Dead Forum

DEAF—DisABILITIES Forum

DECISION—Decision Point Forum

DELL—Dell Computer Corporation

DELRINA—Delrina Corporation

DELTAPOINT—Delta Point

DELTATAO—Delta Tao

DEMOCRACY—CNN Newsroom Online

DENEBA—Deneba Software

DES—DeskMate

DESIGNSONLINE—Designs Online

DESKMATE—DeskMate

DFFOOD—Destination Florida: Restaurants and Nightlife

DFOUT—Destination Florida: Outdoors

DFPARKS—Destination Florida: Attractions

DFROOMS—Destination Florida: Places to Stay

DFSHOP—Destination Florida: Shopping

DFSPORTS—Destination Florida: Sports

DFX—Digital F/X

DIALOGUE—American Dialogue

DIAMOND—Diamond Computer Systems

DIGISOFT—DYA/Digisoft Innovations

DIGITAL—Digital Vision

DIGITALECLIPSE—Digital Eclipse

DIGITALRESEARCH—Novell Desktop Systems

DIGITALTECH—Digital Technologies

DILBERT—Dilbert Cartoon area

DINE—Wine & Dine Online

DIPLOMATS—Diplomats in the Classroom

DIRECT—Direct Software

DIRECTORY—Member Directory

DIROFSERVICES—Directory of Services

DISABILITY—DisABILITIES Forum

DISCOVERAOL—Discover AOL

DISCOVERY—The Discovery Channel

DISNEY—Disney Adventures Magazine

DISNEYSOFTWARE—Disney / Buena Vista Software

DOL—Designs Online

DOLBY—Dolby Audio/Video Forum

DOS—DOS Forum

DOS6—MS-DOS 6.0 Resource Center

DOWNLOADGAMES—Free online game downloading *

DRDOS—DOS Forum

DREAMWORLD—Dreamworld

DRI—Novell Desktop Systems

DTP—Desktop Publishing area [M/PC]

DTSPORTS—DataTimes Sports Reports

DUBLCLICK—Dubl-Click Software

DYNAWARE—Dynaware USA

DYNO—Portfolio Systems, Inc.

E

EARTH—Environmental Forum

EARTH—Network Earth

EBBS—EBBS

ECON—Econ Technologies

ECS—Electronic Courseware

EDITPROFILE—Edit your member profile *

EDMARK—Edmark Technologies

EDTECH—Assoc. for Supervisor & Curriculum Development

EDTV—KIDSNET Forum

EDUCATION—Education department

EFF—Electronic Frontier Foundation

ELECTRICIMAGE—Electric Image

ELECTRONICCOURSEWARE— Electronic Courseware

ELECTRONICPUBLISHING— EPub Resource Center

ELECTRONICS—Gadget Guru Electronics Forum

EMAIL—Post Office

EMERGENCY—Emergency Response Club

EMIGRE—Emigre Fonts

EN/X—Energy Express

ENCYCLOPEDIA—Encyclopedia

ENDNOTE—Niles and Associates

ENERGYEXPRESS—Energy Express

ENGLISH—Nat'l Council of Teachers of English

EPUB—EPub Resource Center

ESH—Electronic Schoolhouse

ETHICS—Ethics and Religion Forum

EUN—Electronic University Network

EXAMPREP—Exam Prep Center

EXCHANGE—The Exchange

EXPERT—Expert Software, Inc

EXTRA—EXTRA: Television's Entertainment Show

F

FANTASYBASEBALL—The Grandstand's Fantasy Baseball

FANTASYBASKETBALL—The Grandstand's Fantasy Basketball

FANTASYFOOTBALL—The Grandstand's Fantasy Football

FANTASYHOCKEY—The Grandstand's Fantasy Hockey

FANTASYLEAGUES—The Grandstand's Fantasy & Simulation Leagues

FARALLON—Farallon

FAX—Fax/Paper Mail [MacAOL and PC/GEOS only; not accessible via WAOL]

FELLOWSHIP—Fellowship of Online Gamers/RPGA Network

FFGF—Free-Form Gaming Forum

FIFTH—Fifth Generation

FILESEARCH—Search database of files

FINANCE—Personal Finance department

FLIGHT—Flight Sim Resource Center

FLORIDA—Destination Florida

FLOWERSHOP—Flower Shop

FLYING—*Flying* Magazine

FOCUS—Focus Enhancements

FONTBANK—FontBank

FOOD—Cooking Club

FOOL—The Motley Fool

FORMZ—auto_des_sys, Inc.

FRACTAL—Fractal Design

FRANKLIN—Franklin Quest

FREE—Member Services *

FRIEND—Sign on a friend to AOL *

FTP—Internet FTP

FULLWRITE—FullWrite

FUNDS—Morningstar Mutual Funds

FUTURELABS—Future Labs, Inc.

G

GADGETGURU—Gadget Guru Electronics Forum

GALLERY—Portrait Gallery

GAMEBASE—Game Base

GAMEDESIGN—Game Designers Forum

GAMEROOMS—Games Parlor

GAMES—Entertainment department

GAMESFORUM—Games Forum [M/PC]

GAMETEK—Gametek

GAMEWIZ—Dr. Gamewiz: Game Master Extraordinaire

GAMING—Online Gaming Forums

GARDENING—The Exchange

GATEWAY2000—Gateway 2000, Inc

GBL—The Grandstand's Simulation Baseball

GCC—GCC Technologies

GCS—Gaming Company Support

GENEALOGY—Genealogy Club

GENERALMAGIC—General Magic

GEOGRAPHIC—*National Geographic* Online

GEOWORKS—GeoWorks

GERALDO—The Geraldo Show

GGL—The Grandstand's Simulation Golf

GIFCONVERTER—GIF Converter

GIFTED—Giftedness Forum

GIX—Gaming Information Exchange

GLCF—Gay & Lesbian Community Forum

GLOBAL—Global Village Communication

GMAT—Kaplan Online/GMAT, Business School

GOLF—Sports department

GOLFCOURSES—Golf Courses & Resort Information

GOPHER—Internet Gopher & WAIS

GRADUATESCHOOL—Kaplan Online/GRE, Graduate School

**GRANDSTAND—The Grand-
stand**

GRAPHICSIMULATIONS—
Graphic Simulations

GRAPHISOFT—Graphisoft

GRAVIS—Advanced Gravis

GRE—Kaplan Online/GRE,
Graduate School

GROUPWARE—GroupWare
SPECIAL INTEREST GROUP

GRYPHON—Gryphon Software

GSARTS—The Grandstand's
Martial Arts (The Dojo)

GSAUTO—The Grandstand's
Motor Sports (In The Pits)

GSBASEBALL—The
Grandstand's Baseball (Dug-
out)

GSBASKETBALL—The
Grandstand's Basketball (Off
the Glass)

GSBOXING—The Grandstand's
Boxing (Squared Circle)

GSCOLLECTING—The
Grandstand's Collecting
(Sports Cards)

GSDL—The Grandstand's
Simulation Basketball

GSFOOTBALL—The
Grandstand's Football (50
Yard Line)

GSFL—The Grandstand's
Simulation Football

GSGOLF—The Grandstand's
Golf (On The Green)

GSHL—The Grandstand's
Simulation Hockey

GSHOCKEY—The Grandstand's
Hockey (Blue Line)

GSHORSE—The Grandstand's
Horse Sports (Post Time)

GSMAG—*GS+* Magazine

GSOTHER—The Grandstand's
Other Sports (Whole 9 Yards)

GSS—Global Software Suport

GSSOCCER—The Grandstand's
Soccer (The Kop)

GSSOFTWARE—The
Grandstand's Sports Software
Headquarters

GSSPORTSMART—The
Grandstand's Sports Products
(Sportsmart)

GSWINTER—The Grandstand's
Winter Sports (The Chalet)

GSWRESTLING—The
Grandstand's Wrestling
(Squared Circle)

GUIDEPAGE—Page a Guide

GWA—The Grandstand's
Simulation Wrestling

HALLOFFAME—Downloading
Hall of Fame

HAM—Ham Radio Club

HANDLE—Add, change or delete screen names

HARDWARE—Hardware Forum [M/PC]

HARLEY—Cycle World Online

HATRACK—Hatrack River Town Meeting

HBSPUB—Harvard Business School Publishing

HCSSOFTWARE—HSC Software

HDC—hDC Corporation

HEADLINES—Today's News department

HEALTH—Better Health & Medical Forum

HELIOS—Helios USA

HELP—Member Services *

HELPWANTED—Search Help Wanted—USA

HERITAGEFOUNDATION— Heritage Foundation area

HIGHLIGHTS—AOL Highlights Tour

HISPANIC—The Exchange

HOBBIES—Clubs & Interest Department

HOCKEY—Sports department

HOLIDAY—AOL Holiday Central

HOLLYWOOD—Hollywood Online

HOMEOFFICE—*Home Office Computing* Magazine

HOMEOWNER—Homeowner's Forum

HOMEPC—*HomePC* Magazine

HOMETHEATER—Stereo Review Online magazine

HOMEWORK—Academic Assistance Center

HOOVERS—Hoover's Business Resources

HOROSCOPE—Horoscopes

HORSERACING—The Grandstand

HOT—What's Hot This Month showcase

HROSSPEROT—Ross Perot/ United We Stand area

HURRICANE—Tropical Storm and Hurricane Info

HSC—HSC Software

HYPERCARD—HyperCard Forum

I

IBM—IBM Forum

IBMOS2—OS/2 Forum

IBVA—IBVA Technologies

IA—Instant Artist Resource Center

IC—Industry Connection

ICF—International Corporate Forum

ICOM—Viacom New Media

ICRS—The Grandstand's Simulation Auto Racing

ICS—International Correspondence Schools

IES—Interactive Education Services

IIN—Redate/IIN Online

IMAGING—Advanced Color Imaging Forum

IMH—Issues in Mental Health

IMPACTII—IMPACT II: The Teachers Network

IMPROV—The Improv Forum

INCIDER—*inCider*

INFOCOM—Infocom

INLINE—Inline Design

INSIDEMEDIA—Cowles/SIMBA Media Information Network

INSIDETECH—Inside Technology

INSIGNIA—Insignia Solutions

INTEL—Intel Corporation

INTELLIMATION— Intellimation

INTERACTIVEED—Interactive Education Services

INTERCON—InterCon Systems Corporation

INTERNATIONAL—International House

INTERNET—Internet Connection department

INTERPLAY—Interplay

INTHENEWS—Mercury Center In the News area

INVESTORS—Investors Network

IOMEGA—Iomega Corporation

ISIS—ISIS International

ISLAM—Religion & Ethics Forum

ISLANDGRAPHICS—Island Graphics Corporation

IYM—IYM Software Review

J

JLCOOPER—JLCooper Electronics

JOBS—Job Listings Database

JPEGVIEW—JPEGView

JUDAISM—Religion & Ethics Forum

K

KAPLAN—Kaplan Online

KEEFE—Mike Keefe Cartoons

KENSINGTON—Kensington Microware, Ltd.

KENTMARSH—Kent-Marsh

KIDDESK—Edmark Technologies

KIDSNET—KIDSNET Forum

KIWI—Kiwi Software, Inc.

KNOWLEDGEBASE—Microsoft Knowledge Base

KOALA—Koala/MacVision

KODAK—Kodak Photography Forum

KOMANDO—Kim Komando's Komputer Clinic

KOOL—Kids Only Online

KPT—HSC Software

L

LABNET—TERC LabNet

LANGUAGESYS—SYS Language Systems

LAPIS—Lapis Technologies

LAPUB—LaPub

LASTCALL—Last Call Talk Show

LAWRENCE—Lawrence Productions

LAWSCHOOL—Kaplan Online/ LSAT, Law School

LEADERSHIP—Leadership Journal

LEADERTECH—Leader Technologies

LEADINGEDGE—Leading Edge

LEARN—Education department

LEGAL—Legal SPECIAL INTEREST GROUP

LETRASET—Letraset

LETTER—A Letter from Steve Case *

LIBERTARIAN—Libertarian Party Forum

LIBRARY—Library of Congress Online

LIFETIME—Lifetime Television

LINKS—Access Software

LINKSWARE—LinksWare, Inc.

LISTINGS—TMS TV Source

LITERACY—Adult Literacy Forum

LOCALNEWSPAPERS—Local Newspapers

LONGEVITY—*Longevity* Magazine Online

LUCAS—LucasArts Games

M

MAC—Mac Computing department

MAC500—Mac Shareware 500

MACART—Graphic Art & CAD Forum

MACBIBLE—The Macintosh Bible/Peachpit Forum

MACBUSINESS—Business Forum

MACDEVELOPMENT—Mac Development Forum

MACDTP—Mac Desktop Publishing/WP Forum

MACEDUCATION—Mac Education Forum

MACGAME—Mac Games Forum

MACHACK—MacHack area

MACHARDWARE—Mac Hardware Forum

MACHOME—MacHome Journal

MACHYPERCARD—Mac HyperCard Forum

MACMULTIMEDIA—Mac Multimedia Forum

MACMUSIC—Mac Music & Sound Forum

MACOS—Mac Operating Systems Forum

MACROMEDIA—MacroMedia, Inc.

MACSOFTWARE—Mac Software Center

MACSPEAKERZ—True Image Audio [MacAOL and PC/GEOS only; not accessible via WAOL]

MACTECH—*MacTech* Magazine

MACTELECOM—Mac Communications Forum

MACTIVITY—Mactivity '94 Forum

MACUTILITIES—Mac Utilities Forum

MACVISION—Koala/MacVision

MACWORLD—*MacWorld* Magazine

MACWORLDEXPO—MacWorld Expo Center

MADA—MacApp Developers Association

MAGAZINES—The Newsstand

MAGICLINK—Sony Magic Link

MAILGATEWAY—Mail Gateway

MAILINGLISTS—Internet Mailing Lists

MAINSTAY—Mainstay

MALLARD—Mallard Software

MANHATTANGRAPHICS—Manhattan Graphics (RSG)

MARKETINGPREFS—Marketing Preferences *

MARKETFIELD—Marketfield Software

MARKETMASTER—Market Master

MARKETNEWS—Market News area

MARRIAGEPARTNERSHIP—Marriage Partnership

MARTINSEN—Martinsen's Software

MASS—Massachusetts Governor's Forum

MASTERWORD—MasterWord

MAXIS—Maxis

MCAFEE—McAfee Associates

MCAT—Kaplan Online/MCAT, Medical School

MCBUSINESS—Mercury Center Business & Technology area

MCENTERTAINMENT—Mercury Center Entertainment area

MCINTIRE—Univ. of VA Alumni/McIntire School of Commerce

MCLAUGHLIN—The McLaughlin Group

MCLIBRARY—Mercury Center Newspaper Library

MCLIVING—Mercury Center Bay Area Living area

MCM—Communications Forum

MCMARKET—Mercury Center Advertising

MCNEWS—Mercury Center In the News area

MCO—Military City Online

MCSPORTS—Mercury Center Sports area

MCTALK—Mercury Center Conference area

MECC—MECC

MEDICALSCHOOL—Kaplan Online/MCAT, Medical School

MEDICINE—Better Health & Medical Forum

MEMBERS—Member Directory

MEN—The Exchange

MENSA—Giftedness Forum

MERCURY—Mercury Center

MERIDIAN—Meridian Data

MESSAGEPAD—Newton Resource Center

METROWERKS—Metrowerks

METZ—Metz

MGX—Micrografx, Inc.

MHM—Members Helping Members message board *

MICHIGAN—Michigan Governor's Forum

MICRODYNAMICS—Micro Dynamics, Ltd.

MICROFRONTIER—MicroFrontier, Ltd.

MICROGRAFX—Micrografx, Inc.

MICROJ—Micro J Systems, Inc.

MICROMAT—MicroMat Computer Systems

MICRON—Xceed Technology

MICROPROSE—MicroProse

MICROSEEDS—Microseeds Publishing, Inc.

MICROSOFT—Microsoft Resource Center

MIDI—Graphics and Sound Forum

MIRROR—Mirror Technologies

MMWCAFE—Multimedia World Online's Cafe [PC only]

MMWCLINIC—Multimedia World Online's Clinic [PC only]

MMWGOLDMINE—Multimedia World Online's Goldmine [PC only]

MMWLIBRARY—Multimedia World Online's Library [PC platform]

MMWNEWS—Multimedia World Online's News [PC platform only]

MMWOFFICE—Multimedia World Online's Office [PC only]

MMWORLD—Multimedia World Online [PC only]

MMWPAVILION—Multimedia World Online's Pavilion [PC only]

MMWTESTTRACK—Multimedia World Online's Test Track [PC only]

MMWWAREHOUSE—Multimedia World Online's Warehouse [PC only]

MMWWELCOME—Multimedia World Online's Welcome area [PC only]

MOBILE—Mobile Office Online

MODEMHELP—Modem Help area * [PC platform only]

MONSTERISLAND—Adventures by Mail

MONTESSORI—Montessori Schools

MORAFFWARE—MoraffWare

MORNINGSTAR—Morningstar Mutual Funds

MORPH—Gryphon Software

MOTORCYCLE—Motorcycle menu

MOVIES—Movies menu

MSA—Management Science Associates

MSBC—Microsoft Small Business Center

MSFORUM—Microsoft Product Support

MSKB—Microsoft Knowledge Base

MSTATION—Bentley Systems, Inc.

MTC—Communications Forum

MTV—MTV Online

MULTIMEDIA—The Multimedia Exchange

MUSIC—Rocklink

MUSIC&SOUND—Graphics and Sound Forum [M/PC]

MUSTANG—Mustang Software

MW—MasterWord

N

NAESP—National Principals Center

NAME—Add, change, or delete screen names

NAMI—National Alliance of Mentally Ill

NAPC—Employment Agency Database

NAQP—National Association of Quick Printers area

NATURE—The Nature Conservancy

NBC—NBC Online

NBR—The Nightly Business Report

NCLEX—Kaplan Online/ NCLEX, Nursing School

NEAONLINE—National Education Association

NEC—NEC Technologies

NEOLOGIC—NeoLogic

NETWORKEARTH—Network Earth

NETWORKING—Communications/Telecom/Networking Forum [M/PC]

NEW—New Features & Services showcase

NEWAGE—Religion & Ethics Forum

NEWAOL—New AOL Information area *

NEWERA—Tactic Software

NEWREPUBLIC—*The New Republic* Magazine

NEWS&FINANCE—News & Finance Department

NEWSBYTES—Newsbytes

NEWSGROUP—Internet Usenet Newsgroup area

NEWSPAPER—Local Newspapers

NEWSPLUS—NewsPlus area

NEWSSEARCH—Search News Articles

NEWTON—Newton Resource Center

NEWWORLD—New World Computing

NIKON—Nikon Electronic Imaging

NILES—Niles and Associates

NINTENDO—Video Games area

NMAA—National Museum of American Art

NMAH—National Museum of American History

NMSS—National Multiple Sclerosis Society

NOHANDS—No Hands Software

NOMADIC—Nomadic Computing Discussion SPECIAL INTEREST GROUP

NORTON—Symantec

NOVELL—Novell Desktop Systems

NOW—Now Software

NPR—National Public Radio Outreach

NSDC—National Staff Development Council

O

OBJECTFACTORY—Object Factory

OFFICE—Penny Wise Office Products Store

OGF—Online Gaming Forums

OLDUVAI—Olduvai Software, Inc.

OLT—OnLine Tonight

OMNI—*OMNI* Magazine Online

ON—ON Technology

ONYX—Onyx Technology

OPCODE—Opcode Systems, Inc.

OPTIMAGE—OptImage Interactive Services

OPTIMAS—OPTIMAS Corporation

ORIGIN—Origin Systems

OS2—OS/2 Forum

OTTER—Otter Solution

OUTDOORS—The Exchange

P

PACEMARK—PaceMark Technologies, Inc.

PACKER—Packer Software

PAGAN—Religion & Ethics Forum

PALM—Palm Computing

PAP—Applications Forum

PAPERMAIL—Fax/Paper Mail

PAPYRUS—Papyrus

PARENT—Parents' Information Network

PARENTALCONTROL— Parental Controls

PARLOR—Games Parlor

PASSPORT—Passport Designs

PASSWORD—Change your password *

PC—People Connection

PCAPPLICATIONS—PC Applications Forum

PCCATALOG—PC Catalog

PCCLASSIFIEDS—Browse the PC Catalog

PCDESKMATE—DeskMate

PCDEV—PC Development Forum

PCEXPO—Redgate Online > PC Expo area

PCFORUMS—PC Computing department

PCGAMES—PC Games Forum

PCGRAPHICS—PC Graphics Forum

PCHARDWARE—PC Hardware Forum

PCHELP—Beginners' Forum

PCLIBRARIES—PC Software Center

PCM—PC Telecom/Networking Forum

PCMU—PC Music and Sound Forum

PCNOVICE—*PC Novice & PC Today* Online

PCPC—Personal Computer Peripherals

PCSTUDIO—PC Studio

PCUTILITIES—DOS Forum

PCWORLD—*PCWorld* Online

PDA—Personal Digital Assistant's Forum

PEACHPIT—The Macintosh Bible/Peachpit Forum

PEACHTREE—Peachtree Software

PENPAL—Edmark Technologies

PENTIUM—Intel Corporation

PERFORMA—Apple Club Performa

PERSONALFINANCE—Personal Finance area

PET—Pet Care Club

PFSOFTWARE—Personal Finance Software Center

PFSS—Personal Finance Software Support

PHOTOFOCUS—Graphics and Photo Focus area

PHOTOGRAPHY—Photography Area

PHOTOSHOP—Photoshop interest group

PHW—PC Hardware Forum

PICTURES—Pictures of the World

PIN—Parents' Information Network

PIXAR—Pixar

PIXEL—Pixel Resources

PLACES—P.L.A.C.E.S. Interest Group

PLAYER—Viewer Resource Center

PLAYMATION—Playmation

PORTABLE—Mobile Office Online

PORTFOLIO—Your Stock Portfolio

PORTFOLIOSOFTWARE— Portfolio Systems, Inc.

POWERBOOK—PowerBook Resource Center

POWERMAC—Power Mac Resource Center

POWERUP—Power Up Software

PPI—Practical Peripherals, Inc.

PRAIRIESOFT—PrairieSoft, Inc.

PRESS—AOL Press Release Library

PREVENTION—Substance Abuse Forum

PRINCETONREVIEW—Student Access Online

PRINCIPALS—National Principals Center

PRODIGY—Prodigy Refugees Forum

PRODUCTIVITY—Applications/ Business/Productivity Forum [M/PC]

PROFILE—Edit your member profile *

PROGRAMMERU—Programmer University

PROGRAMMING—Development Forum [M/PC]

PROGRAPH—Prograph International, Inc.

PROVUE—ProVUE Development

PS1—IBM Connection

PSION—Psion

PSYCHICLABS—IBVA Technologies

Q

QUALITAS—Qualitas

QUARK—Quark, Inc.

QUE—The Quantum Que and Graffiti community message boards

QUEST—Adventures by Mail

QUICKFIND—Search database of files [M/PC]

QUICKPRINTERS—National Association of Quick Printers area

QUILTING—The Exchange: Needlecrafts/Sewing Center

QUOTE—Stock Market Timing & Charts area

R

RADIUS—Radius, Inc.

RAILROADING—The Exchange

RASTEROPS—RasterOps

RAYDREAM—Ray Dream

RDI—Free-Form Gaming Forum

REACTOR—Reactor

REALESTATE—Real Estate Online

REDGATE—Redgate/IIN Online

REFERENCE—Reference Desk department

REFERENCEHELP—Reference Desk Help area

REGISTRATION—IES Registration Center

RELIGION—Ethics and Religion Forum

RENDERING—3D Resource Center

RENDERMAN—Pixar

REPRISE—Warner/Reprise Records Online

RESEARCH—Academic Assistance Center

RESNOVA—ResNova Software (RESNOVASOFTWARE)

RICKILAKE—The Ricki Lake Show

ROAD—*Road & Track* Magazine

ROCKLAND—Rockland Software

ROGERWAGNER—Roger Wagner Publishing

ROLEPLAYING—Role-Playing Forum

ROMANCE—Romance Connection message boards

ROTUNDA—Rotunda Forum Auditorium

RPGA—Fellowship of Online Gamers/RPGA Network

S

SABRE—EAASY SABRE

SALIENT—Salient Software

SANJOSE—Mercury Center

SAT—Kaplan Online/SAT, ACT, College

SATREVIEW—*Saturday Review* Online

SCHOLASTIC—Scholastic Network/Scholastic Forum

SCHOOLHOUSE—Electronic Schoolhouse

SCIFICHANNEL—The Sci-Fi Channel

SCOUTS—Scouting Forum

SCUBA—Scuba Club

SEARCHNEWS—Search news articles

SEGA—Video Games area

SENIOR—SeniorNet

SERIUS—Serius

SERVICES—Directory of Services

SF—Science Fiction Forum

SIM—The Simming Forum

SHAREWARESOLUTIONS— Shareware Solutions

SHIVA—Shiva Corporation

SHOPPERSEXPRESS—Shoppers Express

SHOPPING—Marketplace department

SHORTHAND—Online Shorthands

SIERRA—Sierra On-Line

SIGNUP—IES Registration Center

SILICON—Hardware

SKI—Ski Reports

SMITHSONIAN—Smithsonian Online

SOFTARC—SoftArc

SOFTDISK—Softdisk Superstore [PC platform only]

SOFTSYNC—Expert Software, Inc.

SOFTWARE—Software Center [M/PC]

SOFTWARECREATIONS— Software Creations

SOFTWARESUPPORT—Personal Finance Software Support

SOFTWARETOOLWORKS— Software Toolworks

SOLIII—Sol III Play-by-Email Game

SONY—Sony Magic Link area

SOPHCIR—Sophisticated Circuits

SOS—Wall Street SOS Forum

SPACE—National Space Society

SPECTRUM—Spectrum HoloByte

SPECULAR—Specular International

SPEEDY—Designs Online

SPORTS—Sport News area

SPORTSBOARDS—The Grandstand's Sports Boards

SPORTSCHAT—The Grandstand's Chat Rooms

SPORTSLIBRARIES—The Grandstand's Libraries

SPORTSLINK—Sports department

SSI—Strategic Simulations

SSSI—SSSi

STAC—STAC Electronics

STAMPS—The Exchange

STARTREK—"Star Trek" Club

STEREOREVIEW—*Stereo Review* Online magazine

STF—STF Technologies

STOCK—Stock Market Timing & Charts area

STOCKPORTFOLIO—Your Stock Portfolio

STOCKTIMING—Decision Point Forum

STORE—Travel & Shopping Department

STRATA—Strata, Inc.

STRATEGIC—Strategic Simulations

STUDENT—Student Access Online

STUDY—Study Skills Service

STUFFIT—Aladdin Systems, Inc.

SUGGESTION—Suggestion boxes *

SUPERCARD—Hardware

SUPERDISK—Alysis Software

SUPERMAC—SuperMac

SUPPORT—Member Services *

SURVIVOR—Survivor Software

SWC—Software Creations

SYMANTEC—Symantec

SYNEX—Synex

SYSTEM7—Mac Operating Systems Forum

T

TACTIC—Tactic Software

TALENT—Talent Bank

TALKSHOW—Future Labs, Inc.

TANDY—Tandy Headquarters

TAX—Tax Forum [seasonal]

TCW—*Today's Christian Woman*

TEACHER—Teachers' Information Network

TEACHERPAGER—Teacher Pager

TEACHERU—Teachers' University

TECHHELPLIVE—Tech Help Live *

TECHWORKS—Technology Works

TEEN—Teen Scene message boards

TEKNOSYS—Teknosys Works

TELECOM—Communications/ Telecom/Networking Forum [M/PC]

TELESCAN—Telescan Users Group Forum

TELEVISION—Soap Opera Summaries

TENNIS—Sports department

TGS—Prograph International, Inc.

THREESIXTY—Three-Sixty Software

THRUSTMASTER— Thrustmaster

THUNDERWARE— Thunderware

TI—Texas Instruments

TIA—True Image Audio

TICKET—Ticketmaster

TICKETMASTER—Chicago Online Ticketmaster

TIGER—TIGERDirect, Inc.

TIME—*Time* Magazine Online

TIMESART—@times: Art & Photography

TIMESARTS—@times: The Arts

TIMESBOOKS—@times: Books of The Times

TIMESDINING—@times: Dining Out & Nightlife

TIMESLEISURE—@times: Leisure Guide

TIMESMOVIES—@times: Movies & Video

TIMESMUSIC—@times: Music & Dance

TIMESREGION—@times: In The Region

TIMESSPORTS—@times: Sports & Fitness

TIMESSTORIES—@times: Top Stories

TIMESTHEATER—@times: Theater

TIMESLIPS—Timeslips Corporation

TIPS—Advice & Tips

TITF—Daily calender of forum activity

TLC—The Learning Channel

TMAKER—T/Maker

TMS—TMS TV Source

TNC—The Nature Conservancy

TNEWS—Teachers' Newsstand

TNPC—The National Parenting Center

TOMORROW—Tomorrow's Morning newspaper

TOOLWORKS—Software Toolworks

TOS—Terms of Service *

TOUR—AOL Highlights Tour

TOURGUIDE—AOL Products Center

TRAINING—Career Development Training

TRAVEL—Travel & Shopping Department

TRAVELADVISORIES—US State Department Travel Advisories

TRAVELER—Travel Forum

TRAVELERSCORNER—Traveler's Corner

TRAVELHOLIDAY—*Travel Holiday* Magazine

TREK—"Star Trek" Club

TRIB—*Chicago Tribune*

TRIBADS—Chicago Online Classifieds

TRIVIA—Trivia Club

TRUEIMAGEAUDIO—True Image Audio

TSENG—Tseng

TSHIRT—AOL Products Center

TTALK—Teachers' Forum

TUNEUP—Tune Up Your PC

TUTORING—Academic Assistance Center

TV—Television

TVGOSSIP—TV Gossip

TVGUIDE—TMS TV Source

TWI—Time Warner Interactive

u

UA—Unlimited Adventures

UCPA—United Cerebral Palsy Association, Inc.

UGF—User Group Forum

UHA—Homeowner's Forum

UNIVERSITY—Electronic University Network

UNLIMITEDADVENTURES— Unlimited Adventures

UPGRADE—Upgrade to the latest version of AOL *

USENET—Internet Usenet Newsgroup area

USERLAND—Userland

USF—University of San Francisco

USMAIL—Fax/Paper Mail

USNEWS—U.S. & World News area

UTAH—Utah Forum

v

VB—Visual Basic Support

VDISC—Videodiscovery

VERONICA—Internet Gopher & WAIS

VERTISOFT—Vertisoft

VETS—Military and Vets Club

VIACOM—Viacom New Media

VIDEODISC—Videodiscovery

VIDEOGAMES—Video Games area

VIDEOSIG—Video SPECIAL INTEREST GROUP

VIDI—VIDI

VIEWER—Viewer Resource Center

VIEWPOINT—Viewpoint DataLabs

VIREX—Datawatch

VIRGINIA—Virginia Forum

VIRTUS—Virtus Walkthrough

VIRUS—Virus Information Center SPECIAL INTEREST GROUP

VISIONARY—Visionary Software

VISUALBASIC—Visual Basic Support

VOYAGER—The Voyager Company

VOYETRA—Voyetra Technologies

VR—Virtual Reality Resource Center

VRLI—Virtual Reality Labs, Inc.

W

WAIS—Internet Gopher & WAIS

WARNER—Warner/Reprise Records Online

WASHINGTON—Capital Connection

WEATHER—Weather

WEATHERMAPS—Color Weather Maps

WEIGAND—Weigand Report

WEISSMANN—Traveler's Corner

WESTWOOD—Westwood Studios

WHCSB—White House Conference on Small Business

WIN—Windows Forum

WIN500—Windows Shareware 500

WINDOWS—Windows Forum

WINDOWSMAG—*Windows* Magazine

WINDOWWARE—Wilson Windowware

WINE—Wine & Dine Online

WINNEWS—Windows News area

WIRED—*Wired* Magazine

WIRELESS—Wireless Communication

WOMANSDAY—*Woman's Day*

WOMEN—The Exchange

WOODSTOCK—Woodstock Online

WORDPERFECT—WordPerfect Support Center

WORKING—Working Software

WORLDNEWS—U.S. & World News area

WORTH—*Worth* Magazine Online

WORTHPORTFOLIO—*Worth* Magazine Online Portfolio

WPMAG—*WordPerfect* Magazine

WRITERS—Writer's Club

WWIR—*Washington Week in Review* magazine

X, Y, and Z

XAOS—Xaos Tools

XCEED—Xceed Technology

YOURCHURCH—Your Church

YOURMONEY—Your Money area

ZEDCOR—Zedcor, Inc.

Chapter 24

About That Disk...

> **In This Chapter**
>
> ➤ What disk is this, I think I know...
>
> ➤ Getting the stuff off the disk and using it
>
> ➤ Growing your own Mac or DOS disk

Well, this may be the moment you've been waiting for. Finally, the scoop on that little square of plastic glued in the back of the book. I'll remind you up front that the disk is aimed at Windows users (although CompuShow 2000! is DOS-based, not a Windows application). For Mac and DOS AOL users, there's a section at the end of the chapter that tells you how to cobble together a disk of your own fabulous AOL add-ons.

Dissecting the Disk

Some of the software on the disk is *freeware*: you can use it, give it to friends, and think nothing of it. Some of it is *shareware*: if you like it, use it, and plan to keep it, you need to send the program's author a registration fee. (Chapter 12 talks about freeware and shareware in more detail.) When you pay the fee, you get the latest copy of the software and (in some cases) a full manual, and you quit getting those annoying "Are you ever going to pay for this?" messages.

Here's what's on the disk (in alphabetical order):

➤ **CompuShow 2000!** by Bob Berry at Canyon State Systems and Software. It's a DOS-based graphics viewing and editing program. You can use it to look at and tinker with most of those wild and crazy graphics files you'll be downloading from AOL. It's shareware, and the registration fee is $33.

➤ **VBRUN300.DLL** from Microsoft Corporation. It's a Windows add-in that lets you use programs written in Visual Basic even if you don't own a copy of Visual Basic. You'll need it if you want to use WAOL PAL, ZipShell Pro, and/or You've Got Mail!, all of which are described below. It's free!

Any bit of software (like VBRUN300) that allows you to use stuff written for or with an application without having to own the original application, is called a **run-time version** (just in case you hear the term bandied about).

➤ **WAOL PAL**, by Sam Hazan. It will help you keep track of all your new digital pals online. It's shareware, and the registration fee is $7.50.

➤ **Wedge**, by Tundra Slosek. Wedge is a freeware utility to help you squeeze into a chat room that's full using sneaky and devious methods. It's free!

➤ **ZipShell Pro**, by Jonathan Griffin of NewVision. This is an incredibly handy shareware utility that lets Windows users easily compress and decompress files for up- or downloading (or just for storage, to save space on your hard drive). It's shareware, and the registration fee is $29.95 (but there's a money-saving coupon at the back of the book).

➤ **You've Got Mail!** by Roald Oines and Rachel Barnot. It's a very helpful mail utility to help simplify the process of reading, answering, and sending your mail. It's shareware, and the registration fee is $19.95, plus shipping.

➤ *Zounds,* **there's sounds!** There's a small but very cranky collection of .WAV files you can use to make your feelings known in any chat room online. You can kiss 'em or slap 'em with these files. I created these files just for you, so they're free.

Each of the items on the disk is in its own, self-extracting archive (if you've read Chapter 12, you know what that means). That's so you can pick and choose what you actually want to install on your computer, instead of having it all dropped there in a lump. (I hate it when that happens.) What you might want to do is read through this chapter and decide what you want to try out. When you've decided, you can come back and follow the step-by-step stuff for the items you want to use. Just a suggestion.

Step One

To begin, you're going to need to create a directory on your hard drive. To do that:

1. Start your computer and launch Windows.

2. From the Program Manager, double-click the **File Manager** icon (it's in the Main program group).

3. When the File Manager opens, click on the icon of the hard drive in which you want to create the directory (I'd guess C:, but what do I know—you may have other ideas). Then click on the drive's root directory (for drive C:, it's the one called C:\).

4. Select Create Directory from the File menu. The Create Directory dialog box appears.

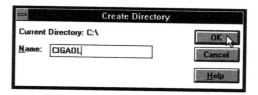

I can name that directory in three notes.

5. In the Name: box, type **CIGAOL** as the name for your directory.

6. Click **OK**.

Your directory is created. Wipe the sweat from your brow—it wasn't *that* difficult. You'll still need the File Manager, so don't exit it just yet.

Copy This

Now we'll copy the stuff you want from the disk to your new directory. Carefully remove the disk from its little plastic sheath (I love that word, "sheath") at the back of the book and pop it (the disk, not the sheath) into your A: drive.

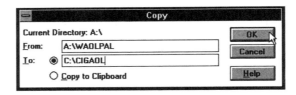 If you're using drive B: or a different disk drive, remember to substitute its drive letter wherever I say "A:" okay?

Still in the File Manager? Good. Click on the icon for drive A:. Your PC moans and groans for a second as it reads the directory information. Then you'll see a listing of all the folders (six of them, one for each item on the disk).

In the list box on the right side of the file display, click on the first folder you want to copy to your new CIGAOL directory. That selects it. Select Copy from the File menu to access the Copy dialog box. In the To: box (where it says C:\CIGAOL in the next figure), type the drive letter and name of the directory you just created. Click **OK**.

Copy
Current Directory: A:\
From: A:\WAOLPAL
To: ⦿ C:\CIGAOL
○ Copy to Clipboard
OK Cancel Help

Copying a folder with the File Manager.

If it asks if you really want to copy the folder and its contents, click **OK** again. Windows copies the folder from the disk into your new directory. Repeat the process for each of the folders you want to copy to your hard drive.

Naturally, if you want to copy all of the folders from the disk to your directory, you can select all of the files at once; simply click on the first file, press and hold down **Shift**, and click on the last file. Then select Copy from the File menu, and you can do them all at once. You already knew that, though, didn't you?

Once you have the folders copied to your hard drive, you can read the installation directions for each one in the following sections.

ZipShell Pro

Let's do ZipShell Pro first. That way, if you care to, you can use it to unzip the rest of these puppies, even though you don't have to.

Decompressing ZipShell Pro

To decompress ZipShell Pro, use the File Manager to navigate to the ZSHELL folder in your CIGAOL directory and double-click on it. That opens the screen shown below. In the text box at the bottom of the screen (where it says C:\ZSHELL—yours will probably say C:\CIGAOL\ZSHELL), you can edit the path if you want ZipShell installed somewhere else on your hard drive. It isn't necessary, but you can if you want to. When that's set, click **Extract** (which is just another way of saying "decompress").

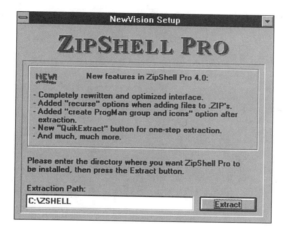

ZipShell will extract itself and set itself up as a Windows application.

When you click Extract, ZipShell does its thing for a minute or two (you'll see a thermometer-like display so you know what's happening), and then it asks if you want it to set up a Program Group. Click **Yes**. It finishes the installation and opens the new program group (called NewVision ZipShell Pro).

In the meantime, a registration screen pops up, giving you the opportunity to enter your name and a serial number. Click **Skip** for now; you don't have a serial number yet. You'll get it when you register your copy of ZipShell. That screen goes away, and ZipShell opens.

Using ZipShell Pro

To use ZipShell Pro to extract/decompress an archive, click on the **Open** button. That gives you a standard Windows Open dialog box. For the sake of practice, use it to navigate to the WAVS folder inside your CIGAOL folder. Double-click on the **WAVS** folder. You probably won't see any files inside the folder. If not, click on the down arrow where it says List Files of Type and select **All Files [*.*]**. The file WAVS.EXE appears.

Click once on the file **WAVS.EXE** to select it, and then click the **OK** button. ZipShell displays a window listing all of the .WAV files in the archive.

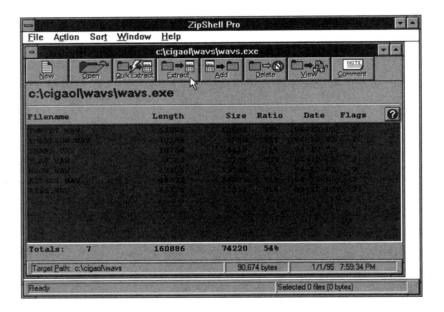

What's inside that archive.

Click on any one of the .WAV files to select it, and then click the **Extract** button. ZipShell thinks about it for a second and then gives you the following screen. The .WAV file you selected is listed in the window labeled "Files to be extracted." The other files in the archive are listed in the other window, called "Files NOT to be extracted."

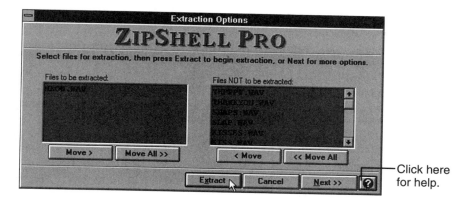

Click here for help.

Decompress one or all of the .WAV files.

You can add any of the other .WAV files to the list of files to be extracted by clicking on the file name, and then clicking the **<Move** button. To add all the other .WAV files, click the **<<Move All** button. Then click **Extract**. Those files are decompressed and ready for your use.

If you want to skip this intermediate "pick a file, any file" step, click the **Quick Extract** button, which automatically decompresses everything in the archive.

Creating an archive is just as easy. Click the **New** button to create an empty, untitled archive. You then click the **Add** button to add to the archive the files you want to compress. First you'll be asked to specify a location and enter a name (including a file extension; for now, use .ZIP until you've had a chance to read the online help files in the Help menu) for the archive in a standard Windows Save dialog box.

Then you select the files to add to the archive (this is similar to the Extraction Options screen in the last figure). Click the **Add** button, and everything is compressed nice as you please.

For more detailed information, read the related help files available in ZipShell's Help menu.

.WAV Goodbye

To decompress the .WAV files (if you didn't follow along with the ZipShell demonstration), you need the File Manager again. Navigate to your CIGAOL directory and double-click on it. When the directory opens, you'll see folders for each item you copied. Double-click on the **WAVS** folder.

Inside, you'll find a file called WAVS.EXE. Double-click on it. File Manager launches the file, and it decompresses itself. After a moment, you'll have seven additional files in that folder (Kiss, Kisses, Meow (for catty remarks), Slap, Snaps, Thankyou, and Thpppt) all with the .WAV extension. You can double-click individual files if you want to hear what they sound like. That opens Windows multimedia player. Just click on the **Play** button to hear the sound.

In order to use the files online, use the File Manager to move or copy the files into your AOL folder (probably called WAOL20 or something similar). The next time you sign on, you can use these sounds in a chat room, as described in Chapter 10.

Just as a reminder, for someone else to hear these sounds online, she must also have them installed in her WAOL folder. Feel free to share these sounds with your online friends. Send them the files attached to email (Chapter 9 tells you how).

VBRUN, Do Not Walk...

The process for decompressing the file VBRUN.DLL is just the same as the process for decompressing the sounds. In a nutshell:

1. Use the File Manager to navigate to the VBRUN folder in your CIGAOL directory and double-click on it.

2. Double-click on the **VBRUN.EXE** file inside the folder. The file extracts itself, and you'll find a file called VBRUN300.DLL in the folder when it's finished.

3. Copy or move VBRUN300.DLL into your Windows System folder (probably C:\WINDOWS\SYSTEM).

You'll need to quit and restart Windows for VBRUN to kick in, and you'll want it working if you plan to use WAOL PAL or You've Got Mail!. Once it's installed in your Windows System folder and you restart Windows, you can forget about it. You'll never have to worry about it again.

What a (WAOL)PAL!

To decompress WAOL PAL (you'll be doing this in your sleep tonight), use the File Manager to navigate to the WAOLPAL folder in your CIGAOL folder. Double-click on the **WAOLPAL** folder to open it, and double-click on the **WAOL-PAL.EXE** file inside. WAOL PAL extracts itself. Before it puts anything anywhere, WAOL PAL asks you nicely if it's okay. If it is, press **Y**, and it continues.

When it's done and you're back at the File Manager, locate the file called **SETUP.EXE** in the WAOL PAL folder and double-click on it. Like most Setup programs, it painlessly installs WAOL PAL in Windows and gives you a program group named **SNR Software** (shown in the following figure). Just double-click the program group to open it, and then double-click on the **WAOL PAL** application icon.

WAOL PAL is one of the applications that requires VBRUN300.DLL. Make sure you decompress and install VBRUN300.DLL before you try to install WAOL PAL (or You've Got Mail!, for that matter).

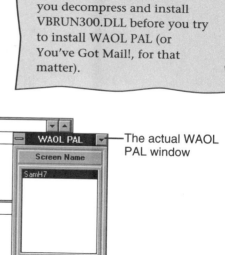

Application icon

The actual WAOL PAL window

Click to select a function, and then double-click a screen name above.

Manual in Write format

WAOL PAL and its program group.

When you launch WAOL PAL, it opens into the narrow window shown above. This gives you an easy way to send an IM, address a letter, or see if a friend of yours is online. Just click on the radio button in front of what you want to do, and then double-click on the screen name of the friend you want to contact. WAOL PAL does the rest.

To see one or more new screen names on the list, click the **More** button to expand the WAOL PAL window. Then click the **New** button, and the New Pal window opens.

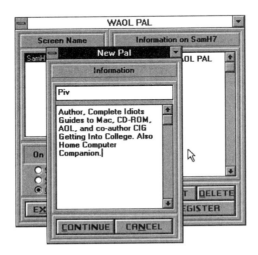

Adding a pal.

Type your Pal's screen name at the top of the window. Enter any information you'd like to have handy (partner's name, children's names, birthday, and so on) below that, and click **Continue**. Your pal is added to your list, and you can track him or her down whenever you're online.

Give Yourself a WEDGEie

Wedge automates the process of squeezing into a full chat room. It's very convenient if you need to get into a particular room and just won't be satisfied with a numbered clone (for instance, "Lobby 23" when you want "Lobby"). If you don't know what that means, you haven't read Chapter 10 yet. You might want to do that before you try to use Wedge.

Decompressing Wedge

Like all the other self-extracting archives on the disk, you decompress Wedge using the File Manager. Inside your CIGAOL folder, double-click on the **Wedge** folder. That opens the folder and magically reveals the WEDGE.EXE file within.

Double-click on the **WEDGE.EXE** file, and it decompresses itself. When it's done, you'll have two additional files in the folder: WEDGE.EXE and a read-me file called WEDGE.TXT. Whenever you get a read-me text file with a program, it's a good idea to read it. Feel free to move Wedge wherever it is convenient for you to have it—but remember where it is.

Using Wedge

To use Wedge, use the File or Program Manager to navigate to WEDGE.EXE and double-click on it to launch it. When it launches, you may not even notice it—it's a little bar down toward the bottom of your screen (see the next figure).

Click here to start wedging.———[Wedge]

Wedge yourself into a chat room.

After launching Wedge, launch WAOL. Log on and do whatever you need or want to do. When you go to the People Connection, click on the **Rooms** button. Find the room you'd like to enter. If the room's full (it's got 23 people in it), click the room's name once to select it, and then click on the left side of the Wedge bar (the button with the wedge in it). Then just sit back and let Wedge worm you into the Chat room. If your PC is sound-capable, Wedge makes a sound when it gets you into the room.

To shut Wedge down, click on the Wedge bar to activate it, and then press **Alt+F4**. Wedge goes away, waiting to serve you another day.

You've Got Mail!

You've Got Mail! is a mail utility that can simplify the process of reading, saving, and replying to your mail online and off.

Decompressing You've Got Mail!

Like just about everything else we've looked at, you'll use the File Manager to decompress it. Navigate to the YGM folder and double-click on it. Inside, double-click on the file **YGM12.EXE**, and the file decompresses.

To use You've Got Mail! (YGM for short), double-click on the **YGM.EXE** file. The first thing you'll see when it launches is a little window that says "Welcome to You've Got Mail!. Please Enter Your Screen Name." Type your AOL screen name in the box and press **Enter**.

The window changes to one that says "Setup You've Got Mail!," and a text box shows the screen name you entered. If it's correct (no typos), click **Add *Screen Name***, and you'll move on. If the screen name is wrong for some reason, click **Cancel**, and you'll move back to the first window.

Next you need to set your preferences for this screen name (you can have several different sets, depending on the number of screen names you and your family use). The preferences screen, shown below, asks for three kinds of information: mail stuff, online stuff, and WAOL stuff.

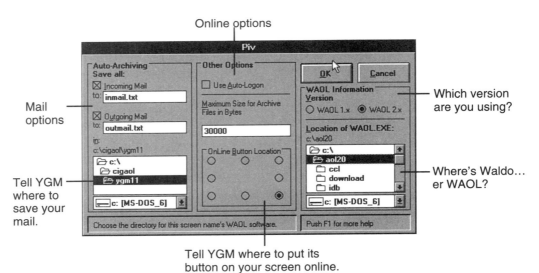

You've Got Mail! Preferences.

The mail stuff is in the column labeled Auto-Archiving. You can tell YGM to save your incoming mail or outgoing mail, or both. You also tell it where to save it.

The Other Options column lets you set YGM to automatically log on to AOL (the Auto-Logon feature), set the maximum size for your mail archives, and control where the YGM button appears on your screen so you can call it up while online. The settings will be fine as they appear until you get used to it. You may want to tinker with them later.

Finally, the column labeled WAOL Information asks for the scoop on your AOL software, specifically what version you are using and where it's located on your hard drive.

When you've provided all that information, click **OK**. You've Got Mail! launches. It looks like the figure below, and you already have a piece of mail from the authors of the program.

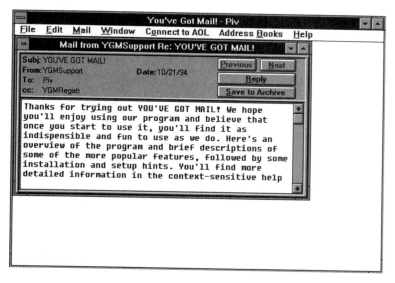

Hey, you've really got mail!

Once you get YGM set up to your liking, it's a pretty straightforward program and it's easy to use. You may want to read some of the online help files (available in the Help menu) before you use it the first time. Drop me a note.

Using You've Got Mail!

To use You've Got Mail! (YGM for short), launch it by double-clicking on the file **YGM.EXE** in the File Manager. It starts right up. Then launch America Online; you can either launch it normally (by double-clicking the AOL icon in its program group), or you can use the Logon command under the Connect to AOL menu (which launches AOL and signs you on to the service). In order to use the Logon command, you need to have stored your passwords with AOL. Chapter 6 tells you how.

When you connect to AOL, You've Got Mail! puts a teeny-tiny window with buttons down at the bottom of your screen. You can see it in the figure below. If you click on the Copy button, YGM copies an open piece of mail to your You've Got Mail! mail archive. If you click on the Log Off button, you will be disconnected from AOL.

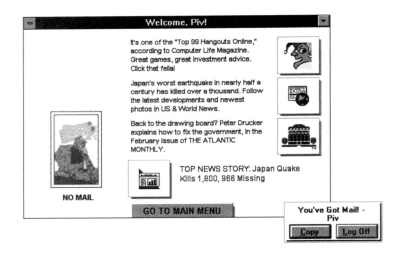

How You've Got Mail! looks online.

YGM does most of its stuff offline though. To read mail you've saved (or even small text files), select the **Open** command from the **File** menu. You'll get a standard Open dialog box that you can use to navigate to your mail archive.

To compose mail, select **Write a Letter** from the Mail menu. You'll get a mail window like the one following. Just enter a subject, the screen name of the person to whom it's addressed (in the To: box), and the screen names of anyone you want to receive copies (in the cc: box).

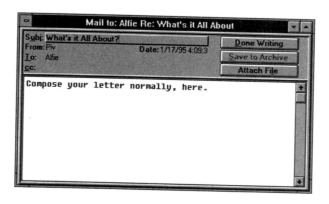

Writing a letter with YGM.

Click once in the big text box at the bottom to put the cursor there, and then type away. You can also attach a file by clicking on the Attach File button. When you're done, click **Done Writing**, and You've Got Mail! saves your letter for later delivery.

YGM also gives you the option of keeping multiple address books. To create one, select **Create Address List** from the **Address Books** menu. First you'll be asked to name the address list. It gives you an editing window like the one here. In the box labeled Address, type the screen name of the person you want to add, and in the Comments box, type a brief description (maybe her real name). Then click **Add**. The screen name and description are added to your list. When you're finished adding names, click **OK**.

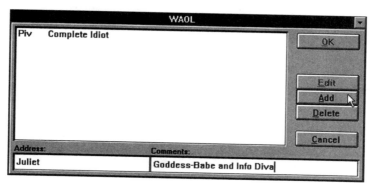

Creating a YGM address book.

For more detailed instructions, read the online help files available in the Help menu.

CompuShow 2000!

No, it's not a movie being shown on "Mystery Science Theater 3000" (even if it sounds like one). CompuShow 2000! is a graphics program that enables you to look at, print, and tinker with the graphics files you'll probably be downloading from America Online. To start (all together now), you'll use the File Manager to decompress the files. In your CIGAOL folder, double-click on the **2SHOW** folder. That expands the files.

Installing CompuShow 2000!

Don't panic, now. To install CompuShow, you'll need to use the MS-DOS prompt. You'll find its icon in the Main program group. Double-click on it to launch it.

1. With the MS-DOS Prompt running, at the C:\ prompt, type **CD CIGAOL\2SHOW** and press **Enter**. That changes you to the 2Show directory (a folder under Windows).

2. Type **2SHOWA** and press **Enter** to start the installation process.

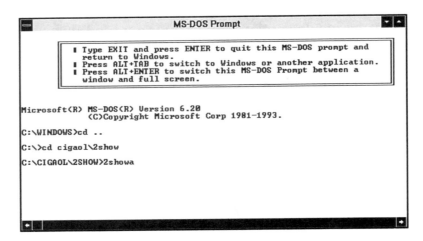

Installing CompuShow from the MS-DOS Prompt.

3. The installer asks if you want to install to a floppy disk (it might be a good idea, until you decide if you like CompuShow). If you do, press **Y**; if not, press **N**.

4. If you're installing to a floppy, insert a disk in your A: or B: drive. The installer asks which drive to use. Enter the drive letter and press **Enter**.

   If you're installing to your hard drive, the installer asks you to enter the letter of the drive you want to use (probably C). Enter the drive letter and press **Enter**.

5. The installer asks if you want to install the novice or expert versions. Press **N** and then **Enter** to install the novice version. (You can always reinstall the expert version when you really are an expert.)

   And that's it! Your PC installs CompuShow 2000!. When it's complete, you can launch it by typing **2Show** at the command prompt for the appropriate drive (A:\, B:\, or C:\).

Although you may install CompuShow from the MS-DOS Prompt in Windows, do *not* run the application in the MS-DOS Prompt—even though that's what's shown in the figure on the next page. (How do you think I discovered the problem?) CompuShow and Windows will squabble over whose video drivers to use, and the application will probably crash. Quit Windows before attempting to run CompuShow. As always, I screw up so you don't have to.

Using CompuShow 2000!

CompuShow works like any DOS-based program. You'll use the File menu to open the file you want. Then you make your adjustments and save the changed file (also with the File menu).

As you can see in the figure on the next page, CompuShow has an extensive amount of help available (under the Help menu, oddly enough). Before you begin playing with the program, at least read the Basic Instructions and Terms. Before you try, it will help if you sign on to AOL and download some graphics files to look at.

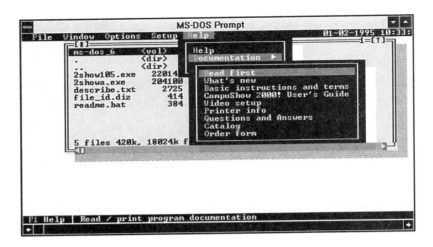

The CompuShow 2000! screen.

Use your mouse to access CompuShow's menus, or press the **F10** key and use your arrow keys to select menu items. The Setup menu lets you set up CompuShow to use your monitor and video display card to their best advantage.

To view a graphics file, use the directory display to navigate to the directory that contains your image files. If you just downloaded some, they're probably in your AOL/DOWNLOADS subdirectory. If you need to change to another drive, press the **F2** key or select **Drive** from the File menu.

Use your arrow keys or mouse to select the file you want to open, and then press **Enter**. CompuShow checks the image and tries to select the appropriate resolution and number of colors. To accept its choice, just press **Enter**. Otherwise, select another from the list and press **Enter**. After a moment, the image is displayed.

Press **Esc** (or **Enter**) to make the image go away; that returns you to the Display Options screen. You can try another resolution (just select one and press **Enter**) or press C to return to the directory screen and select another graphic to view.

For more detailed information about using CompuShow 2000!, consult the online documentation by selecting the appropriate item(s) from the **Documentation** submenu in the **Help** menu. Happy viewing!

Mac and DOS Grow Your Own Disk

I don't want anyone to feel left out because his or her kind of disk is excluded from this book. So here are some places to look for cool files of your own. Before you start looking around, you may want to read through Chapter 12, which explains searching for and downloading files in detail.

Mac Stuff

For Mac users starting out with America Online, there's no cooler forum or library than The Help Desk (Keyword: HELP DESK). The Help Desk's information files and file library (shown in the figure below) will have you up and tinkering with your AOL software faster than you can say "Jack Robinson."

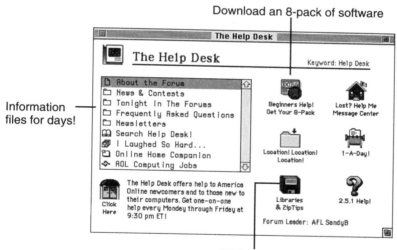

Download an 8-pack of software

Information files for days!

Click here for cool files.

The Macintosh Help Desk—tons of help.

The file library includes collections of sounds, utilities, and even starter kits that include a couple of popular applications to help you out online and off. You can also download helpful text files that tell you how to do funky stuff like replace those "Welcome!" and "You've Got Mail!" sounds with ones of your own (or ones you've downloaded).

If you want a graphics program similar to the one on the disk, I recommend Kevin Mitchell's great shareware program GIFConverter. Search for it by name.

DOS and GeoWorks

The fastest way to find add-ons for the DOS version of AOL is to do a file search. Here's how:

1. Select **Search Software Libraries** from your Go To menu.

2. For the search string, type **AOL** or **AOL Add-ons**.

3. Press **Enter**.

AOL searches its libraries and comes back with a lot of potential candidates. Start browsing for stuff that suits your needs. Did I mention (*wink, wink*) that you, too, can use CompuShow 2000! from the disk? It isn't a Windows application, it's for DOS.

The Least You Need to Know

Picking software for someone else to use is chancy at best. I mean, what do I know about what you'll be doing online? I hope you find some of the software from the disk useful; if you don't, you can always find your own.

➤ All the items on the disk are compressed in individual self-extracting archives. You must decompress them before you can use them.

➤ You can install one, all, or a combination of software from the disk. That's why they're individually compressed. Just follow the directions for each application.

➤ Some of the items on the disk are free (Wedge and the sounds); use them till you burst. The others are shareware. If you keep them and use them, you're expected to pay the registration fees to the authors. It's *very* rude not to.

➤ Mac and DOS users can put together a similar set of AOL add-ons just by looking in the right places online.

Speak Like a Geek: The Complete Archive

⌘ The symbol used to represent the Macintosh *Command* key.

.arc Short for archive. File extension you'll find on some PC files that have been *compressed* (for example, DOCUMENT.arc). See also *compression*.

.sea Short for Self-Extracting Archive. File extension you'll find on some Macintosh files that have been *compressed*. You don't have to have additional software to decompress self-extracting files. See also *compression*.

.sit Short for StuffIt, a compression utility. You'll find .sit at the end of some Macintosh file names (*i.e.* Information.sit) that have been *compressed*. See also *compression*.

.zip Short for PKZip, a compression utility, .zip is a file extension you find on some PC file names (*i.e.* DOCUMENT.zip) that have been *compressed*. See also *compression*.

BCC See *blind carbon copy*.

blind carbon copy A method of sending email to multiple recipients without letting them know the screen names of the other recipients.

boolean The method of searching a database (such as Compton's Encyclopedia online) that lets you include "and" or "not" between two search words to expand (*and*) or narrow (*not*) your search.

CC   An old business term that stands for Carbon Copy. The term is still used with email to show who is getting a copy of the letter.

chat   Talking online through typed conversation.

chat room   An online area set up specifically for people to gather and talk. Most chat rooms are in the People Connection, but many forums have their own chat rooms.

compatible   When computer equipment is *compatible* to another similar piece of equipment, it means they work pretty much the same. An IBM-compatible computer works pretty much the same as a computer actually made by IBM, and a modem by one manufacturer is much the same as one made by another.

compression   A method of making computer files smaller so they take up less space on your hard drive and require less time to upload and download. It's accomplished with compression software that replaces repetitive data with little placeholders. See also *decompression*.

Ctrl   Abbreviation used to represent a computer's *Control* key. It's part of most IBM-compatible keyboard shortcuts.

cyberspace   A word coined by science fiction author William Gibson in his novel *Neuromancer* (a "must read" for true geek wannabes). When computer users on opposite sides of the country meet and talk in real-time, the ethereal, computer-generated place they meet is *cyberspace*.

database   A great big pile of information that you can look through (search) according to a search string (a key word or phrase). There are many searchable databases available on America Online.

decompression   Before you can use a file that has been compressed, you must decompress it with software that swaps the original data for the placeholders in the file, returning the file(s) to their original size.

desktop publishing   Using computers, page layout software, and laser printers to create both large and small-scale publications without having to resort to typesetters and other old-fashioned publishing tools.

dialog box   When you ask AOL (or any software) to do something, if it needs more information to do what you've asked, it will ask for that information by way of a dialog box. It's called a dialog box because it asks a question that you answer (that's dialog), and it's box-shaped.

download time   How long it will take to transfer a file from the AOL computer to yours. The times are approximate and can vary either way.

downloading   Retrieving a file from a remote computer for use on your own. See also *uploading*.

dtp   See *desktop publishing*.

email   Electronic mail; there's no paper involved unless you decide to print it out. Email gets where it's going almost immediately, which is why I use it more than regular mail.

emoticons   Contraction for *emotion icons*. See also *smiley*.

expansion card   A circuitry board that fits into an expansion slot inside your computer.

expansion slot   Part of your computer that will accept an expansion card/board that adds new functions and/or features to your computer.

export   The capability of an application to save a file in the format of another application (or one that another application can *import*, at least). For example, Microsoft Word can save files in a number of formats (like WordPerfect) for both Macintosh and IBM-compatible computers. See also *import*.

FAQ   Frequently Asked Question. Before you post a "Help Me" question, you should always scout around to see if there's a topic (in a message area) or a file (in a file library) of FAQs. Your answer may already be there, and folks can get a little cranky answering the same question over and over.

flame   When someone's posts to a message board are more about name-calling and anger-venting than about actually discussing something, the message(s) are called flames. Writing such a message is called flaming. If someone posts a message like that about something you posted, you've been flamed.

FlashSession   An automated method for retrieving your email and selected files from America Online.

folder drift   When a message thread starts off talking about "Travel Tips for Pets" and ends up talking about how little "Muffy" is so cute when she chases her tail, that thread is suffering from folder drift. That's where, over time, the original gist of the thread gets lost and/or buried under tangential comments.

font The name for the typefaces used by computers. Much of the terminology of computerized type is borrowed/adapted from the language of typesetting.

Forum A self-contained area online devoted to one broad topic. Generally, all AOL forums have informational text you can read, a file library, a message area, and often a chat room.

freeware Freeware is *free software*. You can download it, use it, and give copies to your friends, and never spend anything more for it than the cost of the phone call and online charges incurred while downloading it.

FTP The way files are sent and received via the Internet. It stands for *file transfer protocol*. It also is the name of the application you use to move those files.

gateway A connection between two different computer services. It allows you to access information from the other service without having to disconnect from the host service (in this case, AOL). For example, AOL has a gateway to the Internet.

GeoWorks Ensemble A DOS-shell application, like Windows, that gives you the benefits of a graphical user interface (GUI, pronounced "goo-ey"). However, unlike Windows, GeoWorks will run on even the lowliest XT IBM-compatible with minimum RAM.

GIF Graphics Interchange Format. A picture file format that is supposed to work on all computer platforms.

gopher A way of browsing through tons of information quickly on the Internet. Member organizations and individuals set up Gopher servers that contain nothing but menus of items. Double-clicking on the menu item retrieves the item: sometimes it's a text file, sometimes it's another set of menus.

GUI Pronounced "goo-ey," it stands for Graphical User Interface. See also *interface*.

Guide Part of AOL's service staff. Guides moderate some chat rooms (such as Lobbies and Help rooms), answer questions, and generally keep things moving. In emergency situations, you can use the Keyword: GUIDEPAGER to summon a Guide online.

Hayes-compatible   A term that identifies a modem that conforms to the standard set of modem commands developed by the Hayes Corporation. Hayes compatibility is fairly standard among modems.

IM   See *instant message*.

Instant Message   IM, for short; a message sent between members who are both online. Unlike mail, it is delivered instantly, hence the name. When you receive an IM, you'll hear a musical tone, and the message (usually) jumps to the front of your monitor where you can read and reply to it.

import   The capability of an application to open a file created in another application with a minimum of fuss. In the process, the application translates the file into its own format so you never have to bother with it again. See also *export*.

interface   The middle ground between a user and a computer operating system, where both interact. You tell your computer to do stuff through the interface. And the computer asks you questions (Where do you want that file saved?) also through the interface. Windows and the Mac OS are both interfaces that rely on pictures (icons) to represent features and functions of the interface. That's why they're called *GUIs* or graphical user interfaces.

Internet   An International network of computers that let people exchange information, files, email, and bad, bad jokes with each other.

JPEG   A graphic file format in which images can contain millions of colors and still take up minimal space on a disk. The files are automatically compressed to save that space. However, the more the files are compressed, the worse they look; they lose detail and get splotchy looking.

keyboard shortcut   A combination of two or more keys that have the same effect as selecting a command from a menu. Crtl+N and ⌘-N are the DOS and Mac keyboard shortcuts for the New command with AOL.

keyword   A one-word way of navigating to a particular area of AOL. You use a Keyword by pressing Ctrl+K on an IBM-compatible (Windows or DOS) or ⌘-K on a Mac. Type in the Keyword and press Enter.

launch   Another way of saying "start" an application.

local access number   America Online's central computers are located in Vienna, Virginia. Calling in would be a long distance call for most people. Instead of socking you with long distance charges, you access AOL by calling (usually) a local phone number; the computer at that location (called a *node*, if you care) connects you to America Online.

lurker   Someone who enters a chat room and drifts off into a corner, not speaking to anyone publicly or participating in any way in the chat.

macro   A key combination that invokes a more complicated sequence of keystrokes already stored in a macro program. Forum hosts, game hosts, and Guides often use macros so they don't have to continually type the same word or phrase over and over.

master account   The very first screen name you created, the first time you logged onto America Online, is called your master account.

message archive   To save space on the message boards, old or inactive message threads will be turned into text files for storage, and you can download them from the forum's library. These are called *message* or *thread archives*.

modem   A device that turns the information and commands from your computer into sounds that can travel through telephone lines to another modem-equipped computer at a remote location.

Network   In most cases, two or more computers and/or peripherals (printers, maybe) hooked together so they can communicate. With AOL, the "network" of Network & Modem Setup refers to the telephone network (SprintNet, Tymnet, and so on) that you use to connect to America Online.

newbies   A term used for new users of AOL.

newsgroup   The Internet equivalent of a message area on AOL, where various people post and respond to each other's messages.

node   A term borrowed from the language of networking. When you dial your local access number, you're actually calling an intermediary computer (the local node) that in turn connects you to AOL.

offline   You *are not* connected to America Online (or any other online service).

online   You *are* connected to AOL (or any other online service).

PBX   A type of telephone system used in some hotels and business locations. They're high-powered and digital and may damage your modem. Ask before you plug into a strange phone system.

PKZip   The file compression utility that is the standard for IBM-compatible computers on AOL. See also *compression*.

post   A message added to a message board is sometimes called a "post," and message and post may be used interchangeably. The act of adding a message to a board is also known as *posting*.

protocol   A procedure for asking questions and making comments in an online event room. It's comparable to being in school and having to raise your hand (and be recognized by the teacher) before you open your mouth. It makes online events move along nicely, with little confusion.

punt   Slang term for suddenly being disconnected from America Online. You've been treated like a football and drop-kicked from the service.

queue   The order of people waiting to send comments or questions in a chat room using a protocol.

run-time   Any bit of software (like VBRUN300, on the disk) that allows you to use stuff written for (or with) a particular application (Microsoft Visual Basic, for VBRUN300) even if you don't own the original application, is called a *run-time version*.

screen name   Literally, it's the name that appears on your screen (and other members' screens) whenever you speak in a chat room. It's also your email address on AOL.

sign off   Disconnecting from an online service.

sign on   Connecting to an online service, like America Online.

smiley   A facial expression used in chat rooms that's created with your computer's punctuation keys. ;-)

StuffIt   Compression software created by Aladdin Systems. It's the Macintosh standard for file compression on AOL.

system requirements   The least amount of computer stuff you need to have before you can use a product (whether it's hardware or software) with your computer. Generally it includes a specific kind of computer (486, Mac Quadra, etc.) with a certain amount of random-access memory (say, 4 megabytes of RAM), other hardware (like a color monitor, hard drive, and/or modem), and a version of your computer's operating system (DOS 6.2 or Mac OS 7.5). Matching your system to the system requirements is the easiest way to tell if you can use a particular product.

technical support   The part of a hardware or software company that is devoted to answering technical questions about its products. There's almost always a technical support number listed in your manual, usually in the section devoted to troubleshooting.

template   A fill-in-the blanks version of a particular kind of publishing file. Instead of finding graphics and text in a template, you'll find placeholders that tell you where to put your graphics and text that says "insert your graphic here." Templates really speed up the design process because you don't have to start from scratch.

thread   A group of messages on a related topic is called a message thread, or just thread. You can follow the series of messages from start to finish. See also *message archive*.

thread archive   See *message archive*.

troubleshooting   A Rambo-sounding term that means figuring out what's going wrong and fixing it. There's no real shooting involved.

uploading   Sending a file to a remote computer for storage or distribution.

version number   The system that software manufacturers use to identify the latest greatest versions of their product. Version 2.0 is newer than version 1.0. Version 2.5.1 is newer than version 2.5.

virus   A bit of computer code hidden inside another file. Computer viruses are passed like the viruses that cause colds and AIDS; when you use an infected file, it infects your computer. The virus may be harmless (flashing an amusing message on your screen), or it may be harmful (destroying all of the data on your hard drive). Practice safe computing. Use antivirus software.

WAIS   Wide Area Information Server, pronounced "ways." A method for quickly searching through tons of information, originally developed for use on huge supercomputers.

Index

Symbols

* (asterisk), keywords, 262
. (period) keyboard shortcut, 40
@TIMES keyword, 263
1-800-FLOWERS (shopping online), 189
2Market
  billing information, 188
2Market (shopping online), 185-189
3D keyword, 263
3DSIG keyword, 263
5THGENERATION keyword, 263
9600 keyword, 263

A

AAC (Academic Assistance Center), 159-161
ABC Classroom, 165
Academic Assistance Center (AAC), 159-161
Academic Message Boards, 162
academic programming, 159-167
Academic Research Service, 162
  Newton MessagePad, 162
  PDAs (Personal Digital Assistants), 162
access numbers
  finding, 212-218
  troubleshooting, 242

access
  home, 218
  remote, 211-212
accessing
  email, 41
  Industry Connection, 155
  message boards (forums), 128-130
account balances (Member Services), 235
Account Security (Member Services), 236
Activate FlashSession Now command (Mail menu), 256
AD&D Neverwinter Nights (The Marketplace), 183
AD&D Online, 85
Add Message button (e-mail), 254
add-ons, 309-310
adding newsgroups, 203
Address Book (e-mail), 101-103
Address Book menu commands, 305
Address Group dialog box, 102
addressing (Internet), 198
AIDS (HIV+/AIDS Support Group), 230-231
air travel, 219
  EAAsy Sabre, 189-193
America Online
  Address Book (e-mail), 101-103
  assumptions, 26-27
  billing and payment information, 31-32
  Boolean searches, 164
  budgeting, 252

chat rooms, 5-6, 105-120
connections (troubleshooting), 243
cost, 4-5, 252
departments, 79-82
disconnecting from, 244
DOS requirements, 9
e-mail, 5, 92-94
educational programming, 159-167
etiquette, 4
features, 43-44
files, 135-150
FlashSessions, 98-101, 256-257
forums, 121-133, 224-228
Go To menu, customizing, 258-259
hardware requirements, 3, 7-9
Highlights feature, 43
home access, 218
installation, 15-22
Internet, 195-208
Internet Connection, 196-198
keyboard shortcuts, 259
keywords, 5
launching, 23-24
local access numbers, 27-29
location files, 215-218
logging (chat rooms), 118-119
Macintosh requirements, 9
Main Menu, 77-78
Member Services, 233-238
memory, 8

G